DERIVATIVES

CFA® Program Curriculum
2025 • LEVEL II • VOLUME 7

WILEY

ISBN 978-1-961409-27-9 (paper)
ISBN 978-1-961409-38-5 (ebook)
August 2024

SKY07B90A48-567B-4CA4-8907-A3D64AF62D15_072224

Please visit our website at
www.WileyGlobalFinance.com.

CONTENTS

How to Use the CFA Program Curriculum   v
    CFA Institute Learning Ecosystem (LES)   v
    Designing Your Personal Study Program   v
    Errata   vi
    Other Feedback   vi

Derivatives

Learning Module 1 **Pricing and Valuation of Forward Commitments**   3
    Introduction   3
        Principles of Arbitrage-Free Pricing and Valuation of Forward
           Commitments   4
        Pricing and Valuing Generic Forward and Futures Contracts   5
    Carry Arbitrage   10
        Carry Arbitrage Model When There Are No Underlying Cash Flows   10
        Carry Arbitrage Model When Underlying Has Cash Flows   18
    Pricing Equity Forwards and Futures   21
        Equity Forward and Futures Contracts   21
        Interest Rate Forward and Futures Contracts   24
    Pricing Fixed-Income Forward and Futures Contracts   33
        Comparing Forward and Futures Contracts   38
    Pricing and Valuing Swap Contracts   39
        Interest Rate Swap Contracts   42
    Pricing and Valuing Currency Swap Contracts   48
    Pricing and Valuing Equity Swap Contracts   56
    Summary   *61*
    Practice Problems   *65*
    Solutions   *73*

Learning Module 2 **Valuation of Contingent Claims**   81
    Introduction   82
        Principles of a No-Arbitrage Approach to Valuation   82
    Binomial Option Valuation Model   84
    One-Period Binomial Model   86
    Two-Period Binomial Model: Call Options   93
    Two-Period Binomial Model: Put Options   97
    Two-Period Binomial Model: Role of Dividends   100
    Interest Rate Options and Multiperiod Model   106
        Multiperiod Model   109
    Black-Scholes-Merton (BSM) Option Valuation Model   109
        Introductory Material   110
        Assumptions of the BSM Model   110
    BSM Model: Components   112
    BSM Model: Carry Benefits and Applications   116

Black Option Valuation Model and European Options on Futures   120
    European Options on Futures   120
Interest Rate Options   122
Swaptions   126
Option Greeks and Implied Volatility: Delta   128
    Delta   129
Gamma   132
Theta   135
Vega   136
Rho   137
Implied Volatility   138
Summary   *142*
Practice Problems   *145*
Solutions   *152*

Glossary   **G-1**

How to Use the CFA Program Curriculum

The CFA® Program exams measure your mastery of the core knowledge, skills, and abilities required to succeed as an investment professional. These core competencies are the basis for the Candidate Body of Knowledge (CBOK™). The CBOK consists of four components:

> A broad outline that lists the major CFA Program topic areas (www .cfainstitute.org/programs/cfa/curriculum/cbok/cbok)

> Topic area weights that indicate the relative exam weightings of the top-level topic areas (www.cfainstitute.org/en/programs/cfa/curriculum)

> Learning outcome statements (LOS) that advise candidates about the specific knowledge, skills, and abilities they should acquire from curriculum content covering a topic area: LOS are provided at the beginning of each block of related content and the specific lesson that covers them. We encourage you to review the information about the LOS on our website (www.cfainstitute.org/programs/cfa/curriculum/study-sessions), including the descriptions of LOS "command words" on the candidate resources page at www.cfainstitute.org/-/media/documents/support/programs/cfa-and -cipm-los-command-words.ashx.

> The CFA Program curriculum that candidates receive access to upon exam registration

Therefore, the key to your success on the CFA exams is studying and understanding the CBOK. You can learn more about the CBOK on our website: www.cfainstitute .org/programs/cfa/curriculum/cbok.

The curriculum, including the practice questions, is the basis for all exam questions. The curriculum is selected or developed specifically to provide candidates with the knowledge, skills, and abilities reflected in the CBOK.

CFA INSTITUTE LEARNING ECOSYSTEM (LES)

Your exam registration fee includes access to the CFA Institute Learning Ecosystem (LES). This digital learning platform provides access, even offline, to all the curriculum content and practice questions. The LES is organized as a series of learning modules consisting of short online lessons and associated practice questions. This tool is your source for all study materials, including practice questions and mock exams. The LES is the primary method by which CFA Institute delivers your curriculum experience. Here, candidates will find additional practice questions to test their knowledge. Some questions in the LES provide a unique interactive experience.

DESIGNING YOUR PERSONAL STUDY PROGRAM

An orderly, systematic approach to exam preparation is critical. You should dedicate a consistent block of time every week to reading and studying. Review the LOS both before and after you study curriculum content to ensure you can demonstrate the knowledge, skills, and abilities described by the LOS and the assigned reading. Use the LOS as a self-check to track your progress and highlight areas of weakness for later review.

Successful candidates report an average of more than 300 hours preparing for each exam. Your preparation time will vary based on your prior education and experience, and you will likely spend more time on some topics than on others.

ERRATA

The curriculum development process is rigorous and involves multiple rounds of reviews by content experts. Despite our efforts to produce a curriculum that is free of errors, in some instances, we must make corrections. Curriculum errata are periodically updated and posted by exam level and test date on the Curriculum Errata webpage (www.cfainstitute.org/en/programs/submit-errata). If you believe you have found an error in the curriculum, you can submit your concerns through our curriculum errata reporting process found at the bottom of the Curriculum Errata webpage.

OTHER FEEDBACK

Please send any comments or suggestions to info@cfainstitute.org, and we will review your feedback thoughtfully.

Derivatives

1

Pricing and Valuation of Forward Commitments

by Adam Schwartz, PhD, CFA.

Adam Schwartz, PhD, CFA is at Bucknell University (USA).

CFA Institute would like to thank Robert Brooks, PhD, CFA and Barbara Valbuzzi, CFA for their contributions to earlier versions of this reading.

LEARNING OUTCOMES

Mastery	The candidate should be able to:
☐	describe how equity forwards and futures are priced, and calculate and interpret their no-arbitrage value
☐	describe the carry arbitrage model without underlying cashflows and with underlying cashflows
☐	describe how interest rate forwards and futures are priced, and calculate and interpret their no-arbitrage value
☐	describe how fixed-income forwards and futures are priced, and calculate and interpret their no-arbitrage value
☐	describe how interest rate swaps are priced, and calculate and interpret their no-arbitrage value
☐	describe how currency swaps are priced, and calculate and interpret their no-arbitrage value
☐	describe how equity swaps are priced, and calculate and interpret their no-arbitrage value

INTRODUCTION

1

| ☐ | describe how equity forwards and futures are priced, and calculate and interpret their no-arbitrage value |

Forward commitments include forwards, futures, and swaps. A forward contract is a promise to buy or sell an asset at a future date at a price agreed to at the contract's initiation. The forward contract has a linear payoff function, with both upside and downside risk.

A swap is essentially a promise to undertake a transaction at a set price or rate at several dates in the future. The technique we use to price and value swaps is to identify and construct a portfolio with cash flows equivalent to those of the swap. Then, we can use tools, such as the law of one price, to determine swap values from simpler financial instruments, such as a pair of bonds with a cash flow pattern similar to those of our swap.

Look out for the big picture: value additivity, arbitrage, and the law of one price are important valuation concepts.

Forwards and swaps are widely used in practice to manage a broad range of market risks. As well, more complex derivative instruments can sometimes be understood in terms of their basic building blocks: forwards and option-based components. Here are just some of the many and varied uses for forwards, futures, and swaps that you might encounter in your investment career:

- Use of equity index futures and swaps by a private wealth manager to hedge equity risk in a low tax basis, concentrated position in his high-net-worth client's portfolio.
- Use of interest rate swaps by a defined benefits plan manager to hedge interest rate risk and to manage the pension plan's duration gap.
- Use of derivatives (total return swaps, equity futures, bond futures, etc.) overlays by a university endowment for tactical asset allocation and portfolio rebalancing.
- Use of interest rate swaps by a corporate borrower to synthetically convert floating-rate debt securities to fixed-rate debt securities (or vice versa).
- Use of VIX futures and inflation swaps by a firm's market strategist to infer expectations about market volatility and inflation rates, respectively.

Principles of Arbitrage-Free Pricing and Valuation of Forward Commitments

In this section, we examine arbitrage-free pricing and valuation of forward commitments—also known as the no-arbitrage approach to pricing and valuing such instruments. We introduce some guiding principles that heavily influence the activities of arbitrageurs, who are price setters in forward commitment markets.

There is a distinction between the pricing and the valuation of forward commitments. Forward commitment pricing involves determining the appropriate forward commitment price or rate when initiating the forward commitment contract. Forward commitment valuation involves determining the appropriate value of the forward commitment, typically after it has been initiated.

Our approach to pricing and valuation is based on the assumption that prices adjust to prevent arbitrage profits. Hence, the material will be covered from an arbitrageur's perspective. Key to understanding this material is to think like an arbitrageur. Specifically, the arbitrageur seeks to make a profit following two rules:

Rule #1: Do not use your own money; and

Rule #2: Do not take any price risk.

To make a profit, subject to these restrictions, the arbitrageur may need to borrow or lend money and buy or sell assets. The no-arbitrage approach considers the contract's cash flows from contract initiation (Time 0) to contract maturity (Time T). If an initial investment requires an outflow of 100 euros, then we will present it as a –100 euro cash flow. Cash inflows to the arbitrageur have a positive sign, and outflows are negative.

Pricing and valuation tasks based on the no-arbitrage approach imply an inability to create a portfolio that earns a risk-free profit without making a positive net investment of capital. In other words, if cash and forward markets are priced correctly with respect to each other, we cannot create such a portfolio. That is, we cannot create money today with no risk or future liability. This approach is built on the **law of one price**, which states that if two investments have equivalent future cash flows regardless of what will happen in the future, then these two investments should have the same current price. Alternatively, if the law of one price is violated, someone could buy the cheaper asset and sell the more expensive asset, resulting in a gain at no risk and with no commitment of capital. The law of one price can be used with the value additivity principle, which states that the value of a portfolio is simply the sum of the values of each instrument held in the portfolio.

Throughout this discussion of forward commitments, the following key assumptions are made: (1) replicating instruments are identifiable and investable; (2) market frictions are nil; (3) short selling is allowed with full use of proceeds; and (4) borrowing and lending are available at a known risk-free rate.

Our analyses will rely on the **carry arbitrage model**, a no-arbitrage approach in which the underlying instrument is either bought or sold along with establishing a forward position—hence the term "carry." Carry arbitrage models are also known as cost-of-carry arbitrage models or cash-and-carry arbitrage models. Carry arbitrage models account for costs to carry/hold the underlying asset. Carry costs include financing costs plus storage and insurance costs (for physical underlying, like gold). The carry arbitrage model must also adjust for any carry benefits (i.e., negative carry costs), including dividends and interest (such as bond coupons) received. Typically, each type of forward commitment will result in a different model, but common elements will be observed. Carry arbitrage models are a great first approximation to explaining observed forward commitment prices in many markets.

The central theme here is that forward commitments are generally priced so as to preclude arbitrage profits. Section 3 demonstrates how to price and value equity, interest rate, fixed-income, and currency forward contracts. We also explain how these results apply to futures contracts.

Pricing and Valuing Generic Forward and Futures Contracts

In this section, we examine the pricing of forward and futures contracts based on the no-arbitrage approach. The resulting carry arbitrage models are based on the replication of the forward contract payoff with a position in the underlying that is financed through an external source. Although the margin requirements, mark-to-market features, and centralized clearing in futures markets result in material differences between forward and futures markets in some cases, we focus mainly on cases in which the particular carry arbitrage model can be used in both markets.

Forwards and Futures

Forward and futures contracts are similar in that they are both agreements in which one party is legally obligated to sell and the other party is legally obligated to buy an asset (financial or otherwise) at an agreed price at some specific date in the future. The main difference is that a futures contract is an exchange-traded financial instrument. Contracts trading on an organized exchange, such as the Chicago Mercantile Exchange (CME), incorporate standard features to facilitate trading and ensure both parties fulfill their obligations. For example, a gold futures contract traded on the CME (COMEX) features a standard contract size of 100 ounces, agreed upon deliverable assets (gold bars, perhaps), and a limited choice of maturity dates. To ensure performance of the long and the short parties, the futures exchange requires the posting and daily maintenance of a margin account.

A forward contract is an agreement to buy or sell a specific asset (financial or otherwise) at an agreed price at some specific date in the future. Forward contracts are bilateral non-exchange traded contracts, offering flexibility in terms of size, type of the underlying asset, expiration date, and settlement date. This customization comes at a price of potential credit risk and ability to unwind the position. Since the financial crisis, best practices for OTC contracts suggest daily settlement and margin requirements for forward contracts similar to those required by futures exchanges. Without daily settlement, a forward contract may accumulate (or may lose) value over time. Some of the differences and similarities between forwards and futures are summarized in Exhibit 1.

Exhibit 1: Characteristics of Futures and Forward Contracts

Futures	Forwards
Exchange-traded	Negotiated between the contract counterparties
Standardized dates and deliverables	Customized dates and deliverables
Trades guaranteed by a clearinghouse	Trading subject to counterparty risk
Initial value = 0	Initial value = 0 (Typically, but not required)
An initial margin deposit specified by the exchange is required. The margin account is adjusted for gains and losses daily. If daily losses cause the margin balance to drop below a limit set by the futures exchange (i.e., maintenance margin), additional funds must be deposited, or the position will be closed.	Margin requirements may be specified by the counterparties.
Daily settlement marks the contract price equal to the market price and contract value = 0.	Contract may outline a settlement schedule. The forward may accumulate (or lose) value between settlement periods or until maturity (if no early settlements are required).

Forward price (F) or **futures price** (f) refers to the price that is negotiated between the parties to the forward or futures contract, respectively.
Our notation will be as follows, let:

S_t represent spot price (cash price for immediate delivery) of the underlying instrument at any time t,

F_t represent forward price at any time t, and

f_t represent futures price at any time t.

Therefore, S_0, F_0, and f_0 denote, respectively, the spot, forward, and futures price, respectively, established at the initiation date, 0. The initial forward price is established to make the contract value zero for both the long and short parties. The forward (delivery) price does not change during the life of the contract. Time T represents the time at which the contract expires and the future transaction is scheduled to take place. Thus, S_T, F_T, and f_T are the spot, forward, and futures price, respectively, at expiration time T. Between initiation at time 0 and expiration at time T, the spot price of the underlying asset may fluctuate to a new value, S_t. The price of a newly created forward or futures contract at time t with the same underlying and expiration (at time T) may differ from the price agreed to at time 0. So, our forward or futures contract established at time 0 may have a positive or negative value at time t. V_t and v_t will later be used to describe, respectively, the value of a forward and futures contract at any time t.

As we approach expiration, the price of a newly created forward or futures contract will approach the price of a spot transaction. At expiration, a forward or futures contract is equivalent to a spot transaction in the underlying. This property is often called **convergence**, and it implies that at time T, both the forward price and the futures price are equivalent to the spot price—that is,

Convergence property: $F_T = f_T = S_T$.

The convergence property is intuitive. For example, the one-year forward price of gold (that is, the price set today to purchase gold one year from now) might be very different from the spot price of gold. However, the price to buy gold one hour in the future should be very close to the spot price. As the maturity of the forward or futures contract approaches, the forward or futures price will converge to the spot price. If the forward or futures price were higher than the spot at maturity, an arbitrageur would:

1. Sell the forward or futures contract.
2. Borrow funds using a loan to buy the asset.
3. Make delivery at expiration of the contract, repay the loan, and keep the profit.

As market participants exploit this arbitrage opportunity, the forward or futures price will fall due to selling pressure.

If the futures price is below spot price, an arbitrageur would short sell the asset, invest the short-sale proceeds at the risk-free rate, and then enter into a long futures contract. He or she would take delivery of the asset at the futures contract expiration and use it to cover the short. The profit is simply the difference between the short-sale price and the futures price, after adjusting for carrying and financing costs. These actions on the part of arbitrageurs would act to enforce the convergence property.

Prior to expiration, the price of a newly created futures or forward contract will usually differ from the spot price. The forward and futures prices may even differ slightly from each other. For example, when the possibility of counterparty default exists or when the underlying asset price (such as a bond) is correlated with interest rates (which might impact the financing costs for daily settlement), the futures price might vary slightly from the forward price. For most cases, the generalist may assume the price of a futures contract and a forward contract will be same. That is $F_t = f_t$ before expiration.

Exhibit 2 shows the convergence property for a stock index futures/forward contact under continuous compounding and varying dividend yields. To carry a stock index, we must forego the interest rate that could be otherwise earned on our money, but we will collect dividend payments. As shown in Exhibit 2, the convergence path to the spot price at maturity depends on the costs and benefits of carrying the underlying asset. Here the stock index pays a dividend yield, which is a carry benefit. To hold the stock index, we must forego interest that could otherwise be earned on the investment. This financing rate (interest rate, r_c), assumed to be 2% in the following graph, is a cost to carry the index.

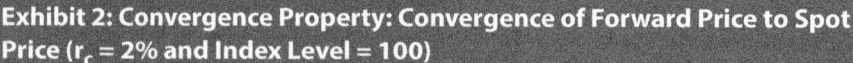

Exhibit 2: Convergence Property: Convergence of Forward Price to Spot Price (r_c = 2% and Index Level = 100)

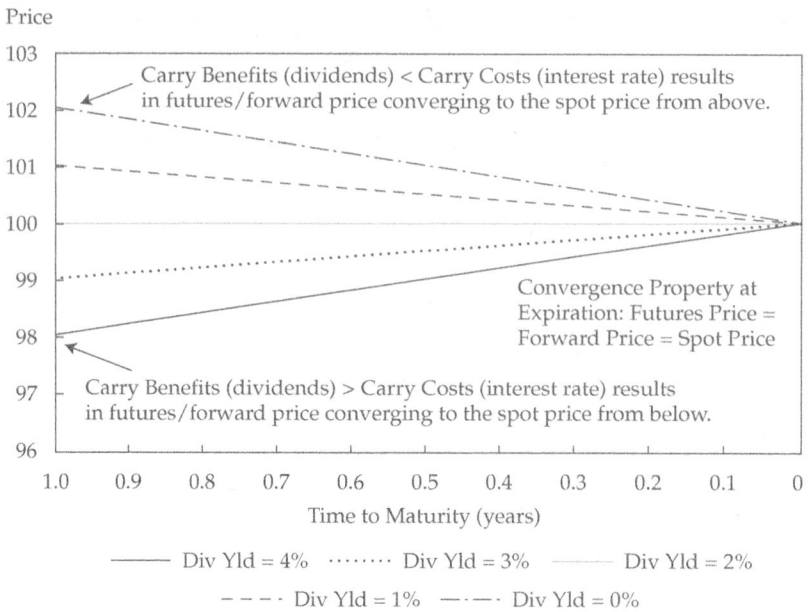

As maturity of the contract approaches (at time = T), the price of a newly created forward or futures contract will approach the spot price so that at expiration $F_T = f_T = S_T$, according to the convergence property. Prior to expiration, the forward/futures prices may be above, below, or nearly equal to the current spot price S_t. For futures contracts, the difference between the spot price and the futures price is the **basis**. As the maturity date nears, the basis converges toward zero. According to the convergence property, the future price approaches the spot price as we move toward expiration. At expiration, the futures price is equal to the price today for delivery today (i.e., spot price). If the convergence property does not hold, arbitrage will force the prices to be equal at contract expiration. The nature of the pricing relationship between the spot and forward/futures prices shown here will be explained shortly using the carry arbitrage model. For example, carry arbitrage will help us understand why assets with carry benefits (dividends) greater than carry costs (costs to finance and store the underlying) will have forward prices that converge to the spot price from below.

As market prices change, the value of existing futures and forward positions will change also. The market value of the forward or futures contract, termed **forward value** or **futures value**, respectively, and sometimes just value, refers to the monetary value of an existing forward or futures contract. When the forward or futures contract is established, the price is negotiated so that the value of the contract on the initiation date is zero. Subsequent to the initiation date, the value can be significantly positive or negative.

For example, an industrial firm requires platinum to manufacture certain components used in automobile manufacturing. The firm enters a long forward contract on 10 March. Under the terms of the contract, the firm agrees to buy 4,500 ounces of platinum on 10 September for $900 per ounce from a metal producer. From the firm's point of view, this is effectively a six-month long forward contract at a price of $F_0 =$ $900. If the price (technically, the September forward price) of platinum increases to $1,100 in May, the firm will be happy to have locked in a purchase price of $900 (long forward contract value is positive). If the price of platinum decreases to $800, the firm must still honor the forward agreement to buy platinum at $900 (long forward contract value is negative). To describe the value of a forward contract, let V_t be the value of the forward contract at any time t.

When the forward contract is established, the forward price is negotiated so that the market value of the forward contract on the initiation date is zero. Most forward contracts are structured this way and are referred to as **at market contracts**. Again, we assume no margin requirements. No money changes hands, meaning that the initial value is zero, so, $V_0 = 0$.

At expiration, the value of a forward contract V_T is realized and, as shown next, is straightforward to compute. Remember, the profit on any completed transaction is the sale price minus the purchase price. The profit or value of the forward contract at expiration is also the sale price minus the purchase price. At initiation, a forward or futures contract allows for either a future purchase price or a future sale price, F_0, to be known at time 0. In a long forward, a buyer can lock in a purchase price, F_0. In a short forward, a seller can lock in a sale price, F_0. Again, a forward contract allows a buyer or a seller to fix an initial price F_0, either the purchase price (long forward) or the sale price (short forward). The party long the forward effectively agrees to buy an asset in the future (at time T) at a price set today (at time 0), F_0.

At expiration, the asset can be sold in the spot market at a price S_T. Therefore, a *long* position in a forward contract has a value at expiration of:

$$V_T = S_T - F_0.$$

A short position effectively locks in a sale price of F_0. It is the negative of the long position. Therefore, the value of a short forward position at expiration is the sale price minus the purchase price of the asset:

$$-V_T = -(S_T - F_0) = F_0 - S_T.$$

For example, in January a fund manager agrees to sell a bond portfolio in May for F_0 = £10,000,000. The fund manager locks in the sale price, F_0. If the spot price of the bond portfolio at expiration (S_T) is £9,800,000, then the short forward contract will have an expiration value to the fund manager of:

$$-V_T = £10,000,000 - £9,800,000 = £200,000.$$

The fund manager makes a profit by selling at a higher price than the market price at expiration.

Value may accumulate or diminish with the passage of time in forward contracts, which is why forward contracts require the posting of collateral. Futures contract values, on the other hand, are settled by margining at the end of each trading day when the contract is marked-to-market. The gains and losses in the position over time accumulate in the futures traders' margin accounts. Prior to daily settlement, during the trading hours the market value of a long position in a futures contract is the current futures price less the future price at the last time the contract was marked-to-market times the multiplier, N_f (the multiplier is the standard contract size set by the futures exchange).

For a long futures contract, the value accumulated during the trading day (v_t) is:

$$v_t = \text{Multiplier} \times (\text{Current futures price} - \text{Previous settlement price}) \text{ or}$$

$$v_t = N_f \times (f_t - f_{t-1}).$$

Assume an investor is long one contract (N_f = 100 ounces/contract) of June gold, which settled at $1,300/ounce on the previous trading day. So, the investor is effectively agreeing to purchase 100 ounces of gold in June for $1,300 per ounce or $130,000 total. The trader need not pay the entire $130,000 today but must post a deposit in a margin account to guarantee his/her performance. During the current trading day, the price of June gold increases to $1,310. Before marking-to-market, the value of the long contract is $100 \times (\$1{,}310 - \$1{,}300) = +\$1{,}000$. After marking-to-market, the gain or loss is reflected in the trader's margin account and the new contract price is set equal to the settlement price. The futures contract value after daily settlement is 0 or $v_t = 0$.

2   CARRY ARBITRAGE

☐ | describe the carry arbitrage model without underlying cashflows and with underlying cashflows

We first consider a generic forward contract, meaning that we do not specify the underlying as anything more than just an asset. As we move through this section, we will continue to address specific additional factors to bring each carry arbitrage model closer to real markets. Thus, we will develop several different carry arbitrage models, each one applicable to a specific forward commitment contract. We start with the simpler of the two base cases, carry of an asset without cash flows to the underlying, then move to the more complex case of forwards on assets with underlying cash flows, such as bonds with coupon payments or stocks that pay dividends.

Carry Arbitrage Model When There Are No Underlying Cash Flows

Carry arbitrage models receive their name from the literal interpretation of carrying the underlying asset over the life of the forward contract. If an arbitrageur enters a forward contract to sell an underlying instrument for delivery at time T, then to offset this exposure, one strategy is to buy the underlying instrument at time 0 with borrowed funds and carry it to the forward expiration date (time T). The asset can then be sold (or even delivered) under the terms of a forward contract. The risks of this scenario are illustrated in Exhibit 3.

Exhibit 3: Cash Flows from Carrying an Underlying Asset and Offsetting Short Forward Position

	Time 0	Time T
Borrowing Funds to Purchase and Carry an Underlying Asset		
Underlying	$-S_0$ (purchase)	$+S_T$ (sale)
Borrowed funds	$+S_0$ (inflow)	$-FV(S_0)$ (repayment)
Net Cash Flow	$+S_0 - S_0 = 0$	$+ST - FV(S_0)$
Short Forward Position		
Short Forward	$V_0 = 0$	$V_T = F_0 - S_T$
Overall Position: Long Asset + Borrowed Funds + Short Forward		
	$+S_0 - S_0 + V_0 = 0$	$+S_T - FV(S_0) + V_T = 0$
		$+S_T - FV(S_0) + (F_0 - S_T) = 0$
		$+F_0 - FV(S_0) = 0$
Net	0	$F_0 = FV(S_0)$

The underlying asset is bought for S_0 with borrowed funds. The asset can be sold at time T for a price, S_T. At time T, the borrowed funds must be repaid at a cost of $FV(S_0)$; note that FV stands for the future value function. Clearly, when S_T is below (above) $FV(S_0)$, our underlying transaction will suffer a loss (earn a profit). A short forward position can be added to our long position in the underlying asset to offset any profit or loss in the underlying. Both positions have no initial (time 0) cash flow. To prevent arbitrage, the overall portfolio (Asset + Borrowed funds + Short forward) should have a value of zero at time T. If the cost to finance the purchase of the asset, $FV(S_0)$, is equal to the initially agreed upon forward price, F_0, then there is no arbitrage profit. So, we should have $F_0 = FV(S_0)$.

For now, we will keep the significant technical issues to a minimum. When possible, we will just use FV and PV to denote future value and present value, respectively. At this point we are not yet concerned about compounding conventions, day count conventions, or even the appropriate risk-free interest rate proxy.

Carry arbitrage models rest on the no-arbitrage assumptions. Therefore, the arbitrageur does not use his or her own money to acquire positions but borrows to purchase the underlying. Borrowing (if the underlying asset is purchased) and lending the proceeds (if the underlying asset is sold) are done at the risk-free interest rate. Furthermore, the arbitrageur offsets all transactions, meaning he/she does not take any price risk. We do not consider other risks, such as liquidity risk and counterparty credit risk, as they would unnecessarily complicate our basic presentation.

If we assume continuous compounding (r_c), then $FV(S_0) = S_0 exp^{r_c T}$. If we assume annual compounding (r), then $FV(S_0) = S_0(1 + r)^T$. Note that in practice, observed interest rates are derived from market prices. For example, a T-bill price implies the T-bill rate. Significant errors can occur if the quoted interest rate is used with the wrong compounding convention. When possible, we just use basic present value and future value representations to minimize confusion.

To help clarify, we first illustrate the price exposure solely from holding the underlying asset. Exhibit 4 shows the cash flows from carrying the underlying, a non-dividend-paying stock, assuming $S_0 = 100$, r = 5%, and T = 1. For illustration purposes, we allow the stock price at expiration to go down to $S_T^- = 90$ or up to $S_T^+ = 110$. The initial transactions will generate cash flows shown at times 0 and T. In practice, the set of transactions (market purchases, bank transactions) are executed simultaneously at each time period, not sequentially. Here are the two transactions at time 0 that produce a levered equity purchase.

Step 1   Purchase one unit of the underlying at time 0 (an outflow).

Step 2   Borrow the purchase price at the risk-free rate (an inflow).

Exhibit 4: Cash Flows for Long Financial Position

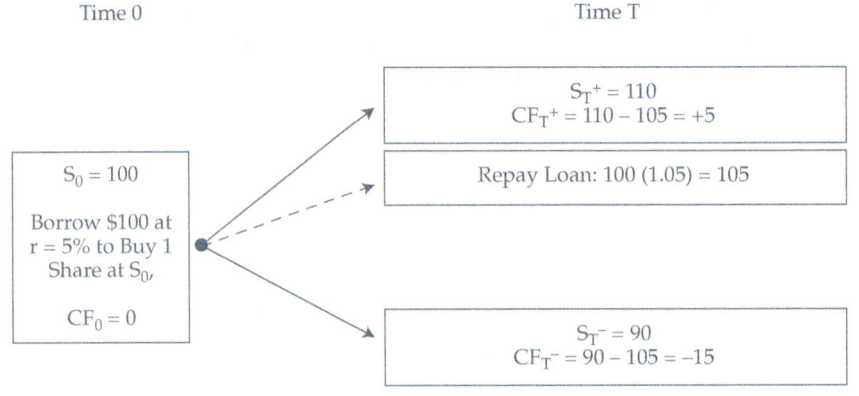

At time T ($= 1$), the stock price can jump up to $S_T^+ = 110$ or jump down to $S_T^- = 90$. Because the two outcomes are different, the strategy at this point has price risk. After the loan is repaid, the net cash flow will be $+5$ if the stock jumps up to 110 or -15 if the stock price jumps down to 90. To eliminate price risk, we must add another step to our list of simultaneous transactions. As suggested by Exhibit 3, we sell (go short) a forward contract to set a price today for the future sale of our underlying, and that price ($F_0 = FV(S_0)$) is 105.

> Step 1   Sell a forward at $F_0 = 105$. For a short forward contract, F_0 is the price agreed to at time 0 to sell the asset at Time T.

The resulting portfolio with its offsetting transaction is illustrated in Exhibit 5.

Exhibit 5: Cash Flow for Long Financial Position with Short Forward Contract

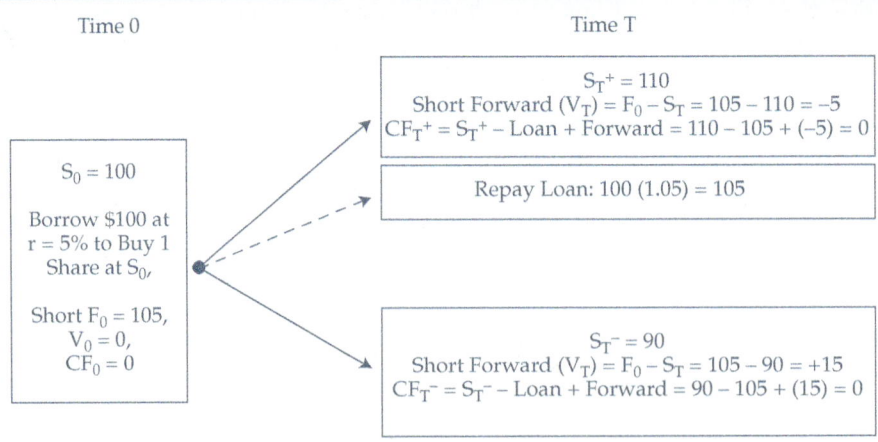

Regardless of the value of the underlying at maturity, we owe 105 on the loan. Notice that at expiration the underlying is worth 90 or 110. Since we agreed to sell the asset at 105, the forward contract value is either 15 or -5, respectively. If the asset is selling for 90 at time T, the forward contract allows us to sell our underlying position for 15 more ($105 - 90$) than in the spot market. The combination of the proceeds from the sale of the underlying and the value of the short forward at maturity is always 105 ($=$

90 + 15 or 110 − 5), which is precisely the amount necessary to pay off the loan. So, there is zero net cash flow at expiration under any and all circumstances. Since this transaction has no risk (no uncertainty about value at time T), we require that the no-arbitrage forward price (F_0) is simply the future value of the underlying growing at the risk-free rate, or

$$F_0 = \text{Future value of underlying} = FV(S_0). \tag{1}$$

In our example, $F_0 = FV(S_0) = 105$. In fact, with annual compounding and $T = 1$, we have simply $F_0 = S_0(1 + r)^T = 100(1 + 0.05)^1$. The future value refers to the amount of money equal to the spot price invested at the compounded risk-free interest rate during the time period. It is not to be confused with or mistaken for the mathematical expectation of the spot price at time T.

Without market frictions, arbitrage may be possible when mispricing occurs. To better understand the arbitrage mechanics, suppose that $F_0 = 106$. Based on the prior information, we observe that the forward price is higher than the price suggested by the carry arbitrage model—recall $F_0 = FV(S_0) = 105$. Because the carry arbitrage model value is lower than the market's forward price, we conclude that the market's forward price is too high and should be sold. An arbitrage opportunity exists, and it will involve selling the forward contract at 106 (Step 1). Step 2 occurs when a second transaction is needed to borrow funds to undertake Step 3, purchase of the underlying instrument so that gains (or losses) in the underlying will offset losses (or gains) on the forward contract. Note, the second step ensures the arbitrageur does not use his or her own money. The third transaction, the purchase of the underlying security, guarantees the arbitrageur does not take any market price risk. Note that all three transactions are done simultaneously. To summarize, the arbitrage transactions for $F_0 > FV(S_0)$ can be represented in the following three steps:

Step 1   Sell the forward contract on the underlying.

Step 2   Borrow the funds to purchase the underlying.

Step 3   Purchase the underlying.

Exhibit 6 shows the resulting cash flows from these transactions. This strategy is known as carry arbitrage because we are carrying—that is, we are long—the underlying instrument. At time T, we earn an arbitrage profit of +1. We do not use any of our own money and make a profit no matter the price of the underlying at maturity (i.e., 110, 90, or anything else). Since the profit of +1 at maturity occurs under every circumstance, it is considered risk-free. Any situation that allows a risk-free profit with no upfront cost will not be available for very long. It represents a clear arbitrage opportunity, one that will be pursued until forward prices fall and eliminate the arbitrage opportunity.

Note that if the forward price, F_0, were 106, the value of the forward contract at time 0 would be the PV of the +1 cash flow at Time T. Thus, at time 0, the value of our short forward is $V_0 = PV[F_0 − FV(S_0)] = (106 − 105)/(1 + 0.05)^1 = 0.9524$.

Exhibit 6: Cash Flow with Forward Price Greater Than Carry Arbitrage Model Price

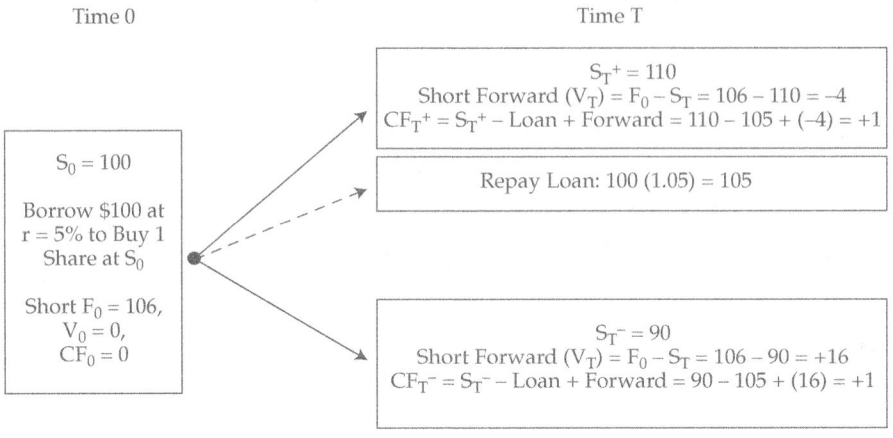

Suppose instead we observe a lower forward price, $F_0 = 104$. Based on the prior information, we conclude that the forward price is too low when compared to the forward price determined by the carry arbitrage model of $F_0 = FV(S_0) = 105$. Since the forward price is too low, Step 1 is to buy the forward contract, and the value at T is $S_T - F_0$. The arbitrageur does not want any price risk, so Step 2 is to sell short the underlying instrument. To accomplish Step 2, we must borrow the asset and sell it. Note that when an arbitrageur needs to sell the underlying, it must be assumed that he/she does not hold it in inventory and thus must sell it short. If the underlying were held in inventory, the investment in it would not be accounted for in the analysis. When the transaction calls for selling a derivative instrument, such as a forward contract, it is always just selling—technically, not short selling.

The long forward contract will allow us to cover our short later. The arbitrageur will then lend the short sale proceeds of 100 at the risk-free rate (Step 3). The deposit of 100 will grow to 105 at time T. Clearly, we will have a profit of +1 when we buy the asset at 104 and deliver it to clear the short. Again, to summarize, the arbitrage transactions when the forward price is too low—that is, $F_0 < FV(S_0)$—involve the following three steps:

Step 1   Buy the forward contract on the underlying.

Step 2   Sell the underlying short.

Step 3   Lend the short sale proceeds.

We must replace the asset at a price of S_T, but we have +105 from the loan and a long forward at 104. Remember, the value of a long forward at time T is $V_T = S_T - F_0$. So, using the prior information, the value of the forward at expiration will be $90 - 104 = -14$ (if $S_T^- = 90$) or $110 - 104 = +6$ (if $S_T^+ = 110$). Thus, the cash flows at maturity will be $CF^- = +105 - 14 - 90 = +1$ or $CF^+ = +105 + 6 - 110 = +1$. Again, we make a profit equal to the mispricing of +1 regardless of the stock value at time T. It is an arbitrage profit, since it was done with no money invested and with no risk.

Note that this set of transactions is the exact opposite of the prior case in Exhibit 6. This strategy is known as **reverse carry arbitrage** because we are doing the opposite of carrying the underlying instrument; that is, we are selling short the underlying instrument.

Therefore, unless $F_0 = FV(S_0)$, there is an arbitrage opportunity. Notice that if $F_0 > FV(S_0)$, then the forward contract is sold and the underlying is purchased. Thus, arbitrageurs drive down the forward price and drive up the underlying price until $F_0 = FV(S_0)$ and a risk-free positive cash flow today (i.e., in PV terms) no longer exists. Further, if $F_0 < FV(S_0)$, then the forward contract is purchased and the underlying is sold short. In this case, the forward price is driven up and the underlying price is driven down. Absent market frictions, arbitrageurs' market activities will drive forward prices to equal the future value of the underlying, bringing the law of one price into effect once again. Most importantly, if the forward contract is priced at its equilibrium price, there will be no arbitrage profit.

EXAMPLE 1

Forward Contract Price

An Australian stock paying no dividends is trading in Australian dollars for A\$63.31, and the annual Australian interest rate is 2.75% with annual compounding.

1. Based on the current stock price and the no-arbitrage approach, which of the following values is *closest* to the equilibrium three-month forward price?

    A. A\$63.31

    B. A\$63.74

    C. A\$65.05

Solution:

B is correct. Based on the information given, S_0 = A\$63.31, r = 2.75% (annual compounding), and T = 0.25. Therefore,

$$F_0 = FV(S_0) = 63.31(1 + 0.0275)^{0.25} = A\$63.7408.$$

2. If the interest rate immediately falls 50 bps to 2.25%, the three-month forward price will:

    A. decrease.

    B. increase.

    C. be unchanged.

Solution:

A is correct, because the forward price is directly related to the interest rate. Specifically,

$$F_0 = FV(S_0) = 63.31(1 + 0.0225)^{0.25} = A\$63.6632.$$

Therefore, we see in this case that a decrease in interest rates resulted in a decrease in the forward price. This relationship between forward prices and interest rates will generally hold so long as the underlying is not also influenced by interest rates.

As we see in Example 1, the quoted forward price does not directly reflect expectations of future underlying prices. The only factors that matter are the current price (S_0), the interest rate and time to expiration, and, of course, the absence of arbitrage. Other factors will be included later as we make the carry arbitrage model more realistic, but we will not be including expectations of future underlying prices. So, if we can carry the asset, an opinion that the underlying will increase in value, perhaps even substantially, has no bearing on the forward price.

We now turn to the task of understanding the value of an existing forward contract. There are many circumstances in which, once a forward contract has been entered, one wants to know the contract's fair value. The goal is to calculate the position's value at current market prices. The need may arise from market-based accounting, for example, in which the accounting statements need to reflect the current fair value of various instruments. Finally, it is simply important to know whether a position in a forward contract is making money or losing money (that is, the profit or loss from exiting the contract early).

The forward value prior to maturity is based on arbitrage. A timeline to help illustrate forward valuation is shown in Exhibit 7. Suppose the first transaction involves buying a forward contract with a price of F_0 at Time 0 with expiration at Time T. Now consider selling a new forward contract with price F_t at Time t, again with expiration at Time T. Exhibit 7 shows the potential cash flows. Remember the equivalence at expiration between the forward price, the futures price, and the underlying price will hold: $F_T = f_T = S_T$. Note that the middle of the timeline, "Time t" is the valuation date of the forward contract. Note also that we are seeking the forward value; therefore, this set of transactions would result in cash flows only if it is executed. We need not actually execute the transactions; we just need to see what they would produce if we did. This point is analogous to the fact that if we are holding a liquid asset, we need not sell it to determine its value; we can simply observe its market price, which gives us an estimate of the price at which we could sell the asset.

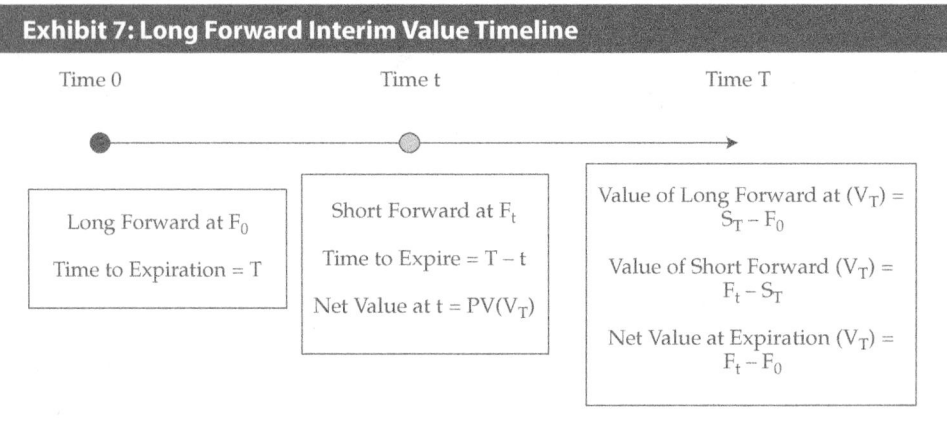

Exhibit 7: Long Forward Interim Value Timeline

Time 0

Long Forward at F_0

Time to Expiration = T

Time t

Short Forward at F_t

Time to Expire = T – t

Net Value at t = $PV(V_T)$

Time T

Value of Long Forward at $(V_T) =$
$S_T – F_0$

Value of Short Forward $(V_T) =$
$F_t – S_T$

Net Value at Expiration $(V_T) =$
$F_t – F_0$

Importantly, there are now three different points in time to consider: Time 0, Time t, and Time T. Note that once the offsetting forward is entered at time t, the net position is not subject to market risk. That is, the S_T terms cancel (in Exhibit 7), so the cash flow at Time T is not influenced by what happens to the spot price. The position is completely hedged. Therefore, the value observed at Time t of the original forward contract initiated at Time 0 and expiring at Time T is simply the present value of the difference in the forward prices, $PV(F_t – F_0)$, at Time t. To be clear, the PV discounts the time T cash flow at the risk-free rate, r, to Time t. Equation 2 shows the long forward value at time t under annual compounding.

Value of Long Forward Contract Prior to Maturity (Time t) =

V_t (long) = Present value of the difference in forward prices:

$$V_t = PV\left[F_t - F_0\right] = \frac{[F_t - F_0]}{(1+r)^{T-t}} \tag{2}$$

where F_t is the current forward price and F_0 is the initial forward price.

Alternatively,

$$V_t = S_t - PV[F_0] = S_t - \frac{F_0}{(1+r)^{T-t}}. \tag{3}$$

Equation 3 can be derived from Equation 2. Assuming annual compounding,

$$F_t = S_t(1+r)^{(T-t)}, \text{ so } PV[F_t] = PV[S_t(1+r)^{(T-t)}]$$

$$= S_t(1+r)^{(T-t)} / (1+r)^{(T-t)} = S_t.$$

While both are correct, Equation 2 may be useful in cases when market frictions may cause the observed forward price, F_t, to differ slightly from the correct arbitrage-free price. Equation 3 may be more intuitive and has the advantage that the spot price, S_t, may be more readily observed than the forward price, F_t.

As in Equation 2, the long forward contract value can be viewed as the present value, determined using the given interest rate, of the difference in forward prices—the initial one and the new one that is priced at the point of valuation. If we know the underlying price at Time t, S_t, we can estimate the forward price, $F_t = FV(S_t)$, and we can then solve for the forward value as in Equation 2.

The interim valuation of a short forward contract is determined in a similar fashion. The short position value is also the present value of differences in forward prices and simply the negative of the long position value. So that,

Value of short forward contract prior to maturity (Time t) = $-V_t$

$$-V_t = PV\left[F_0 - F_t\right] = \frac{[F_0 - F_t]}{(1+r)^{T-t}},$$

or alternatively,

$$= PV\left[F_0\right] - S_t = \frac{F_0}{(1+r)^{T-t}} - S_t$$

EXAMPLE 2

Forward Contract Value

1. Assume that at Time 0 we entered into a one-year long forward contract with price $F_0 = 105$. Nine months later, at Time t = 0.75, the observed price of the underlying stock is $S_{0.75} = 110$ and the interest rate is 5%. The value of the existing forward contract expiring in three months will be *closest* to:

   A. −6.34.

   B. 6.27.

   C. 6.34.

Solution:

B is correct. Note that, $S_{0.75} = 110$, r = 5%, and T − t = 0.25.

Therefore, the three-month forward price at Time t is equal to $F_t = FV(S_t) = 110(1 + 0.05)^{0.25} = 111.3499$.

Based on $F_0 = 105$, we find that the value of the existing forward entered at Time 0 and valued at Time t using the difference method (Equation 2) is:

$$V_t = PV[F_t - F_0] = (111.3499 - 105)/(1 + 0.05)^{0.25} = 6.2729.$$

Alternatively, using Equation 3 we have,

$$V_t = S_t - PV[F_0] = 110 - [105/(1 + 0.05)^{0.25}] = 6.2729.$$

Now that we have the basics of forward pricing and forward valuation, we introduce some other realistic carrying costs that influence pricing and valuation.

Carry Arbitrage Model When Underlying Has Cash Flows

We have seen that forward pricing and valuation are driven by arbitrageurs seeking to exploit mispricing by either carrying or reverse carrying the underlying instrument. Carry arbitrage, when $F_0 > FV(S_0)$, requires paying the interest cost from borrowing to fund purchase of the underlying, whereas reverse carry arbitrage, when $F_0 < FV(S_0)$, results in receiving the interest benefit from lending the proceeds from short-selling the underlying. For many instruments, there are other significant carry costs and benefits. We will now incorporate into forward pricing various costs and benefits related to the underlying instrument. For this reason, we need to introduce some notation.

Let CB denote the **carry benefits**: cash flows the owner might receive for holding the underlying assets (e.g., dividends, foreign currency interest, and bond coupon payments). Let CB_T denote the future value of underlying carry benefits at time T and CB_0 denote the present value at time 0 of underlying carry benefits. Let CC denote the **carry costs**. For financial instruments, carry costs are essentially zero. For commodities, however, carrying costs include such factors as waste, storage, and insurance. Let CC_T denote the future value of underlying carry costs at time T and CC_0 denote the present value of underlying carry costs at time 0. We do not cover commodities in this reading, but you should be aware of these costs. Moreover, you should note that carry costs are similar to financing costs. Holding a financial asset does not generate direct carry costs, but it does result in the opportunity cost of the interest that could be earned on the money tied up in carrying the spot asset. Remember, the financing costs at the risk-free rate are included in the calculation of $F_0 = FV[S_0]$. Other carrying costs that are common to physical assets (such as storage and insurance) are equivalent concepts. For example, to buy and hold gold, money is taken out of the bank (opportunity cost = r, the risk-free rate) to purchase the asset, and money must be paid to store and insure it. The cost to finance the spot asset purchase, the cost to store it, and any benefits that may result from holding the asset will all play a part in determination of the forward price.

The key forward pricing equation can be expressed as:

F_0 = Future value of the underlying adjusted for carry cash flows

$$= FV[S_0 + CC_0 - CB_0] \tag{4}$$

Equation 4 relates the forward price of an asset to the spot price by considering the cost of carry. It is sometimes referred to as the **cost of carry model** or future-spot parity. Carry costs and a positive rate of interest increase the burden of carrying the underlying instrument through time; hence, these costs are added in the forward pricing equation. Conversely, carry benefits decrease the burden of carrying the underlying instrument through time; hence, these benefits are subtracted in the forward pricing equation.

Based on Equation 4, $F_0 = FV(S_0 + CC_0 - CB_0)$, if there are no explicit carry costs ($CC_0 = 0$) as with many financial assets, then we have:

$$F_0 = FV(S_0) - FV(CB_0) = FV(S_0) - FV(\text{Benefits}).$$

For a stock paying a dividend (D), a benefit, prior to maturity of the forward contract, we have the forward contract price (F_0):

$$F_0 = FV(S_0 - PV(D)) = FV(S_0) - FV(D).$$

In words, the initial forward price (F_0) is equal to the future value of carrying the underlying (S_0) minus the future value of any ownership benefits, (FV(D)), for a dividend paying stock, prior to expiration. Note the FV computation for the stock price will likely use a different time period than the FV computation for the dividends. This is because the dividend FV is only compounded from the time the dividend is collected until the expiration of the forward contract. So, FV(PV(D)) for a dividend collected at time t and held to expiration at time T would be $FV(PV(D)) = FV(D/(1 + r)^t) = (1 + r)^T \times [(D/(1 + r)^t) = D(1 + r)^{T-t}$. The calculation of F_0 for a dividend paying stock is illustrated in Example 3.

EXAMPLE 3

Forward Contract Price with Underlying Cash Flows

A US stock paying a $10 dividend in two months is trading at $1,000. Assume the US interest rate is 5% with annual compounding.

---

1. Based on the current stock price and the no-arbitrage approach, which of the following values is *closest* to the equilibrium three-month forward price?

   A. $1,002.23

   B. $1,022.40

   C. $1,025.31

Solution:

A is correct. Based on the information given, we know $S_0 = \$1,000$, r = 5% (annual compounding), and T = 0.25. After 2 months, we will receive the benefit of a $10 dividend, which earns interest for 1 month. Therefore,

$$F_0 = FV(S_0) - FV(D) = 1{,}000(1 + 0.05)^{3/12} - 10(1 + 0.05)^{1/12}$$

$$= \$1{,}012.2722 - \$10.0407 = \$1{,}002.2315.$$

Using Equation 4, we could have arrived at the same result. Here $CC_0 = 0$, and CB_0 is the PV of the dividend at time 0 = $10/(1 + 0.05)^{2/12} = \$9.919$. Then,

$$F_0 = FV(S_0 + CC_0 - CB_0) = FV(1{,}000 + 0 - 9.919)$$

$$= (990.081) \times (1 + 0.05)^{3/12} = \$1{,}002.23.$$

---

2. If the dividend is instead paid in one month, the three-month forward price will:

   A. decrease.

   B. increase.

   C. be unchanged.

Solution:

A is correct. The benefit of the dividend occurs one month earlier, so we can collect interest for one additional month. The future value of the dividend would be slightly higher. So, the forward price would decrease slightly,

$$F_0 = FV(S_0) - FV(D) = 1,000(1 + 0.05)^{3/12} - 10(1 + 0.05)^{2/12}$$

$$= \$1,012.2722 - \$10.0816 = \$1,002.1906.$$

The value for a long forward position when the underlying has carry benefits or carry costs is found in the same way as described previously except that the new forward price (F_t), as well as the initial one (F_0), are adjusted to account for these benefits and costs. Specifically,

V_t = Present value of the difference in forward prices adjusted for carry benefits and costs

$$= PV[F_t - F_0].$$

This equation is Equation 2. The forward value is equal to the present value of the difference in forward prices. The PV discounts the risk-free cash flow [$F_t - F_0$] at time T to time t. The benefits and costs are reflected in this valuation equation because they are incorporated into the forward prices, where $F_t = FV(S_t + CC_t - CB_t)$ and $F_0 = FV(S_0 + CC_0 - CB_0)$. Again, the forward value is simply the present value of the difference in forward prices.

EXAMPLE 4

Forward Contract Price with Carry Costs and Benefits

1. A long one-year forward contract on a productive asset was entered at a forward price of ₵1,000. Now, seven months later, the underlying asset is selling for ₵1,050. The PV of the cost to store, insure, and maintain the asset for the next 5 months is ₵4.00, and the asset will generate income over the next 5 months with a PV of ₵28.00. Assume annual compounding for all costs and benefits and a risk-free rate of 2%.

   Based on the current spot price and the no-arbitrage approach, which of the following values is *closest* to the equilibrium five-month forward value?

   A. ₵34.22

   B. ₵33.50

   C. ₵35.94

Solution:

A is correct. Based on the information given, we know the following: F_0 = 1,000, S_t = 1,050, CC_t = 4, CB_t = 28, t = 7 months, T − t = 5 months, and r = 2%. The new forward price is $F_t = FV(S_t + CC_t - CB_t)$. So, with annual compounding, we have:

$$F_t = (1,050 + 4 - 28)(1 + 0.02)^{5/12} = ₵1,034.50 \text{ and}$$

$$V_t = PV[F_t - F_0) = [₵1,034.50 - ₵1000]/(1 + 0.02)^{5/12} = ₵34.22.$$

Now let us consider stock indexes, such as the EURO STOXX 50 or the US Russell 3000. With stock indexes, it is difficult to account for the numerous dividend payments paid by underlying stocks that vary in timing and amount. A **dividend index point** is a measure of the quantity of dividends attributable to a particular index. It is a useful measure of the amount of dividends paid, a very useful number for arbitrage trading. To simplify the problem, a continuous dividend yield is often assumed. This means it is assumed that dividends accrue continuously over the period in question rather than on specific discrete dates, which is not an unreasonable assumption for an index with a large number of component stocks.

The focus of the carry arbitrage model with continuous compounding is again the future value of the underlying adjusted for carry costs and benefits and can be expressed as:

$$F_0 = S_0 \exp^{(r_c+CC-CB)\,T} \tag{5}$$

(Future value of the underlying adjusted for carry).

Note that in this context, r_c, CC, and CB are continuously compounded rates.

The carry arbitrage model can also be used when the underlying asset requires storage costs, needs to be insured, and suffers from spoilage. In these cases, rather than lowering the carrying burden, these costs make it more expensive to carry and hence the forward price is higher. We now apply these results to equity forward and futures contracts.

PRICING EQUITY FORWARDS AND FUTURES

3

☐ describe how equity forwards and futures are priced, and calculate and interpret their no-arbitrage value

☐ describe how interest rate forwards and futures are priced, and calculate and interpret their no-arbitrage value

We now apply the concepts of arbitrage-free pricing and valuation to the specific types of forward and futures contracts typically used in investment management. We cover, in turn, equity, interest rate, fixed income, and currency forwards and futures. In doing so, we take account of the cash flows generated by the underlying (e.g., dividends, bond coupon payments, foreign currency interest) and the unique features of each of these contracts.

Equity Forward and Futures Contracts

Although we alluded to equity forward pricing and valuation in the last section, we will now illustrate with concrete examples the application of carry arbitrage models to equity forward and futures contracts. Remember that here we assume that forward contracts and futures contracts are priced in the same way. Additionally, remember that it is vital to treat the compounding convention of interest rates appropriately.

If the underlying is a stock, then the carry benefit is the dividend payments as illustrated in the next two examples.

EXAMPLE 5

Equity Futures Contract Price with Continuously Compounded Interest Rates

1. The continuously compounded dividend yield on the EURO STOXX 50 is 3%, and the current stock index level is 3,500. The continuously compounded annual interest rate is 0.15%. Based on the carry arbitrage model, the three-month futures price will be *closest* to:

   A. 3,473.85.

   B. 3,475.15.

   C. 3,525.03.

Solution:

B is correct. Based on the carry arbitrage model (see Equation 4), the futures price is

$$f_0 = S_0 \exp^{(r_c + CC - CB)\,T}.$$

We assume the carry costs (CC) are 0 for a financial asset, such as a stock index. The carry benefit (CB), in this case a 3% continuous dividend yield, is greater than the financing cost r_c (0.15%), so the futures price will be below the spot price. The futures price, the future value of the underlying adjusted for carry (i.e., the dividend payments, over the next 3-months) is:

$$f_0 = 3{,}500 \exp^{(0.0015 + 0 - 0.03)(3/12)} = 3{,}475.15.$$

EXAMPLE 6

Equity Forward Pricing and Forward Valuation with Discrete Dividends

1. Suppose Nestlé common stock is trading for CHF70 and pays a CHF2.20 dividend in one month. Further, assume the Swiss one-month risk-free rate is 1.0%, quoted on an annual compounding basis. Assume that the stock goes ex-dividend the same day the single stock forward contract expires. Thus, the single stock forward contract expires in one month.

   The one-month forward price for Nestlé common stock will be *closest* to:

   A. CHF66.80.

   B. CHF67.86.

   C. CHF69.94.

Solution:

B is correct. In this case, we have $S_0 = 70$, $r = 1.0\%$, $T = 1/12$, and $FV(CB_0) = 2.20 = CB_T$. Therefore,

$$F_0 = FV(S_0 + CC_0 - CB_0) = FV(S_0) + FV(CC_0) - FV(CB_0)$$

$$= 70(1 + 0.01)^{1/12} + 0 - 2.20 = CHF67.86.$$

As shown in Equation 2a, the value of a forward contract is simply the present value (discounted from time T to time t) of the difference in the initial forward price and the current forward price, that is V_t (long) = $PV[F_t - F_0]$. We will employ this basic principal to value various forward and swap contracts. Here, we find the current value (at time t) of an equity forward contract initially entered at time 0. To reiterate, the value prior to expiration is the present value of the difference in the initial equity forward price and the current equity forward price as illustrated in the next example.

EXAMPLE 7

Equity Forward Valuation

Suppose we bought a one-year forward contract at 102, and there are now three months to expiration. The underlying is currently trading for 110, and interest rates are 5% on an annual compounding basis.

Suppose that instead of buying a forward contract, we buy a one-year *futures* contract at 102 and there are now three months to expiration. Today's futures price is 112.35. There are no other carry cash flows.

1. If there are no other carry cash flows, the forward value of the existing contract will be *closest* to:

   A. −10.00.

   B. 9.24.

   C. 10.35.

Solution:

B is correct. For this case, we have $F_0 = 102$, $S_{0.75} = 110$, r = 5%, and T − t = 0.25. Note that the new forward price at t is simply $F_t = FV(S_t) = 110(1 + 0.05)^{0.25} = 111.3499$. Therefore, from Equation 2a we have:

$$V_t = PV[F_t - F_0] = (111.3499 - 102)/(1 + 0.05)^{0.25} = 9.2366, \text{ or}$$

alternatively, using Equation 2b,

$$V_t = S_t - PV[F_0] = 110 - 102/(1 + 0.05)^{0.25} = 9.2366.$$

Thus, we see that the current forward value is greater than the difference between the current underlying price of 110 and the initial forward price of 102 due to interest costs resulting in the new forward price being 111.35.

2. If a dividend payment is announced between the forward's valuation and expiration dates, assuming the news announcement does not change the current underlying price, the forward value will *most likely*:

   A. decrease.

   B. increase.

   C. be the same.

Solution:

A is correct. The old forward price is fixed. The discounted difference in the new forward price and the old forward price is the value. If we impose a new dividend, it would lower the new forward price and thus lower the value of the old forward contract.

3. After marking to market, the futures value of the existing contract will be *closest* to:

   A. −10.35.

   B. 0.00.

   C. 10.35.

Solution:

B is correct. Futures contracts are marked to market daily, which implies that the market value, resulting in profits and losses, is received or paid at each daily settlement. Hence, the equity futures value is zero each day after settlement has occurred.

We turn now to the widely used interest rate forward and futures contracts.

Interest Rate Forward and Futures Contracts

Historically, the most widely used interest rate that served as the underlying for many derivative instruments was Libor, the London Interbank Offered Rate. In 2008, financial regulators and many market participants began to suspect that the daily quoted Libor rates, which were compiled by the British Bankers Association, were being manipulated by certain banks. The manipulation of Libor by some participants resulted in its replacement by a new market reference rate (MRR) in 2021. Replacements for Libor as the MRR include SOFR (Secured Overnight Financing Rate), determined by the Federal Reserve Bank of New York and SONIA (Sterling Overnight Index Average), administered by the Bank of England. We use the generic term MRR for these and other Libor replacements.

Currently, there are active forward and futures markets for derivatives based on MRR. We will use the symbol L_m to represent our spot MRR. Our focus will be on forward markets, as represented by forward rate agreements. In order to understand the forward market, however, let us first look at the MRR spot market.

Assume the following notation:

L_m = MRR spot rate (set at time t = 0) for an m-day deposit

NA = notional amount, quantity of funds initially deposited

NTD = number of total days in a year, used for interest calculations (360 in the MRR market)

t_m = accrual period, fraction of year for an m-day deposit—t_m = m/NTD = m/360 (for the MRR market)

TA = terminal amount, quantity of funds repaid when the MRR deposit is withdrawn

For example, suppose we are considering a 90-day Eurodollar deposit (m = 90). Dollar MRR is quoted at 2%; thus, L_{90} = 0.02. If \$50,000 is initially deposited, then NA = \$50,000. MRR is stated on an actual over 360-day count basis (often denoted ACT/360) with interest paid on an add-on basis. Add-on basis is the convention in the MRR market. The idea is that the interest is added on at the end—in contrast, for example, to the discount basis, in which the current price is discounted based on the amount paid at maturity. Hence, t_m = 90/360 = 0.25. Accordingly, the terminal amount can be expressed as:

TA = NA × $[1 + L_m t_m]$, and the interest paid is TA − NA = NA × $[L_m t_m]$.

In this example, TA = \$50,000 × [1 + 0.02(90/360)] = \$50,250 and the interest is \$50,250 − \$50,000 = \$250.

Now let us turn to the forward market for MRR. A **forward rate agreement** (FRA) is an over-the-counter (OTC) forward contract in which the underlying is an interest rate on a deposit. An FRA involves two counterparties: the fixed-rate payer (long), who is also the floating-rate receiver, and the fixed-rate receiver (short), who is also the floating-rate payer. Thus, a fixed-payer (long) FRA will profit when the MRR rises. If the floating rate is above the rate in the forward agreement, the long position can be viewed as having the benefit of borrowing at below market rates. The long will receive a payment. A long FRA would be well suited for a firm planning to borrow in the future and wishing to hedge against rising rates. A fixed-receiver (short) FRA might be a bank or financial institution hoping to lock in a fixed lending rate in the future. The fixed receiver, as the name implies, receives an interest payment based on a fixed rate and makes an interest payment based on a floating rate. If we are the fixed receiver, then it is understood without saying that we also are the floating payer, and vice versa. Because there is no initial exchange of cash flows, to eliminate arbitrage opportunities, the FRA price is the fixed interest rate such that the FRA value is zero on the initiation date.

FRAs are identified in the form of "X × Y," where X and Y are months and the multiplication symbol, ×, is read as "by." To grasp this concept and the notion of exactly what is the underlying in an FRA, consider a 3 × 9 FRA, which is pronounced "3 by 9." The 3 indicates that the FRA expires in three months. After three months, we determine the FRA payoff based on an underlying rate. The underlying is implied by the difference in the 3 and the 9. That is, the payoff of the FRA is determined by a six-month (180-day) MRR when the FRA expires in three months. The notation 3 × 9 is market convention, though it can seem confusing at first. The rate on the FRA will be determined by the relationship between the spot rate on a nine-month MRR deposit and the spot rate on a three-month MRR deposit when the FRA is initiated. A long FRA will effectively replicate going long a nine-month MRR deposit and short a three-month MRR deposit. Note that although market convention quotes the time periods as months, the calculations use days based on the assumption of 30 days in a month.

The contract established between the two counterparties settles in cash the difference between a fixed interest payment established on the initiation date and a floating interest payment established on the FRA expiration date. The underlying of an FRA is neither a financial asset nor even a financial instrument; it is just an interest payment. It is also important to understand that the parties to an FRA are not necessarily engaged in a MRR deposit in the spot market. The MRR spot market is simply the benchmark from which the payoff of the FRA is determined. Although a party may use an FRA in conjunction with a MRR deposit, it does not have to do so any more than a party that uses a forward or futures on a stock index has to have a position in the stock index.

In Exhibit 8, we illustrate the key time points in an FRA transaction. The FRA is created and priced at Time 0, the initiation date, and expires h days later. The underlying instrument has m days to maturity as of the FRA expiration date. Thus, the FRA payoff is based on the spot m-day MRR observed in h days from FRA initiation. We can only observe spot market reference rates. To price the FRA, we require two spot rates: L_h, which takes us to the expiration of the FRA, and L_T, which takes us to the underlying maturity.

The FRA helps hedge single period interest rate risk for an m-day period beginning h days in the future. After the initial FRA rate (FRA_0) is established, we may also wish to determine a value for our FRA at a later date (Time g). As the MRR changes, our interest rate agreement may take on a positive or negative value.

Exhibit 8: Important FRA Dates, Expressed in Days from Initiation

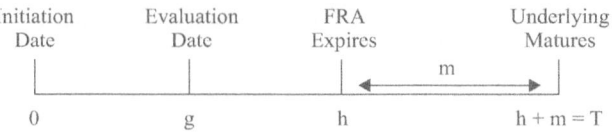

Using the notation in Exhibit 8, let FRA_0 denote the fixed forward rate set at Time 0 that expires at Time h wherein the underlying MRR deposit has m days to maturity at expiration of the FRA. Thus, the rate set at initiation of a contract expiring in 30 days in which the underlying is a 90-day MRR, denoted as a 1 x 4 FRA, will be such a number as 1% or 2.5%. Like all standard forward contracts, no money changes hands when an FRA is initiated, so our objective is to price the FRA, meaning to determine the fixed rate (FRA_0), such that the value of the FRA contract is zero on the initiation date.

When any interest rate derivative expires, there are technically two ways to settle at expiration: "advanced set, settled in arrears" and "advanced set, advanced settled." It is important to note that FRAs are typically settled based on "advanced set, advanced settled," whereas swaps and interest rate options are normally based on "advanced set, settled in arrears." Let us look at both approaches, because they are both used in the interest rate derivatives markets.

In the earlier example of a MRR deposit of $50,000 for 90 days at 2%, the rate was set when the money was deposited, and interest accrued over the life of the deposit. A payment of $50,250 (interest of $250 + principal of $50,000) was made at maturity, 90 days later. Here the term **advanced set** is used because the reference interest rate is set at the time the money is deposited. The advanced set convention is almost always used because most issuers and buyers of financial instruments want to know the rate on the instrument while they have a position in it.

In an FRA, the term "advanced" refers to the fact that the interest rate is set at Time h, the FRA expiration date, which is the time the underlying deposit starts. The term **settled in arrears** is used when the interest payment is made at Time h + m, the maturity of the underlying instrument. Thus, an FRA with advanced set, settled in arrears works the same way as a typical bank deposit as described in the previous example. At Time h, the interest rate is set at L_m, and the interest payment is made at Time T (h + m). Alternatively, when **advanced settled** is used, the settlement is made at Time h. Thus, in an FRA with the advanced set, advanced settled feature, the FRA expires and settles at the same time. Importantly, advanced set, advanced settled is almost always used in FRAs; although we will see advanced set, settled in arrears when we cover interest rate swaps, and it is also used in interest rate options. From this point forward in this discussion, all FRAs will be advanced set, advanced settled, as they are in practice.

The settlement amounts for advanced set, advanced settled are discounted in the following manner:

Settlement amount at h for receive-floating (Long):

$$NA \times \{[L_m - FRA_0] t_m\}/[1 + D_m t_m].$$

Again, the FRA is a forward contract on interest rates; long FRA (floating receiver) wins when rates increase. Note the floating rate (MRR perhaps, L_m) is received and thus has a positive sign. Since floating is received, the fixed rate (FRA_0) is paid (outflow). The FRA rate (fixed at t = 0 for the period m, which runs from time h to time T) is an outflow for the long and has a negative sign. For receive fixed (short), the FRA rate is an inflow and the floating rate L_m is an outflow.

Settlement amount at h for receive-fixed (Short):

$$NA \times \{[FRA_0 - L_m]\, t_m\}/[1 + D_m t_m].$$

The divisor, $1 + D_m t_m$, is a discount factor applied to the FRA payoff. It reflects the fact that the rate on which the payoff is determined, L_m, is obtained on day h from the spot market (advanced set), which uses settled in arrears. The discount factor is, therefore, appropriately applied to the FRA payment because the payment is received in advance, not in arrears. That is, the FRA payment is made early (advanced settled), but the interest on the loan is not due until later (settled in arrears). So, the settlement amount at time h is discounted to account for the fact that interest can be earned for m days on the advanced payment. Often it is assumed at time h that $D_m = L_m$, and we will commonly do so here, but it can be different.

Again, it is important to not be confused by the role played by an MRR spot market in an FRA. In the MRR spot market, deposits are made by various parties that are lending to banks. These rates are used as the benchmark for determining the payoffs of FRAs. The two parties to an FRA do not necessarily engage in any MRR spot transactions. Again, MRR spot deposits are settled in arrears, whereas FRA payoffs are settled in advance—hence the discounting.

EXAMPLE 8

Calculating Interest on MRR Spot and FRA Payments

In 30 days, a UK company expects to make a bank deposit of £10,000,000 for a period of 90 days at 90-day MRR set 30 days from today. The company is concerned about a possible decrease in interest rates. Its financial adviser suggests that it negotiate today a 1 × 4 FRA, an instrument that expires in 30 days and is based on 90-day MRR. The company enters a £10,000,000 notional amount 1 × 4 receive-fixed FRA that is advanced set, advanced settled (note the company is the short-side of this FRA contract). The appropriate discount rate for the FRA settlement cash flows is 2.40%. After 30 days, 90-day MRR in British pounds is 2.55%.

---

1. The interest actually paid at maturity on the UK company's bank deposit will be *closest* to:

   A. £60,000.

   B. £63,750.

   C. £67,500.

Solution:

B is correct. This is a simple deposit of £10,000,000 for 90 days at the prevailing 90-day MRR. Since m = 90, we use L_{90} = 2.55%. Therefore, TA = 10,000,000 × [1 + 0.0255(0.25)] = £10,063,750. So, the interest paid at maturity is £63,750.

---

2. If the FRA was initially priced so that FRA_0 = 2.60%, the payment received to settle it will be *closest* to:

   A. −£2,485.08.

   B. £1,242.54.

   C. £1,250.00.

Solution:

B is correct. In this example, m = 90 (number of days in the deposit), t_m = 90/360 (fraction of year until deposit matures observed at the FRA expiration date), and h = 30 (number of days initially in the FRA). The settlement amount of the 1×4 FRA at h for receive-fixed (the short) is:

$$NA \times \{[FRA_0 - L_m]t_m\}/[1 + D_m t_m]$$

$$= 10,000,000 \times \{[0.0260 - 0.0255](0.25)\}/[1 + 0.0240(0.25)]$$

$$= £1,242.54.$$ Since the short FRA involves paying floating, the short benefited from a decline in rates. Note D_m does not equal L_m in this example.

3. If the FRA was initially priced so that $FRA_0 = 2.50\%$, the payment received to settle it will be *closest* to:

    A. −£1,242.54.

    B. £1,242.54.

    C. £1,250.00.

Solution:

A is correct. The data are similar to those in the previous question, but the initial FRA rate is now 2.50% and not 2.60%. Thus, the settlement amount of the 1×4 FRA at time h for receive-fixed (the short) is:

$$NA \times \{[FRA_0 - L_m]t_m\}/[1 + D_m t_m]$$

$$= 10,000,000 \times \{[0.0250 - 0.0255](0.25)\}/[1 + 0.0240(0.25)]$$

$$= -£1,242.54.$$

The short-side in the FRA suffered from a rise in rates because it is paying floating.

At this point, we highlight a few key concepts about FRAs and how to price and value them:

1. An FRA is a forward contract on interest rates. The long side of the FRA, fixed-rate payer (floating-rate receiver), incurs a gain when rates increase and incurs a loss when rates decrease. Conversely, the short side of the FRA, fixed-rate receiver (floating-rate payer), incurs a loss when rates increase and incurs a gain when rates decrease.

2. The FRA price, FRA_0, is the implied forward rate for the period beginning when the FRA expires to the underlying loan maturity. So, we require two spot rates to determine the initial forward rate. Therefore, pricing an FRA is like pricing a forward contract.

3. Although the interest on the underlying loan will not be paid until the end of the loan, the payoff on the FRA will occur at the expiration of the FRA (advanced settled). Therefore, the payoff of an FRA is discounted back to the expiration of the FRA.

As noted in point 2, the FRA price is the implied forward rate for the period beginning when the FRA expires at time h and running m days to the underlying loan maturity at time T. It is similar to any other forward contract. We wish to identify the appropriate FRA_0 rate that makes the value of the FRA equal to zero on the initiation date. The concept used to derive FRA_0 can be understood through a simple example.

Recall that with simple interest, a one-period forward rate is found by solving the expression $[1 + y(1)] [1 + F(1)] = [1 + y(2)]^2$, where $y(1)$ denotes the one-period yield to maturity and $y(2)$ the two-period yield to maturity. F denotes the forward rate in the next period. We can observe the spot rates $y(1)$ and $y(2)$. The forward rate is implied from those two rates. Borrowing or lending along the 2-year path must cost the same as borrowing or lending along the path using the 1-year spot and the 1-year forward. The solution for $F(1)$ is simply $F(1) = ([1 + y(2)]^2/[1 + y(1)]) - 1$. Assume the one-year spot rate is 3% and the two-year spot rate is 4%. To prevent arbitrage, $F(1) = ([1 + 0.04]^2/[1 + 0.03]) - 1 = 0.0501$. If the forward rate was not 5.01%, an arbitrageur could make a risk-free profit through borrowing along one path and lending along another.

As depicted in Exhibit 9, the rate for an FRA is computed in the same manner. We derive the forward rate (or FRA rate, FRA_0) from two spot rates (such as MRR): the longer rate L_T and the shorter rate L_h. Borrowing or lending at L_T for T days should cost the same as borrowing or lending for h days at L_h and subsequently borrowing or lending for m days at FRA_0.

Exhibit 9: FRA Rates from Spot Market Reference Rate (MRR = MRR)

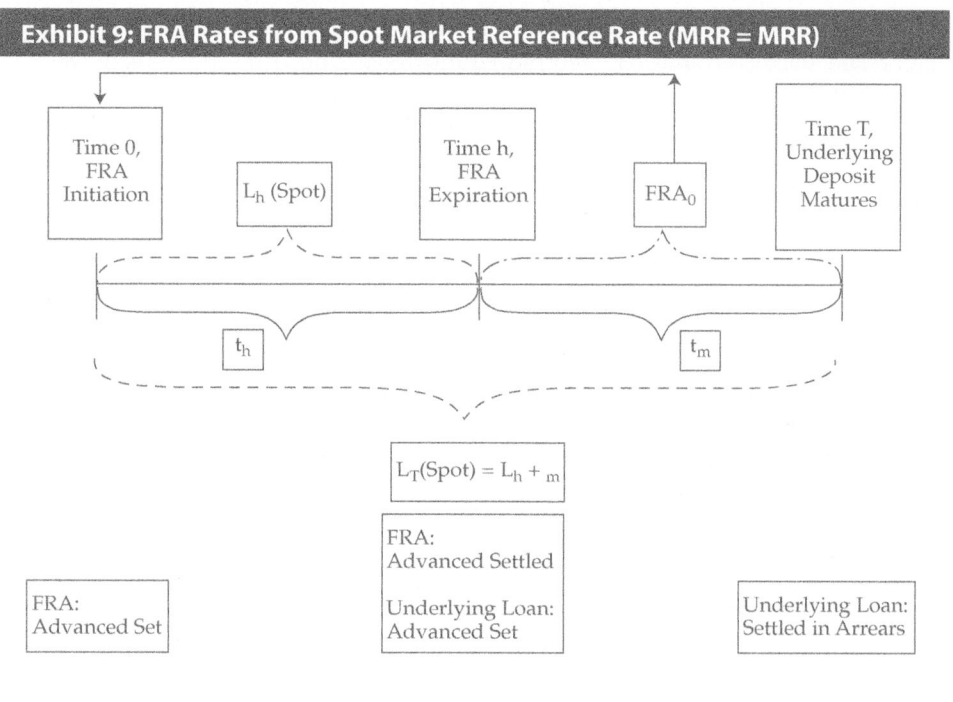

We can solve for the FRA rate by considering that the two paths must be equal to prevent arbitrage or:

$$[1 + L_h t_h][1 + FRA_0 t_m] = [1 + L_T t_T].$$

The solution in annualized form is shown in Equation 6:

$$FRA_0 = \{[1 + L_T t_T]/[1 + L_h t_h] - 1\}/t_m. \tag{6}$$

The result is the forward rate in the term structure.

So, if 180-day MRR is 2.0% and 90-day MRR is 1.5%, then the price of a 3 × 6 FRA would be:

$$FRA_0 = \{[1 + L_T t_{180}]/[1 + L_h t_{90}] - 1\}/t_{90}$$

$$= \{[1 + 0.02(180/360)]/[1 + 0.015(90/360)] - 1\}/(90/360)$$

$$= 0.024907 \text{ or } 2.49\%.$$

This result can be compared with the result from a simple approximation technique. Note that for this FRA, 90 is half of 180. Thus, we can use a simple arithmetic average equation—here, $(1/2)1.5\% + (1/2)X = 2.0\%$—and solve for the missing variable X: X

= 2.5%. Knowing this approximation will always be biased slightly high, we know we are looking for an answer that is a little less than 2.5%. This is a helpful way to check your final answer.

EXAMPLE 9

FRA Fixed Rate

Now consider the following information for problems 2 and 3.

Assume a 30/360-day count convention and the following spot rates:

1-Month USD MRR is 2.48%, 3-Month USD MRR is 2.58%, 6-Month USD MRR is 2.62%, and 1-Year USD MRR is 2.72%.

---

1. Based on market quotes on Canadian dollar (C$) MRR, the six-month C$ MRR and the nine-month C$ MRR rates are presently at 1.5% and 1.75%, respectively. Assume a 30/360-day count convention. The 6 × 9 FRA fixed rate (FRA_0) will be *closest* to:

   A. 2.00%.

   B. 2.23%.

   C. 2.25%.

Solution:

B is correct. Based on the information given, we know $L_{180} = 1.50\%$ and $L_{270} = 1.75\%$. The 6 × 9 FRA rate is thus:

$$FRA_0 = \{[1 + L_T t_T]/[1 + L_h t_h] - 1\}/t_m$$

$$FRA_0 = \{[1 + 0.0175(270/360)]/[1 + 0.015(180/360)] - 1\}/(90/360)$$

$$FRA_0 = [(1.013125/1.0075) - 1]/(0.25) = 0.022333, \text{ or } 2.23\%.$$

---

2. Given these four spot rates in the MRR term structure, how many FRA rates can be calculated?

   A. 4 FRA rates

   B. 6 FRA rates

   C. 12 FRA rates

Solution:

B is correct. Based on the four MRR spot rates given, we can compute six separate FRA rates as follows: 1 × 3, 1 × 6, 1 × 12, 3 × 6, 3 × 12, and 6 × 12 FRA rates.

---

3. The 1 × 3 FRA fixed rate will be *closest* to:

   A. 2.43%.

   B. 2.53%.

   C. 2.62%.

Solution:

C is correct. Based on the information given, we know $L_{30} = 2.48\%$ and $L_{90} = 2.58\%$. The 1×3 FRA rate is thus:

$$FRA_0 = \{[1 + L_T t_T]/[1 + L_h t_h] - 1\}/t_m$$

$$FRA_0 = \{[1 + 0.0258(90/360)]/[1 + 0.0248(30/360)] - 1\}/(60/360)$$

$$FRA_0 = [(1.00645/1.00207) - 1]/(0.1667) = 0.026220, \text{ or } 2.62\%.$$

We can now value an existing FRA (with rate FRA_0) using the same general approach as we did with the forward contracts previously covered. Specifically, we can enter into an offsetting transaction at the new rate that would be set on an FRA that expires at the same time as our original FRA. By taking the opposite position, the new FRA offsets the old one. That is, if we are long the old FRA, we will pay fixed and receive the floating rate L_m at h. We can go short a new FRA and receive fixed (with rate FRA_g) that will obligate us to pay L_m at h.

Consider the following strategy. Let us assume that we initiate an FRA that expires in 90 days and is based on 90-day MRR (so, a 3×6 FRA). The fixed rate at initiation $FRA_0 = 2.49\%$ and $t_m = 90/360$. We are long the FRA, so we will pay the fixed rate of 2.49% and receive floating MRR. Having entered the long FRA, we wish to value our position 30 days later, at Time g, when there are 60 days remaining in the life of the FRA (note that this is now a 2×5 FRA, as one month has passed since FRA initiation). Assume, at this point, the rate on an FRA based on 90-day MRR that expires in 60 days (FRA_g) is 2.59%. Remember, the original FRA has a fixed rate set at 2.49% when it was initiated. Now, 30 days later, a new offsetting FRA can be created at 2.59%. To value the original FRA (at Time g), we short a new FRA that will receive fixed at 2.59% and pay floating MRR at time h. Effectively, we are now receiving fixed at 2.59% and paying fixed at 2.49%. The value of the offset position is 10 bps times (90/360), as follows, times the notional amount, which is then discounted to back to Time g:

10 bps: $FRA_g - FRA_0 = 2.59\% - 2.49\% = 0.10\%$

90/360: $t_m = m/NTD$, as L_m is the 90-day MRR rate underlying both FRAs

Because the cash flows at T are now known with certainty at g, this offsetting transaction at Time g has eliminated any floating-rate risk at Time T. That is, we had a long FRA at time 0 and added a short FRA at time g. Since the notional amounts and times to maturity of the offsetting transaction are the same, the floating portion of the FRA cash flows (L_m) at time T will exactly cancel, $[L_m - FRA_0] + [FRA_g - L_m] = [FRA_g - FRA_0]$.

Our task, however, is to determine the fair value of the original FRA at Time g. Therefore, we need the present value of this Time T cash flow at Time g. That is, the value of the original FRA is the PV of the difference in the new FRA rate and the old FRA rate times the notional amount. Specifically, we let V_g be the value at Time g of the original FRA that was initiated at Time 0, expires at Time h, and is based on m-day MRR, L_m. Note that discounting will be over the period $T - g$. With D_{T-g} as the discount rate and NA as the notional amount. So,

Long FRA value at Time g: $V_g =$

$$NA \times \{[FRA_g - FRA_0] t_m\}/[1 + D_{(T-g)} t_{(T-g)}]. \tag{7}$$

Thus, the Time g value of the receive-floating FRA initiated at Time 0 (V_g) is just the present value of the difference in FRA rates, one entered at Time g and one entered at Time 0. Traditionally, it is assumed that the discount rate, D_m, is equal to the underlying floating rate, L_m, but that is not necessary. Note that here it is $D_{(T-g)}$.

The value of a receive-fixed or short FRA at time g is the negative of the long value ($-V_g$), so we have: $-V_g = -1 \times (NA \times \{[FRA_g - FRA_0]\, t_m\}/[1 + D_{(T-g)}\, t_{(T-g)}])$.

Short FRA value at Time g =

$$NA \times \{[FRA_0 - FRA_g]\, t_m\}/[1 + D_{(T-g)}\, t_{(T-g)}] \tag{8}$$

EXAMPLE 10

FRA Valuation

1. Suppose we entered a receive-floating (long) 6×9 FRA with Canadian dollar notional amount of C\$10,000,000 at Time 0. The six-month spot C\$ MRR was 0.628%, and the nine-month C\$ MRR was 0.712%. Also, assume the 6×9 FRA rate is quoted in the market at 0.877%. After 90 days have passed, the three-month C\$ MRR is 1.25% and the six-month C\$ MRR is 1.35%, which we will use as the discount rate to determine the value at g.

   Assuming the appropriate discount rate is C\$ MRR, the value of the original receive-floating 6×9 FRA will be *closest* to:

   A. C\$14,105.

   B. C\$14,200.

   C. C\$14,625.

Solution:

A is correct. Initially, we have $L_{180} = 0.628\%$, $L_{270} = 0.712\%$, and $FRA_0 = 0.877\%$.

After 90 days (g = 90), we have $L_{90} = 1.25\%$ and $L_{180} = 1.35\%$. Interest rates rose during this period; hence, the FRA has gained value because the position is receive-floating. First, we compute the new FRA rate at Time g and then estimate the fair FRA value as the discounted difference in the new and old FRA rates. The new FRA rate at Time g, denoted FRA_g, is the rate on an FRA expiring in 90 days in which the underlying is 90-day C\$ MRR (so, a 3 x 6 FRA). That rate is found using Equation 6. The shorter spot rate is now for h − g (180 − 90 = 90) days, which is the new time until both FRAs expire. The reference spot rate for the underlying maturity is now in T − g (270 − 90 = 180) days.

$FRA_g = \{[1 + L_{180}\, t_{(T-g)}]/[1 + L_{90}\, t_{(h-g)}] - 1\}/t_m$,

T − g = 180 days and h − g = 90 days, so we have:

$FRA_g = \{[1 + L_{180}\,(180/360)]/[1 + L_{90}\,(90/360)] - 1\}/(90/360)$.

Substituting the values given in this problem, we find:

$FRA_g = \{[1 + 0.0135\,(180/360)]/[1 + 0.0125\,(90/360)] - 1\}/(90/360) = [(1.006750/1.003125) - 1]/0.25$

$= 0.014455$, or 1.445%.

Therefore, using Equation 7, we have:

$V_g = 10,000,000 \times \{[0.01445 - 0.00877]\,(90/360)\}/[1 + 0.0135\,(180/360)]$

$= 14,105$.

We now turn to the specific features of various forward and futures markets. The same general principles will apply, but the specifics will be different.

PRICING FIXED-INCOME FORWARD AND FUTURES CONTRACTS

4

☐ | describe how fixed-income forwards and futures are priced, and calculate and interpret their no-arbitrage value

Fixed-income forward and futures contracts have several unique issues that influence the specifics of the carry arbitrage model. First, in some countries the prices of fixed-income securities (termed "bonds" here) are quoted without the interest that has accrued since the last coupon date. The quoted price is sometimes known as the clean price. Naturally when buying a bond, one must pay the full price, which is sometimes called the dirty price, so the accrued interest is included. Nonetheless, it is necessary to understand how the quoted bond price and accrued interest compose the true bond price and the effect this convention has on derivatives pricing. The quotation convention for futures contracts, whether based on clean or dirty prices, usually corresponds to the quotation convention in the respective bond market. In this section, we will largely treat forwards and futures the same, except in certain places where noted.

In general, accrued interest is computed based on the following linear interpolation formula:

Accrued interest = Accrual period × Periodic coupon amount, or

$$AI = (NAD/NTD) \times (C/n),$$

where NAD denotes the number of accrued days since the last coupon payment, NTD denotes the number of total days during the coupon payment period, n denotes the number of coupon payments per year (commonly n = 2 for semi-annual), and C is the stated annual coupon amount. For example, after two months (60 days), a 3% semi-annual coupon bond with par of 1,000 would have accrued interest of $AI = (60/180) \times (30/2) = 5$. Note that accrued interest is expressed in currency units (not percent), and the number of total days (NTD) depends on the coupon payment frequency. As in the example, semi-annual indicates coupons are paid twice per year, so with 360 days per year, NTD = 360/2= 180.

Second, fixed-income futures contracts often have more than one bond that can be delivered by the seller. Because bonds trade at different prices based on maturity and stated coupon, a mathematical adjustment to the amount required when settling a futures contract, known as the conversion factor (CF), is used to make all deliverable bonds approximately equal in price. According to the Chicago Mercantile Exchange, "A conversion factor is the approximate decimal price at which $1 par of a security would trade if it had a six percent yield-to-maturity." So, the CF adjusts each bond to an equivalent 6% coupon bond (i.e., benchmark bond). Other exchanges use different conversion factors, and these are illustrated later in the text and examples.

Third, when multiple bonds can be delivered for a particular futures contract, a cheapest-to-deliver bond typically emerges after adjusting for the conversion factor. The conversion factor adjustment, however, is not precise. Thus, if there are several candidates for delivery, the bond that will be delivered is the one that is least expensive for the seller to purchase in the open market to settle the obligation.

For bond markets in which the quoted price includes the accrued interest and in which futures or forward prices assume accrued interest is in the bond price quote, the futures or forward price simply conforms to the general formula we have previously discussed. Recall that the futures or forward price is simply the future value of the underlying in which finance costs, carry costs, and carry benefits are all incorporated, or

F_0 = Future value of underlying adjusted for carry cash flows

$= FV(S_0 + CC_0 - CB_0).$

Let Time 0 be the forward contract trade initiation date and Time T be the forward contract expiration date, as shown in Exhibit 10. For the fixed-income bond, let Y denote the time to maturity of the bond at Time T, when the forward contract expires. Therefore, T + Y denotes the underlying instrument's current (Time 0) time to maturity. Let B_0 denote the quoted bond price observed at Time 0 of a fixed-rate bond that matures at Time T + Y and pays a fixed coupon rate.

Exhibit 10: Timeline for Bond Futures and Forwards

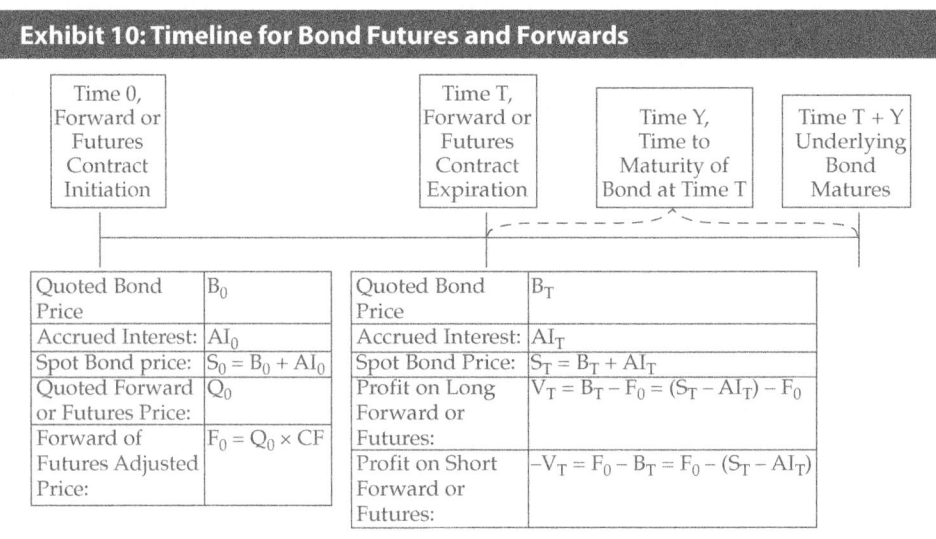

For bonds quoted without accrued interest, let AI_0 denote the accrued interest at Time 0. The carry benefits are the bond's fixed coupon payments, so $CB_0 = PVCI$, meaning the present value of all coupon interest (CI) paid over the forward contract horizon from Time 0 to Time T. The corresponding future value of these coupons paid over the contract horizon to time T is $CB_T = FVCI$. Finally, there are no carry costs, and thus $CC = 0$. To be consistent with prior notation, we have:

S_0 = Quoted bond price + Accrued interest = $B_0 + AI_0$.

We could just insert this price (S_0) into the previous equation, letting $CB_0 = PVCI$, and thereby obtain the futures price the straightforward and traditional way. But fixed-income futures contracts often permit delivery of more than one bond and use the conversion factor system to provide this flexibility. In these markets, the futures price, F_0, is defined as the quoted futures price, Q_0, times the conversion factor, CF. Note that in this section, we will use the letter F to denote either the quoted forward price or the futures price times the conversion factor. In fact, the futures contract settles against the quoted bond price *without* accrued interest. Thus, as shown in Exhibit 10, the total profit or loss on a long position in fixed-income futures at expiration (Time T) is the quoted bond price minus the initial futures price or:

$v_T = B_T - F_0$. Moreover, based on our notation, we can also say,

$v_T = (S_T - AI_T) - F_0$.

The fixed-income forward or futures price including the conversion factor, termed the "adjusted price," can be expressed as:

$F_0 = Q_0 \times CF$

= FV of underlying adjusted for carry cash flows from Times 0 to T

$= FV[S_0 + CC_0 - CB_0] = FV[S_0 + 0 - PVCI] = FV[B_0 + AI_0 - PVCI].$ (9)

In other words, the actual futures price is F_0, but in the market the availability of multiple deliverable bonds gives rise to the adjustment factor. Hence, the price you would see quoted is Q_0, where $Q_0 = F_0/CF$.

Recall that the bracketed term $B_0 + AI_0 - PVCI$ in Equation 9 is just the full spot price S_0 minus the present value of the coupons over the life of the forward or futures contract. The fixed-income forward or futures price (F_0) is thus the future value of the quoted bond price plus accrued interest less any coupon payments made during the life of the contract. Again, the quoted bond price plus the accrued interest is the spot price: It is in fact the price you would have to pay to buy the bond. Market conventions in some countries just happen to break this price out into the quoted price plus the accrued interest.

Why Equation 9 must hold is best understood by illustrating what happens when the futures price is not in equilibrium. In fact, in the following scenario, the futures are overpriced relative to the bond, giving rise to an arbitrage opportunity.

Assume we observe a 3-month forward contract, so T = 0.25, on a bond that expires at some time in the future, T + Y, and this bond is currently quoted (B_0) at 107% of par. There are no coupon payments for this bond over the life of the forward contract, so PVCI = 0.0. Other pertinent details of the bond and futures are presented in Exhibit 11.

Exhibit 11: Bond and Futures Information for Illustrating Disequilibrium and Arbitrage Opportunity

Bond		
Quoted Bond Price	B_0	107.00
PV of Coupon Interest	PVCI	0
Accrued Interest at Time 0	AI_0	0.07
Accrued Interest at Time T	AI_T	0.20
Futures		
Quoted Futures Price	Q_0	135.00
Conversion Factor	CF	0.80
Adjusted Futures Price	$F_0 \ (= Q_0 \times CF)$	108.00
Interest Rate		
For Discounting/Compounding	r	0.20%

We observe that the full spot price of the bond is:

$S_0 = B_0 + AI_0 = 107 + 0.07 = 107.07$.

The futures price (F_0), which is the future value adjusted for carry cash flows (using Equation 9), is:

$F_0 = FV[B_0 + AI_0 - PVCI] = (107 + 0.07 - 0)(1.002)^{0.25} = 107.12$.

Note that the adjusted futures price using the quoted futures price ($Q_0 = 135$) and the conversion factor ($CF = 0.80$) is $F_0 = 108$. Adding the accrued interest at expiration ($AI_T = 0.20$) to the adjusted futures price gives 108.20. Remember, if you are selling a bond you receive the accrued interest; if you are buying a bond you pay the accrued interest. The adjusted futures price plus accrued interest should equal the future value of the full bond price adjusted for any carry cash flows given by Equation 9. Here, the adjusted futures price (including accrued interest) is 108.20, while the cost to buy and carry the bonds is 107.12. This implies that the futures contract is overpriced by $(108.2 - 107.12) = 1.08$, thus there is an arbitrage opportunity. In this case, we would simultaneously: 1) sell the overpriced futures contract; 2) borrow funds to purchase the bonds; and 3) buy the underpriced deliverable bonds.

So, to capture the 1.08 with no risk, an arbitrageur might wish to buy this bond and carry it and short the futures contract at 108. At maturity, the arbitrageur simply delivers the bond to cover the futures contract and repays the loan. Arbitrage should allow for the capture of any over (or under) pricing. Selling the futures contract at 108 involves no initial cash flow. The short futures locks in a sale price of $108 + 0.2 = 108.20$ for the bond just purchased for 107.07. Since there are no carry benefits, it costs the arbitrageur 107.12, $= FV(107.07) = (107.07)(1 + 0.002)^{0.25}$, to carry the bond to expiration. The result is a risk-free profit at expiration of 1.08, $= 108.00 + 0.2 - 107.12$, for which the Time 0 PV is 1.0795, $= 1.08(1.002)^{-0.25}$.

The value of the Time 0 cash flows should be zero to prevent an arbitrage opportunity. This example shows the arbitrage profit as a 1.0795 cash flow at Time 0 or 1.08 at time T per bond. If the value had been negative—meaning the full bond price exceeded the adjusted future price plus accrued interest—then the arbitrageur would conduct the reverse carry arbitrage of short selling the bond, lending the proceeds, and buying the futures (termed reverse carry arbitrage because the underlying is not carried but is sold short).

In equilibrium, the adjusted futures price of the bond plus any accrued interest must equal the cost of buying and holding the spot bond until time T. That is, to eliminate an arbitrage opportunity:

$$F_0 + AI_T = FV[B_0 + AI_0 - PVCI], \text{ which implies, } F_0 = FV(S_0) - AI_T - FVCI.$$

In this example, equilibrium is not met. The adjusted futures price, $F_0 = 108$, promises a profit of $(108 - 106.92) = 1.08$ at expiration, since

$$FV(S_0) - AI_T - FVCI = 107.12 - 0.2 - 0 = 106.92.$$

For clarity, substituting for F_0 and S_0 and solving for the quoted futures price (Q_0) results in Equation 10, the conversion factor adjusted futures price (i.e., quoted futures price):

$$Q_0 = [1/CF] \{FV [B_0 + AI_0] - AI_T - FVCI\} \tag{10}$$

In this example we have,

$$Q_0 = [1/CF] \{FV[B_0 + AI_0] - AI_T - FVCI\}$$

$$= (1/0.8) \{(1 + 0.002)^{0.25}(107 + 0.07) - 0.20 - 0.0\} = 133.65.$$

Recall, a futures price of 135 was used as the quoted price, Q_0 (108 was the adjusted futures price). Any quoted futures price higher than the equilibrium futures price of 133.65 (106.92 adjusted) will present arbitrage opportunities; hence, the arbitrage transaction of selling the futures contract resulted in a riskless positive cash flow.

EXAMPLE 11

Estimating the Euro-Bund Futures Price

1. Euro-bund futures have a contract value of €100,000, and the underlying consists of long-term German debt instruments with 8.5 to 10.5 years to maturity. They are traded on the Eurex. Suppose the underlying 2% coupon (semi-annual payment) German bund is quoted at €108 and has accrued interest of €0.083 (15 days since last coupon paid). The euro-bund futures contract matures in one month (30 days). At contract expiration, the underlying bund will have accrued interest of €0.25; there are no coupon payments due until after the futures contract expires; and the current one-month risk-free rate is 0.1%. The conversion factor is 0.729535.

   In this case, we have the following:

   $T = 1/12$, $CF = 0.729535$, $B_0 = 108$, $FVCI = 0$, $AI_0 = (15/180 \times 2\%/2) = €0.083$, $AI_T = (45/180 \times 2\%/2) = €0.25$, and r

   $= 0.1\%$.

   The equilibrium euro-bund quoted futures price (Q_0) based on the carry arbitrage model will be *closest* to:

   A. €147.57.

   B. €147.82.

   C. €148.15.

Solution:

B is correct. The carry arbitrage model for forwards and futures is simply the future value of the underlying with adjustments for unique carry features. With bond futures, the unique features include the conversion factor, accrued interest, and any coupon payments. Thus, the equilibrium euro-bund futures price can be found using the carry arbitrage model (Equation 10):

$Q_0 = [1/CF]\{FV[B_0 + AI_0] - AI_T - FVCI\}$.

Thus, we have:

$Q_0 = [1/0.729535][(1 + 0.001)^{1/12}(108 + 0.083) - 0.25 - 0] = 147.82$.

Note that the same result can be found by $Q_0 = F_0/CF$, where:

$F_0 = FV(S_0) - AI_T - FVCI = (1 + 0.001)^{1/12}(108 + 0.083) - 0.25 - 0 = 107.84$.

In equilibrium, the quoted euro-bund futures price should be approximately €147.82 based on the carry arbitrage model.

Because of the mark-to-market settlement procedure, the value of a bond future is essentially the price change since the previous day's settlement. That value is captured at the settlement at the end of the day, at which time the value of the bond futures contract, like other futures contracts, resets to zero.

We now turn to the task of estimating the fair value of the bond forward contract at a point in time during its life. Without daily settlement, the value of a forward is not formally realized until expiration. Suppose the first transaction is buying (at Time 0) an at-market bond forward contract priced at F_0 with expiration of Time T. Later (at Time t) consider selling a new bond forward contract priced at F_t, again with expiration of Time T. At the maturity of the forward contracts, we take delivery of the bond under the long forward and use it to make delivery under the short forward. Assuming the same underlying, there is no price risk. The net cash flow at maturity is the difference in the price at which we sold, F_t, and the price we agreed to pay, F_0, or $(F_t - F_0)$. To confirm the price risk on the underlying bond is zero, we could also add the values of the long and the short forward positions at expiration $V_{Long} + V_{Short} = (B_T - F_0) + (F_t - B_T) = F_t - F_0$. Since the position is riskless, the value to the long at time t should be:

V_t = Present value of difference in forward prices at time t = PV $[F_t - F_0]$.

As a simple example of bond forward contract valuation, assume that two forward contracts have been entered as follows: long forward at F_0 = 119.12 and short forward at F_t = 119.92. Time t is one month before expiration, and both forward contracts expire at Time T. Therefore, time to expiration in one-month is T − t = 1/12. Finally, assume the appropriate interest rate for discounting is r = 0.5%.

The forward value observed at Time t for the Time T maturity bond forward contracts is simply the present value of the difference in their forward prices —denoted $PV_{t,T}$ $(F_t - F_0)$. That is, we have:

$V_t = (119.92 - 119.12)/(1 + 0.005)^{1/12} = 0.7997$.

EXAMPLE 12

Estimating the Value of a Euro-Bund Forward Position

1. Suppose that one month ago, we purchased *five* euro-bund forward contracts with two months to expiration and a contract notional value of €100,000 each at a price of 145 (quoted as a percentage of par). The euro-bund forward contract now has one month to expiration. The current annualized one-month risk-free rate is 0.1%. Based on the current forward price of 148, the value of the euro-bund forward position will be *closest* to:

   A. €2,190.

   B. €14,998.

   C. €15,012.

Solution:

B is correct. Because we are given both forward prices, the solution is simply the present value of the difference in forward prices at expiration.

$V_t = PV[F_t - F_0] = (148 - 145)/(1 + 0.001)^{1/12} = 2.99975$.

This is 2.9997 per €100 par value because this forward price was quoted as a percentage of par. Because five contracts each with €100,000 par were entered, we have 0.029997(€100,000)5 = €14,998.75. Note that when interest rates are low and the forward contract has a short maturity, then the present value effect is minimal (about €1.25 in this example).

We conclude this section with some observations on the similarities and differences between forward and futures contracts.

Comparing Forward and Futures Contracts

For every market considered here, the carry arbitrage model provides an approach for both pricing and valuing forward contracts. Recall the two generic expressions:

$F_0 = FV(S_0 + CC_0 - CB_0)$ (Forward pricing)

$V_t = PV[F_t - F_0]$ (Forward valuation)

Carry costs (CC) and financing costs increase the forward price, and carry benefits (CB) decrease the forward price. The arbitrageur is carrying the underlying, and costs increase the burden whereas benefits decrease the burden. The forward value can be expressed as either the present value of the difference in forward prices or as a function of the current underlying price adjusted for carry cash flows and the present value of the initial forward price.

Futures prices are generally found using the same model, but futures values are different because of the daily marking to market. Recall that the futures values are zero at the end of each trading day because profits and losses are taken daily.

In summary, the carry arbitrage model provides a compelling way to price and value forward and futures contracts. Stated concisely, the forward or futures price is simply the future value of the underlying adjusted for any carry cash flows. The forward value is simply the present value of the difference in forward prices at an intermediate time in the contract. The futures value is zero after marking to market. We turn now to pricing and valuing swaps.

PRICING AND VALUING SWAP CONTRACTS   5

☐ describe how interest rate swaps are priced, and calculate and interpret their no-arbitrage value

Based on the foundational concepts we have studied on using the carry arbitrage model for pricing and valuing forward and futures contracts, we now apply this approach to pricing and valuing swap contracts.

A swap contract is an agreement to exchange (or swap) a series of cash flows at certain periodic dates. For example, an interest rate swap might exchange quarterly cash flows based on a floating rate for those based on a fixed rate. An interest rate swap is like an FRA except that it hedges multiperiod interest-rate risk, whereas an FRA only hedges single-period interest-rate risk. Similarly, in a currency swap the counterparties agree to exchange two series of interest payments, each denominated in a different currency, with the exchange of principal payments at inception and at maturity. Swap contracts can be synthetically created as either a portfolio of underlying instruments (such as bonds) or a portfolio of forward contracts (such as FRAs). Swaps are most easily understood as a portfolio of underlying bonds, so we will follow that approach.

Cash flows from a generic receive-floating and pay-fixed interest rate swap are shown in Exhibit 12. The cash flows are determined by multiplying a specified notional amount by a (fixed or floating) reference rate. In a fixed-for-floating interest rate swap (i.e., pay-fixed, receive-floating, also known as a plain vanilla swap), the fixed-rate payer in the swap would make a series of payments based on a fixed rate of interest applied to the notional amount. The counterparty would receive their fixed payments in return for making payments based on a floating rate applied to the same notional amount. The floating rate used as a reference will be referred to as the market reference rate (MRR). In our examples, we will use the MRR.

Exhibit 12: Generic Swap Cash Flows: Pay-Fixed, Receive-Floating

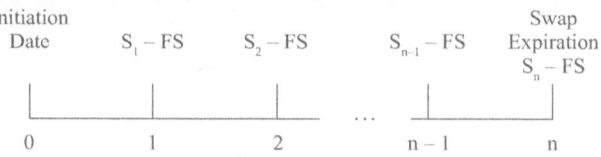

Our generic swap involves a series of n future cash flows at points in time represented simply here as 1, 2, ..., n. Let S_i denote the floating interest rate cash flow based on some underlying, and let FS denote the cash flow based on some fixed interest rate. Notice how the cash flows are netted. If the floating rate S_i increases above the agreed fixed rate FS, so $S_i > FS$, the fixed-rate payer (i.e., floating-rate receiver) will receive positive cash flow. If rates fall, so $S_i < FS$, the fixed-rate receiver (i.e., floating-rate payer) will receive the positive cash flow. We assume that the last cash flow occurs at the swap expiration. Later we will let S_i denote the floating cash flows tied to currency movements or equity movements.

We again will rely on the arbitrage approach for determining the pricing of a swap. This procedure involves finding the fixed rate such that the value of the swap at initiation is zero. Recall that the goal of the arbitrageur is to generate positive cash flows with no risk and no investment of one's own capital. To understand swap valuation, we match the swap cash flows by synthetically creating a replicating portfolio from other instruments. The swap must have the same value as the synthetic portfolio, or arbitrage will result. A pay-fixed, receive-floating swap is equivalent to a short position (i.e., issuer) in a fixed-rate bond and a long position (i.e., investor) in a floating-rate bond. Assuming both bonds were initially priced at par, the initial cash flows are zero and the par payments at maturity offset each other. In other words, the **swap rate** is the rate at which the present value of all the expected floating-rate payments received over the life of the floating-rate bond equal the present value of all the expected fixed-rate payments made over the life of the fixed-rate bond. Thus, the fixed bond payment should be equivalent to the fixed swap payment. Exhibit 13 shows the view of a swap as a pair of bonds. Note that the coupon dates on the bonds match the settlement dates on the swap, and the maturity date matches the expiration date of the swap. As with all derivative instruments, numerous technical details have been simplified here. We will explore some of these details shortly.

Exhibit 13: Receive-Floating, Pay-Fixed as a Portfolio of Bonds

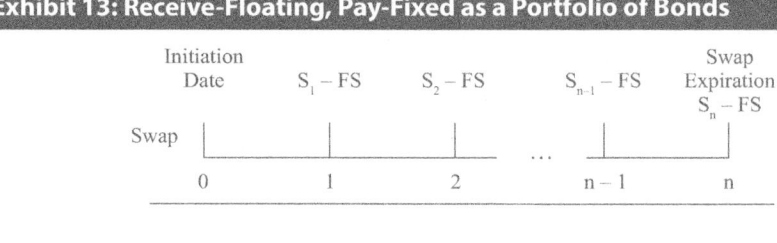

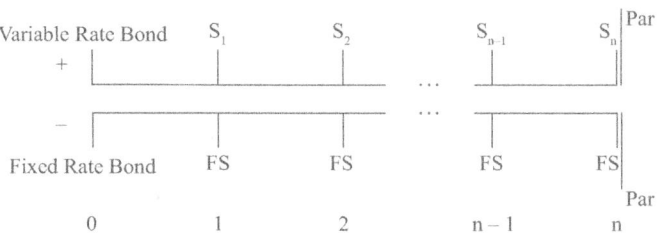

It is worth noting that our replicating portfolio did not need to use a pair of bonds. Swaps can also be viewed as a portfolio of forward or futures contracts. However, in practice futures have standardized characteristics, so there is rarely a set of futures contracts that can perfectly replicate a swap. In addition, because a single forward contract can be viewed as a portfolio of a call and a put (a long call and a short put at the same strike price equal to the swap's fixed rate would replicate the payoffs on a pay-fixed swap), a swap can also be viewed as a portfolio of options. The procedure is fairly straightforward in all cases. Just match the swap cash flows with the cash flows from a portfolio of marketable underlying instruments and rely on the law of one price and the absence of arbitrage to provide a value. Again, bonds are perhaps the best instruments to replicate a swap because they are easy to value.

Market participants often use swaps to transform one series of cash flows into another. For example, suppose that because of the relative ease of issuance, REB, Inc. sells a fixed-rate bond to investors. Based on careful analysis of the interest rate sensitivity of the company's assets, REB's leadership deems a MRR-based variable rate bond to be a more appropriate liability. By entering a receive-fixed, pay-floating interest rate swap, REB can create a synthetic floating-rate bond, as illustrated in Exhibit 15. REB issues fixed-rate bonds and thus must make periodic fixed-rate-based payments to the bond investors, denoted FIX. REB then enters a receive-fixed (FIX) and pay-floating (FLT) interest rate swap. The two fixed-rate payments cancel, leaving on net the floating-rate payments. Thus, we say that REB has created a synthetic floating-rate bond.

Exhibit 14: REB's Synthetic Floating-Rate Bond Based on Fixed-Rate Bond Issuance with Receive-Fixed Swap

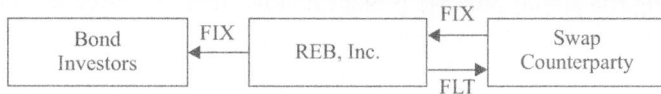

The example in Exhibit 14 is for a swap in which the underlying is an interest rate.

There are also currency swaps and equity swaps. Currency swaps can be used in a similar fashion, but the risks being addressed are both interest rate and currency exposures. Equity swaps can also be used in a similar fashion, but the risk being addressed is equity exposure.

Swaps have several technical nuances that can have a significant influence on pricing and valuation. Differences in payment frequency and day count methods often have a material impact on pricing and valuation. Another issue is identifying the appropriate discount rate to apply to the future cash flows. We turn now to examining three types of swap contracts—interest rate, currency, and equity—with a focus on pricing and valuation.

Interest Rate Swap Contracts

In this section we will focus on the pricing and valuing of interest rate swap contracts. Our approach will view a swap as a pair of bonds, a long position in one bond and a short position in another bond. At inception of a fixed-for-floating swap, a fixed rate is selected so that the present value of the floating-rate payments is equal to the present value of the fixed-rate payments, meaning the swap value is zero for both parties at inception. The fixed rate (FS) is the swap rate. Determining the swap rate is equivalent to pricing the swap. As the market rates change and time passes over the term of the swap, the value of the swap changes. The swap value (the value of the two constituent bonds) can be positive (an asset) or negative (a liability) to the pay-fixed or receive-fixed swap holders.

Swaps are OTC products with many variations. For example, a plain vanilla MRR-based interest rate swap can involve different frequencies of cash flow settlements and day count conventions. In fact, a swap can have both semi-annual payments and quarterly payments as well as actual day counts and day counts based on 30 days per month. Unless stated otherwise, we will assume for simplicity that the notional amounts are all equal to one (NA = 1). Swap values per 1 notional amount can be simply multiplied by the actual notional amount to arrive at the swap's fair market value.

Interest rate swaps have two legs, typically a floating leg (FLT) and a fixed leg (FIX). The floating leg cash flow—denoted S_i because the rate ($r_{FLT,i}$) may change (or float) during each period i—can be expressed as:

$$S_i = AP_{FLT} \times r_{FLT,i} = (NAD_{FLT}/NTD_{FLT}) \times r_{FLT,i}$$

and the fixed leg cash flow (denoted FS) can be expressed as:

$$FS = AP_{FIX} \times r_{FIX} = (NAD_{FIX}/NTD_{FIX}) \times r_{FIX}.$$

AP denotes the accrual period, $r_{FLT,i}$ denotes the observed annual floating rate appropriate for Time i, NAD denotes the number of accrued days during the payment period, NTD denotes the total number of days during the year applicable to each cash flow, and r_{FIX} denotes the fixed annual swap rate. The accrual period accounts for the payment frequency and day count methods. The two most popular day count methods are known as 30/360 and ACT/ACT. As the name suggests, 30/360 treats each month as having 30 days; thus, a year has 360 days. ACT/ACT treats the accrual period as having the actual number of days divided by the actual number of days in the year (365 or 366). Finally, the convention in the swap market is that the floating interest rate is assumed to be advanced set and settled in arrears; thus, $r_{FLT,i}$ is set at the beginning of the period and paid at the end. If we assume constant and equal accrual periods (so, $AP_{FLT} = AP_{FIX}$), the receive-fixed, pay-floating *net* cash flow can be expressed as:

$$FS - S_i = AP \times (r_{FIX} - r_{FLT,i}),$$

and the pay-fixed, receive-floating *net* cash flow can be expressed as:

$$S_i - FS = AP \times (r_{FLT,i} - r_{FIX}).$$

As a simple example, if the fixed rate is 5%, the floating rate is 5.2%, and the accrual period is 30 days based on a 360-day year, the payment of a receive-fixed, pay-floating swap is calculated as:

$$FS - S_i = (30/360) \times (0.05 - 0.052) = -0.000167 \text{ per notional of } 1.$$

Because the floating rate exceeds the fixed rate, the receive-fixed (pay-floating) party would pay this amount (0.000167 per notional of 1) to the pay-fixed (receive-floating) party. In other words, only a single net payment is made by the receive-fixed party to the counterparty. The sign of the net payment is negative as it is an outflow (i.e., negative cash flow) for the receive-fixed (pay-floating) party. Moreover, assuming the notional amount (NA) is £100 million, the net payment made by the receive-fixed party is £16,700 (= −0.000167 x £100,000,000). Finally, if, instead, the fixed rate exceeds the floating rate, the sign of the net payment would be positive as it would be an inflow (i.e., positive cash flow) to the receive-fixed party from the pay-fixed counterparty.

We now turn to swap pricing. Exhibit 15 shows the cash flows for an interest rate swap along with a pair of bonds of equal par value. Suppose (at Step 1) the arbitrageur enters a receive-fixed, pay-floating interest rate swap with some initial value, V_{swap}. Replicating this swap with bonds would entail being long a fixed-rate bond (as the arbitrageur is receiving the fixed-rate coupon) and short a floating-rate bond (as she is paying the floating rate). Therefore, to price this swap, the arbitrageur creates the *opposite* of the replicating portfolio. So, at Step 2 she purchases a floating-rate bond whose value is denoted V_{FLT}. Note that the terms of the variable rate bond are selected to match exactly the floating payments of the swap. Next, a fixed-rate bond is sold short (Step 3)—equivalent to borrowing funds—with terms to match exactly the fixed payments of the swap.

Exhibit 15: Cash Flows for Receive-Fixed, Pay-Floating Swap Offset with Bonds

Position	Step	Time 0	Time 1	Time 2	...	Time n
Swap	Receive-fixed, pay-floating swap	V_{swap}	$+FS - S_1$	$+FS - S_2$	...	$+FS - S_n$
Offsetting Portfolio	Buy floating-rate bond	$-V_{FLT}$	$+S_1$	$+S_2$	...	$+S_n + Par$
	Short-sell fixed-rate bond	$+V_{FIX}$	$-FS$	$-FS$	...	$-(FS + Par)$
	Net Cash Flows	$V_{swap} = -V_{FLT} + V_{FIX} = 0$	0	0	0	0

This portfolio offsets the cash flows from the swap, so the net cash flows from Time 1 to Time n will all be equal to zero. So, in equilibrium we must have $V_{swap} = -V_{FLT} + V_{FIX} = 0$ to prevent an arbitrage opportunity. The value of a receive-fixed, pay-floating swap is:

$$V_{swap} = \text{Value of fixed bond} - \text{Value of floating bond} = V_{FIX} - V_{FLT}. \quad (11)$$

The value of a receive-fixed, pay-floating interest rate swap is simply the value of buying a fixed-rate bond and issuing (i.e., selling) a floating-rate bond. Remember, the fixed-rate and floating-rate bond values are just the PVs of all the expected interest and par payments. Pricing the swap means to determine the fixed rate (r_{FIX}) such that the value of the swap at initiation is zero. Said differently, to price the swap, the value of the fixed bond must equal the value of the floating bond in Equation 11.

As stated earlier, the value of a fixed bond (V_{FIX}) is the sum of the PV(All coupons) + PV(Par). If C is the coupon amount and par is 1, the value of a fixed-rate bond is, V_{FIX} = sum of PV of all coupons (C) + PV of par value, or:

$$\text{Value fixed-rate bond: } V_{FIX} = C\sum_{i=1}^{n} PV_i(1) + PV_n(1). \tag{12}$$

Notice the coupon amount in Equation 12 is multiplied by a summation term. This term includes the present value discount factors, PV(1), for each cash flow (or coupon payment). These PV factors are derived from the term structure of interest rates at the time of valuation. The summation adds up the PV factor for each coupon as it sequentially occurs. The sum of the PV of all the coupons is added to the PV of par at maturity (Time n). The present value expression is based on spot rates and is computed using the formula, $PV_i(1) = \dfrac{1}{1 + Rspot_i\left(\frac{NAD_i}{NTD}\right)}$. Spot interest rates ($Rspot_i$)

will help us value each individual cash flow. As an illustration, consider the following term structure of rates for USD cash flows and the computation of their associated PV factors, as shown in Exhibit 16:

Exhibit 16: Present Value Factors Using the Term Structure

Days to Maturity	US$ Spot Interest Rates (%)	Present Value (US$1)
90	2.10	0.994777
180	2.25	0.988875
270	2.40	0.982318
360	2.54	0.975229
	Sum:	3.941199

The PV factors are computed for each rate in the term structure as:

$$PV_i(1) = \frac{1}{1 + Rspot_i\left(\frac{NAD_i}{NTD}\right)}.$$

Using this formula, we compute the PV factor for a unit cash flow of 1. For example, at 90 days, we have a spot rate of 2.10%, which implies a discount (PV) factor of 0.994777 = $1/[1 + 0.0210 (90/360)]. Similarly, for 360 days, we have a spot rate of 2.54%, which implies a PV factor of 0.975229 = 1/[1 + 0.0254(360/360)].

The present value factors make it straightforward to value a fixed-rate bond under a given term structure. For example, the value of a fixed 4% bond with quarterly interest payments and Par = 1 under the term structure in Exhibit 16 can be computed using Equation 12. The quarterly coupon payment, C, is 4%/4 on par of 1 or 0.01/quarter.

$$V_{FIX} = C\sum_{i=1}^{n} PV_i(1) + PV_n(1) = 0.01(3.941199) + 0.975229(1) = 1.014641.$$

So, using Equation 12 and the PV factors and their sum from Exhibit 16, we can quickly value the bond at 101.464% of par.

To find the fixed rate needed to price a swap, we first make a slight modification to the notation in Equation 12. Since the coupon C is just the fixed interest rate multiplied by Par (and Par is assumed to be 1), we can substitute FS = C, so that:

$$V_{FIX} = FS \sum_{i=1}^{n} PV_i(1) + PV_n(1).$$

The value of a floating-rate bond, V_{FLT}, at the reset date is 1 (par) because the interest payment is set to match the discount rate. Recall that when the YTM (discount rate) of a bond is equal to the coupon rate, the bond sells at par. Here, we assume par is 1. Because the floating rate and the discount rate are initially the same for our floating bond, at the reset date we have V_{FLT} = par = 1.

Setting the value of the fixed bond in Equation 12 equal to 1 (the value of the floating bond at swap initiation, so $V_{FIX} = 1 = V_{FLT}$), we obtain:

$$V_{FIX} = FS \sum_{i=1}^{n} PV_i(1) + PV_n(1) = r_{FIX} \times AP \sum_{i=1}^{n} PV_i(1) + PV_n(1) = 1$$

This expression leads to the swap pricing equation, which sets r_{FIX} for the fixed bond:

$$r_{FIX} = \frac{1 - PV_n(1)}{\sum_{i=1}^{n} PV_i(1)} \times \frac{1}{AP} \qquad (13)$$

The fixed swap rate, the "price" that swap traders quote among one another, is simply one minus the *final* present value term divided by the sum of present values and multiplied by 1/AP. The fixed swap leg cash flow (FS) for a unit of notional amount (NA) is simply the fixed swap rate adjusted for the accrual period, or:

FS = $AP_{FIX} \times r_{FIX}$ (Fixed swap cash flow per unit of NA).

We can multiply FS times the notional amount later to find the cash flow for a swap in practice.

EXAMPLE 13

Solving for the Fixed Swap Rate Based on Present Value Factors

1. Suppose we are pricing a five-year MRR-based interest rate swap with annual resets (30/360 day count). The estimated present value factors, $PV_i(1)$, are given in the following table.

Maturity (years)	Present Value Factors
1	0.990099
2	0.977876
3	0.965136
4	0.951529
5	0.937467

The fixed rate of the swap (r_{FIX}) will be *closest* to:

A. 1.0%.

B. 1.3%.

C. 1.6%.

Solution:

B is correct. Note that the sum of present values is:

$$\sum_{i=1}^{5} PV_i(1) = 0.990099 + 0.977876 + 0.965136 + 0.951529 + 0.937467$$

$$= 4.822107.$$

Since the final cash flow for a bond consists of the nth coupon plus par, we use the PV factor for the last cash flow, here cash flow 5, twice in Equation 13. We sum it with the other PV factors for the individual coupons in the denominator, and we apply it to Par in the numerator. Since the coupons are annual, AP = 1. Therefore, the solution for the fixed swap rate is:

$$r_{FIX} = \frac{1 - 0.937467}{4.822107} \times \frac{360}{360} = 0.012968$$

From pricing a swap in Example 13, we now turn to interest rate swap valuation for a receive fixed (pay floating) swap. As noted previously, the fixed-rate receiver is effectively long a fixed bond and short a floating-rate bond. After initiation, this position will have a positive value when the fixed bond is trading at a premium to par (i.e., interest rates have fallen).

At any time after initiation, the market value of an existing swap can be understood by pricing a new offsetting swap. Assume $r_{FIX,0}$ is the swap rate at initiation. After initiation, the term structure of interest rates will likely imply a different swap rate, $r_{FIX,t}$.

The approach to value a multi-period swap is like the approach to valuing a single period FRA (i.e., multiplying the PV of the difference between the old FRA and the new FRA rates by a notional amount; Equation 6). Valuation is based on arbitrage transactions. Our initial swap position at Time 0 as a floating-rate payer would be offset by a position at Time t as a floating-rate receiver. The floating cash flows from paying and receiving will offset at each date (i), but the fixed payments will be different. We still receive the fixed rate, $r_{FIX,0}$, initially agreed to, but for the purposes of valuation we additionally assume the role as a fixed-rate payer at the new rate, $r_{FIX,t}$. The cash flows per unit of NA at each future date will always be based on the difference between the rate we initially received at Time 0 and the current rate paid at Time t, so $(FS_0 - FS_t) = AP(r_{FIX,0} - r_{FIX,t})$. Thus, the value of a *receive-fixed swap* at some future point in Time (t) is simply the sum of the present values of the difference in fixed swap rates times the stated notional amount (NA), or:

$$V_{SWAP,t} = NA \times (FS_0 - FS_t) \times \sum_{i=1}^{n} PV_i \quad \text{(Value of receive-fixed swap).} \quad (14)$$

In our valuation equation, n is the number of remaining cash flows from time t. Although this n may be different than the number of cash flows initially used to price the swap at time 0, we use the same notation. It is also important to be clear on which side of the swap this value applies. Notice the cash flow FS_0 in Equation 14 is positive. This is because the swap was initially set up (at Time 0) as a receive-fixed (FS_0), pay-floating swap. To establish a value, the swap is offset with a pay-fixed, receive-floating swap at Time t. Thus, when FS_0 has a positive sign, Equation 14 provides the value to the party initially receiving fixed. The negative of this amount is the value to the fixed-rate payer.

Now, since the *fixed-rate payer is effectively long a floating bond and short a fixed bond*, the position will have positive value when the fixed bond is trading at a discount to par (i.e., interest rates have risen). The fixed-rate payer is also the floating receiver and thus benefits as interest rates rise. At any date, the market value of a swap to the *fixed-rate payer* is based on the present value of the difference between the new offsetting fixed cash flow FS_t to be received and the fixed cash flow FS_0 he or she originally agreed to pay. It will be the negative of the receive-fixed swap value ($V_{SWAP,t}$) given by Equation 14, and we can compute it as follows:

$$-V_{SWAP,t} = -1\left[NA \times (FS_0 - FS_t) \times \sum_{i=1}^{n} PV_i\right]$$

$$= \ NA \times \left(FS_t - FS_0\right) \times \sum_{i=1}^{n} PV_i \ \text{(Value of pay-fixed swap)}. \qquad (15)$$

Exhibit 17 provides a summary of the swap legs and the associated replicating and offsetting portfolios for each swap leg. The replicating portfolio (at time 0) provides the same cash flows as our swap. The offsetting portfolio (at time t) will offset the cash flows from our replication of the swap and help us determine a value. Note that the floating cash flows at Time 0 and Time t cancel each other out. For valuation purposes, this allows us to focus on the difference in fixed swap rates. So, the value of a receive-fixed swap at time t is based on the difference between the initial fixed swap rate and the fixed swap rate at time t, or $r_{FIX,0} - r_{FIX,t}$, as shown in the last row of Exhibit 17.

Exhibit 17: Swaps and Related Replicating and Offsetting Portfolios

Swap		Receive-Fixed, Pay-Floating			Pay-Fixed, Receive-Floating		
		Portfolio Position		Rates	Portfolio Position		Rates
Replicating Portfolio	Initiation t = 0	Long Fixed-Rate Bond	Short Floating-Rate Bond	$r_{FIX,0}$ $- r_{FLT,0}$	Long Floating-Rate Bond	Short Fixed-Rate Bond	$r_{FLT,0}$ $- r_{FIX,0}$
Offsetting Portfolio	Time = t	Short Fixed-Rate Bond	Long Floating-Rate Bond	$r_{FLT,t}$ $- r_{FIX,t}$	Short Floating-Rate Bond	Long Fixed-Rate Bond	$r_{FIX,t}$ $- r_{FLT,t}$
Rates for Swap Valuation	Time = t			$r_{FIX,0}$ $- r_{FIX,t}$			$r_{FIX,t}$ $- r_{FIX,0}$

The examples illustrated here show swap valuation only on a payment date. If a swap is being valued between payment dates, some adjustments are necessary. We do not pursue this topic here.

EXAMPLE 14

Solving for Receive-Fixed Swap Value Based on Present Value Factors

Suppose two years ago we entered a €100,000,000 seven-year receive-fixed MRR-based interest rate swap with annual resets. The fixed rate in the swap contract entered two years ago was 2.0%. The estimated present value factors, $PV_i(1)$, are repeated from the previous example.

Maturity (years)	Present Value Factors
1	0.990099
2	0.977876
3	0.965136
4	0.951529
5	0.937467
Sum	4.822107

We know from the previous example that the current equilibrium fixed swap rate is close to 1.30% (two years after the swap was originally entered).

1. The value for the swap party receiving the fixed rate will be *closest* to:

   A. −€5,000,000.

    B. €3,375,000.

    C. €4,822,000.

Solution:

B is correct. $r_{FIX,0} = 2.0\%$, and $r_{FIX,t} = 1.3\%$. We assume annual resets (AP = 360/360 = 1), so the cash flow per unit notional is $FS_0 = 2.0\%$ and $FS_t = 1.3\%$.

The swap value to the fixed-rate receiver is:

$$V_{SWAP,t} = NA \times (FS_0 - FS_t) \times \sum_{i=1}^{5} PV_i$$
$$= €100,000,000 \times (0.02 - 0.013) \times 4.822107 = €3,375,000.$$

2. The value for the swap party paying the fixed rate will be *closest* to:

    A. −€4,822,000.

    B. −€3,375,000.

    C. €5,000,000.

Solution:

B is correct. The equivalent pay-fixed swap value is simply the negative of the receive-fixed swap value:

$$-V_{SWAP,t} = NA \times (FS_t - FS_0) \times \sum_{i=1}^{5'} PV_i$$
$$= €100,000,000 \times (0.013 - 0.02) \times 4.822107$$
$$= -€3,375,000.$$

6   PRICING AND VALUING CURRENCY SWAP CONTRACTS

☐   describe how currency swaps are priced, and calculate and interpret their no-arbitrage value

A currency swap is a contract in which two counterparties agree to exchange future interest payments in different currencies. In a currency swap, one party is long a bond (fixed or floating) denominated in one currency and short a bond (fixed or floating) in another currency. The procedure for pricing and valuing currency swaps is like the pricing and valuation of interest rate swaps. Currency swaps come in a wide array of types and structures. We review a few key features:

1. Currency swaps often involve an exchange of notional amounts at both the initiation of the swap and at the expiration of the swap.

2. The payment on each leg of the swap is in a different currency unit, such as euros and Japanese yen, and the payments are not netted.

3. Each leg of the swap can be either fixed or floating.

Pricing a currency swap involves solving for three key variables: two fixed interest rates (each in a different currency) and one notional amount. We must determine the appropriate notional amount in one currency, given the notional amount in the other currency, as well as two fixed-interest rates such that the currency swap value is zero at initiation.

We will focus on fixed-for-fixed currency swaps, so we essentially trade cash flows on a bond in one currency for cash flows on a bond in another currency. Let k be the currency units, such as euros and yen. Letters are used here rather than numbers to avoid confusion with calendar time. The value of a fixed-rate bond in currency k with par of 1 can be expressed generically as the present value of the coupons plus the present value of par, or:

$$V_k = C_k \sum_{i=1}^{n} PV_i(1) + PV_n\left(Par_k\right).$$

C_k is the coupon in currency k, and Par_k is the Par value paid at maturity in currency k. The value of a fixed-for-fixed currency swap, V_{CS}, is the difference in the price of two bonds. That is, the value of a currency swap is simply the value of a bond in currency a (V_a) less the value of a bond in currency b (V_b), expressed in terms of currency a, as follows:

$$V_{CS} = V_a - S_0 V_b.$$

Here, S_0 is the spot exchange rate at time 0. To make each party indifferent between the two bonds, the par or principal notional amounts are set to reflect the current spot exchange rate. This will lead to the swap having zero value ($V_{CS} = 0$) at inception (to prevent any arbitrage opportunity), so

$$V_a = S_0 V_b.$$

The swap value may change after initiation as the exchange rate and interest rates on the two currencies fluctuate. Currency swap valuation is best understood by considering an example. Exhibit 18 provides an illustration of an at-market 10-year receive-fixed US$ and pay-fixed € swap. The US$ bond has an annual coupon of US$30 and par of US$1,150. The annual coupon amount of the euro-denominated bond is €9 with par of €1,000. Both bonds are assumed to be trading at par (note, this is $1,150 for the US$ bond, not the usual $1,000) and have a 10-year maturity. We proceed as follows:

- Step 1: We enter the receive-fixed US$ and pay-fixed € swap.

  In Steps 2 and 3, we create a portfolio to offset the swap cash flows.

- Step 2 involves short-selling a US bond (so, paying the fixed US$ coupon on the bond) to offset the US dollar inflows from the swap.

- Step 3 involves purchasing a euro bond (so, receiving the fixed € coupon on the bond), which provides offsetting cash flows for the pay-fixed € portion of the swap.

Exhibit 18: Numerical Example of Currency Swap Offset with Bonds

Position	Step	Time 0	Time 1	Time 2	...	Time 10
Swap	1. Receive-fixed US$, pay-fixed euro swap		+$30 − ($1.5/€) x €9 =	+$30 − ($1.1/€) x €9 =	...	+($30 + $1,150) − ($1.2/€) x (€9 + €1,000) =
		0	+$16.5	+$20.1		−$30.8
Offsetting Bond Portfolio	2. Short-sell US$ bond	+$1,150	−$30	−$30	...	−($30 + $1,150)
	3. Buy euro bond	−($1.15/€) x €1,000 = −$1,150	+($1.5/€) x €9 = +$13.5	+($1.1/€) x €9 = +$9.9	...	+($1.2/€) x (€9 + €1,000) = $1,210.8
Offsetting Portfolio Cash Flows		0	−$16.5	−$20.1	...	+$30.8
Overall Net Cash Flows		0	0	0	0	0

The cash flows from the bond portfolio will exactly offset the cash flows from the swap. This illustration assumes a current spot exchange rate (S_0) at which €1 trades for US$1.15, so $S_0 = \$1.15/€1$. Selected future spot exchange rates are $S_1 = \$1.50/€1$, $S_2 = \$1.10/€1$, and $S_{10} = \$1.20/€1$. These future spot exchange rates are used to show the conversion of future euro cash flows into US dollars, but notice that the overall net cash flows are all zero regardless of the future spot exchange rates. In other words, we could have used any numbers for S_1, S_2, and S_{10}. Regardless of exchange rates in the future, the bond portfolio and the swap always have offsetting cash flows. Since the portfolio and swap produce identical (although opposite) cash flows, the law of one price will allow us to determine a value for our swap in terms of a pair of bonds.

Since the net cash flows are 0 at every time t, the portfolio must be worth 0 initially. Exhibit 18 provides the intuition for solving for the notional amount (NA). For a zero cash flow at initiation, the NA (or par value) of the bond denominated in currency a (NA_a) must equal the spot exchange S_0 rate times the notional amount (or par value) of the bond denominated in currency b (NA_b). That is,

$$NA_a = S_0 \times NA_b.$$

The exchange rate is stated as number of units of currency a to buy one unit of currency b. The spot exchange rate in Exhibit 18 is $\$1.15/€1$, so currency a (in the numerator) is US$. At the prevailing exchange rate S_0, it takes $1.15 to buy one euro. $NA_a = \$1,150$ and $S_0 = \$1.15/€1$, so $NA_b = \$1,150/(\$1.15/€1) = €1,000$. Therefore, the swap value at initiation is equal to zero, as it should be:

$$V_{CS} = V_a - S_0 V_b = \$1,150 - (\$1.15/€1) \times €1,000 = 0.$$

At any time during the life (tenor) of the swap shown in Exhibit 18, the opposite cash flows from the offsetting bond transactions result in a zero net cash flow. If the initial swap value is not at market or zero, then there are arbitrage opportunities. If the initial swap value is positive, then a set of arbitrage transactions would be implemented to capture the initial value with no net cash outflow. If the initial swap value is negative, then the opposite set of transactions would be implemented. The goal is to determine the fixed rates of the swap such that the current swap value is zero.

Because the fixed swap rate does not depend on the notional amounts, the fixed swap rates are found in the same manner as the fixed swap rate in an interest rate swap. For emphasis, we repeat the equilibrium fixed swap rate equations for each currency:

$$r_a = \frac{1 - PV_{n,a}(1)}{\sum_{i=1}^{n} PV_{i,a}(1)} \times \frac{1}{AP} \quad \text{and} \quad r_b = \frac{1 - PV_{n,b}(1)}{\sum_{i=1}^{n} PV_{i,b}(1)} \times \frac{1}{AP}. \tag{16}$$

We now have a solution for each of the three swap variables: one notional amount ($NA_a = S_0 \times NA_b$) and two fixed interest rates from Equation 16. Again, the fixed swap rate in each currency is simply one minus the final present value term divided by the sum of present values. We need to be sure that the present value terms are expressed in the appropriate currency. We illustrate currency swap pricing with spot rates by way of an example.

EXAMPLE 15

Currency Swap Pricing with Spot Rates

A US company needs to borrow 100 million Australian dollars (A$) for one year for its Australian subsidiary. The company decides to issue US$-denominated bonds in an amount equivalent to A$100 million. Then, the company enters into a one-year currency swap with quarterly reset (30/360 day count) and the exchange of notional amounts at initiation and at maturity. At the swap's initiation, the US company receives the notional amount in Australian dollars and pays to the counterparty, a swap dealer, the notional amount in US dollars. At the swap's expiration, the US company pays the notional amount in Australian dollars and receives from the counterparty the notional amount in US dollars. Based on interbank rates, we observe the following spot rates today, at Time 0, and compute their PV factors and sums:

Days to Maturity	A$ Spot Interest Rates (%)	Present Value (A$1)	US$ Spot Interest Rates (%)	Present Value (US$1)
90	2.50	0.993789[a]	0.10	0.999750
180	2.60	0.987167	0.15	0.999251[b]
270	2.70	0.980152	0.20	0.998502
360	2.80	0.972763	0.25	0.997506
	Sum:	3.933870	Sum:	3.995009

[a] $A\$0.993789 = 1/[1 + 0.0250(90/360)]$.
[b] $US\$0.999251 = 1/[1 + 0.00150(180/360)]$.

Assume that the counterparties in the currency swap agree to an A$/US$ spot exchange rate of 1.140 (expressed as number of Australian dollars for US$1).

1. The annual fixed swap rates for Australian dollars and US dollars, respectively, will be *closest* to:

   A. 2.80% and 0.10%.

   B. 2.77% and 0.25%.

   C. 2.65% and 0.175%.

Solution:

B is correct. Since the PV factors are given, we do not need to compute them from the spot rates. Using Equation 16, the Australian dollar periodic fixed swap rate is:

$$r_{AUD} = \frac{1 - PV_{n,AUD}(1)}{\sum_{i,AUD}^{4} PV_i(1)} \times AP = \frac{1 - 0.972763}{3.933870} \times \frac{360}{90}$$

$= 0.027695$ or 2.7695%.

The US dollar periodic fixed swap rate is:

$$r_{USD} = \frac{1 - PV_{n,USD}(1)}{\sum_{i,USD}^{4} PV_i(1)} \times AP = \frac{1 - 0.997506}{3.995009} \times \frac{360}{90}$$

$= 0.002497$ or 0.2497%.

The annualized rate is simply (360/90) times the period results: 2.7695% for Australian dollars and 0.2497% for US dollars.

2. The notional amount (in US$ millions) will be *closest* to:

   A. 88.

   B. 100.

   C. 114.

Solution:

A is correct. The US dollar notional amount is calculated as A$100 million divided by the current spot exchange rate, A$1.140/US$1. From $NA_a = S_0 \times NA_b$, we have A$100,000,000 = A$1.14/US$1 $\times N_b$. Solving for N_b we have US$87,719,298 = A$100,000,000/(A$1.14/US$1).

3. The fixed swap quarterly payments in the currency swap will be *closest* to:

   A. A$692,000 and US$55,000.

   B. A$220,000 and US$173,000.

   C. A$720,000 and US$220,000.

Solution:

A is correct. The fixed swap quarterly payments in currency units equal the *periodic* swap rate times the appropriate notional amounts. From the answers to 1 and 2, we have

$FS_{A\$} = NA_{A\$} \times (AP) \times r_{A\$}$

$= A\$100,000,000 \times (90/360) \times (0.027695)$

$= A\$692,375$

and

$FS_{US\$} = NA_{US\$} \times (AP) \times r_{US\$}$

$= US\$87,719,298 \times (90/360) \times (0.002497)$

$= US\$54,759$.

One approach to pricing currency swaps is to view the swap as a pair of fixed-rate bonds. The main advantage of this approach is that all foreign exchange considerations are moved to the initial exchange rate. We do not need to address future foreign currency transactions. Also, note that a fixed-for-floating currency swap (i.e., pay-fixed currency a, receive-floating currency b) is simply a fixed-for-fixed currency swap (i.e., pay-fixed currency a, receive-fixed currency b) paired with a fixed-for-floating interest rate swap (i.e., pay-fixed currency b, receive-floating currency b). Also, we do not technically "price" a floating-rate swap because we do not designate a single coupon rate and because the value of such a swap is par on any reset date. Thus, we have the capacity to price any variation of currency swaps.

We now turn to currency swap valuation. Recall that with currency swaps, there are two main sources of risk: interest rates associated with each currency and their exchange rate. The value of a fixed-for-fixed currency swap at some future point in time, say Time t, is simply the difference in a pair of fixed-rate bonds, one expressed in currency a and one expressed in currency b. To express the bonds in the same currency units, we convert the currency b bond into units of currency a through a spot foreign exchange transaction at a new rate, S_t. The value of a "receive currency a, pay currency b" (fixed-for-fixed) swap at any time t expressed in terms of currency a is the difference in bond values:

$$V_{CS} = V_a - S_t V_b.$$

Substituting the valuation equation for each of the bonds, we have:

$$V_{CS} = \left(FS_a \sum_{i=1}^{n} PV_i(1) + NA_a\, PV_n(1) \right) - S_t \left(FS_b \sum_{i=1}^{n} PV_i(1) + NA_b\, PV_n(1) \right).$$

Note that the fixed swap amount (FS) is the per-period fixed swap rate times the notional amount. Therefore, the currency swap valuation equation can be expressed as:

$$V_{CS} = NA_a \left[AP \times r_{Fix,a} \sum_{i=1}^{n} PV_i(1) + PV_n(1) \right] - S_t NA_b \left[AP \times r_{Fix,b} \sum_{i=1}^{n} PV_i(1) + PV_n(1) \right].$$

(17)

As mentioned, the terms in Equation 17 represent the difference in value of two fixed-rate bonds. The first term in braces is the value of a long position in a bond with face value of 1 unit of currency a, which is then multiplied by the notional amount of the swap in currency a (NA_a). This product represents the value of the cash inflows to the counterparty receiving interest payments in currency a. The second term (after the minus sign) implies outflows and represents the value of a short bond position with face value of 1 unit of currency b, which is multiplied by the product of the swap notional amount in currency b (NA_b) and the current (Time t) exchange rate, S_t (stated in units of currency a per unit of currency b). This gives the value of the payments, in currency a terms, made by the party receiving interest in currency a and paying interest in currency b. V_{CS} is then the value of the swap to the party receiving currency a, while the value of the swap to the party receiving currency b is simply the negative of that amount, $-V_{CS}$.

Equation 17 seems formidable, but it is a straightforward idea. We hold a bond in currency a, and we are short a bond in currency b (which we must express in terms of currency a). It is best understood by an example of a firm that has entered a currency swap and needs to determine the current value.

Example 16 continues the case of the company using a currency swap to effectively convert a bond issued in US dollars into a bond issued in Australian dollars. In studying the problem, take care to identify currency a (implied by how the exchange rate, S_t, is given) and the party receiving interest payments in currency a in the swap.

EXAMPLE 16

Currency Swap Valuation with Spot Rates

This example builds on the previous example addressing currency swap pricing. Recall that a US company needed to borrow 100 million Australian dollars (A$) for one year for its Australian subsidiary. The company decided to borrow in US dollars (US$) an amount equivalent to A$100 million by issuing US-denominated bonds. The company then entered a one-year currency swap with a swap dealer. The swap uses quarterly reset (30/360 day count) and exchange of notional amounts at initiation and at maturity. At the swap's expiration, the US company pays the notional amount in Australian dollars and receives from the dealer the notional amount in US dollars. The fixed rates were found to be 2.7695% for Australian dollars and 0.2497% for US dollars. Initially, the notional amount in US dollars was determined to be US$87,719,298 with a spot exchange rate of A$1.14 for US$1.

Assume 60 days have passed since swap initiation and we now observe the following updated market information:

Days to Maturity	A$ Spot Interest Rates (%)	Present Value (A$1)	US$ Spot Interest Rates (%)	Present Value (US$1)
30	2.00	0.998336	0.50	0.999584
120	1.90	0.993707	0.40	0.998668
210	1.80	0.989609	0.30	0.998253
300	1.70	0.986031	0.20	0.998336
	Sum:	3.967683	Sum:	3.994841

The currency spot exchange rate (S_t) is now A$1.13 for US$1.

1. The current value to the swap dealer in A$ of the currency swap entered 60 days ago will be *closest* to:

    A. −A$13,557,000.

    B. A$637,620.

    C. A$2,145,200.

Solution:

C is correct. The US firm issues $87.7 million of bonds and enters a swap with the swap dealer. The initial exchange rate is given as 1.14A$/1US$, so currency a is A$. The swap dealer is receiving quarterly interest payments in currency a (A$). The swap is diagrammed for Example 15 and Example 16 as shown below:

Swap Cash Flows:

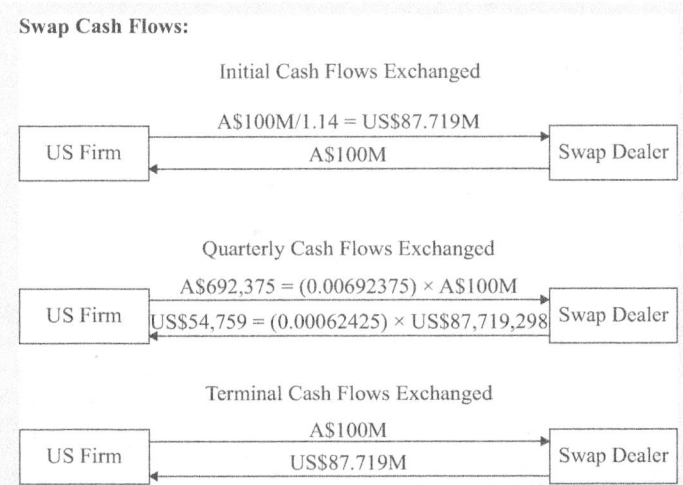

Initial Cash Flows Exchanged

A$100M/1.14 = US$87.719M

US Firm ← A$100M ← Swap Dealer

Quarterly Cash Flows Exchanged

A$692,375 = (0.00692375) × A$100M

US Firm ← US$54,759 = (0.00062425) × US$87,719,298 ← Swap Dealer

Terminal Cash Flows Exchanged

A$100M

US Firm ← US$87.719M ← Swap Dealer

After 60 days, the new exchange rate is 1.13A$/1US$ and the term structure of interest rates has changed in both markets. Equation 17 gives the value of the swap at Time t, V_{CS}. This is the value of the swap to the party receiving interest payments in Australian dollars, which is the swap dealer. Thus, using Equation 14, the value to the swap dealer receiving A$ is:

$$V_{CS} = NA_a \left[AP \times r_{Fix,a} \sum_{i=1}^{n} PV_i(1) + PV_n(1) \right] - S_t NA_b \left[AP \times r_{Fix,b} \sum_{i=1}^{n} PV_i(1) + PV_n(1) \right].$$

V_{CS} = A$100,000,000 × [0.00692375 (3.967683) + 0.986031] − 1.13 (A$/1US$) × (US$87,719,298) × [0.00062425 (3.994841) + 0.998336]

= A$2,145,167.

The first term in Equation 17 represents the PV of the dealer's incoming cash flows in A$, effectively a long position in an A$ bond. Remember, the dealer is receiving quarterly interest payments in A$ and will receive the A$100M terminal payment at swap maturity. To compute the PV of the A$ cash flows, the notional amount is multiplied by a term inside the braces, which represents the periodic interest rate multiplied by the sum of the PV factors for the four payments plus the PV factor for the terminal cash flow (where the PV factors reflect the new term structure). The second term is the PV of the dealer's US$ outflows (effectively a short bond in currency b, here US$). The PV of the quarterly interest payments and terminal payment are calculated using the new term structure and converted into A$ at S_t. Thus, we have the value of the long A$ bond minus the value of short US$ bond (stated in A$ terms). This gives V_{CS}, which is the value of the swap to the party receiving currency a and is the value from the perspective of the swap dealer.

2. The current value to the US firm in US$ of the currency swap entered 60 days ago will be *closest* to:

   A. −$2,673,705.

   B. −$1,898,400.

   C. $334,730.

Solution:

B is correct. In terms of Solution 1, the current value of the swap to the US firm is $-V_{CS}$. This represents the value to the firm making interest payments in currency a (A\$).

$-V_{CS} = -A\$2,145,167$, which when converted to US\$ at S_t is:

$-V_{CS} = -A\$2,145,167 \times (1US\$/1.13A\$) = -US\$1,898,378$.

Note that the US company initially issues a bond in US\$ in their home market and uses the swap to effectively convert to an A\$ bond issue. Understanding the swap as two bonds, the US firm is long a US\$ bond (US\$ is currency b in this example, which the US firm is receiving) and short a bond in A\$ (currency a, which the US firm is paying). The swap offsets the US firm's US\$ bond issue. The swap allows the US firm to make A\$ interest payments to the swap dealer, or to effectively issue a bond in A\$ (currency a). Alternatively, if the exchange rate had been stated as $S_t = 1US\$/1.13A\$$ or equivalently as $S_t = \$0.885/A\$$, then currency a would be US\$. In that case, the swap value, V_{CS}, can be understood in terms of the firm receiving US\$ since the swap gives the US firm the equivalent of a long position in a US\$ bond. The first term in the following equation represents the value of the US\$ bond to the US firm in the swap. The second term is the value of the A\$ bond position (short for the US firm) expressed in US\$ terms.

$$V_{CS} = NA_a\left[AP \times r_{Fix,a} \sum_{i=1}^{n} PV_i(1) + PV_n(1)\right] - S_t NA_b\left[AP \times r_{Fix,b} \sum_{i=1}^{n} PV_i(1) + PV_n(1)\right].$$

$V_{CS} = \$87,719,298 \times [0.00062422 (3.994841) + 0.998336] - (1US\$/A\$1.13) \times (A\$100,000,000) \times [0.00692381 (3.967683) + 0.986031]$

$= -US\$1,898,410$.

The swap value is negative to the US firm due to changes in the term structure and exchange rate. The A\$ has strengthened against the US\$, so now the US firm must pay periodic interest and principal cash flows in A\$ at a rate of 1.13A\$/1US\$. That is, for each US\$ the US firm gets fewer A\$ for making payments to the dealer. The new term structure now offers lower interest rates to A\$ borrowers, and this also contributes to the negative swap value for the US firm. The firm had agreed to pay higher periodic A\$ rates in the swap, but now the present value of those outflows has increased.

---

7   PRICING AND VALUING EQUITY SWAP CONTRACTS

☐ | describe how equity swaps are priced, and calculate and interpret their no-arbitrage value

Drawing on our prior definition of a swap, we define an equity swap in the following manner: An **equity swap** is an OTC derivatives contract in which two parties agree to exchange a series of cash flows whereby one party pays a variable series that will be determined by an equity and the other party pays either (1) a variable series determined by a different equity or rate or (2) a fixed series. An equity swap is used to convert the returns from an equity investment into another series of returns, which, as noted, either can be derived from another equity series or can be a fixed rate. Equity swaps are widely used in equity portfolio investment management to modify returns and risks. Equity swaps allow parties to benefit from returns of an equity or index without owning any shares of the underlying equity. An equity swap may also be used to hedge risk exposure to an equity or index for a certain period.

We examine three types of equity swaps: 1) *receive-equity return, pay-fixed*; 2) *receive-equity return, pay-floating*; and 3) *receive-equity return, pay-another equity return*. Like interest rate swaps and currency swaps, equity swaps have several unique nuances. We highlight just a few. First, the underlying reference instrument for the equity leg of an equity swap can be an individual stock, a published stock index, or a custom portfolio. Second, the equity leg cash flow(s) can be with or without dividends. Third, all the interest rate swap nuances exist with equity swaps that have a fixed or floating interest rate leg.

We focus here on viewing an equity swap as a portfolio of an equity position and a bond. The equity swap cash flows can be expressed as follows:

NA(Equity return – Fixed rate) (for receive-equity, pay-fixed),

NA(Equity return – Floating rate) (for receive-equity, pay-floating), and

NA(Equity return$_a$ – Equity return$_b$) (for receive-equity, pay-equity),

where a and b denote different equities. Note that an equity-for-equity swap can be viewed simply as a receive-equity a, pay-fixed swap combined with a pay-equity b, receive-fixed swap. The fixed payments cancel out, and we have synthetically created an equity-for-equity swap.

The cash flows for an equity leg (S_i) of an equity swap can be expressed as:

$S_i = NA_E R_E$,

where R_E denotes the periodic return of the equity either with or without dividends as specified in the swap contract, and NA_E denotes the notional amount. The cash flows for a fixed-interest rate leg (FS) of an equity swap are the same as those of an interest rate swap, or:

$FS = NA_E \times AP_{FIX} \times r_{FIX}$,

where AP_{FIX} denotes the accrual period for the fixed leg (for which we assume the accrual period is constant) and r_{FIX} here denotes the annual fixed rate on the equity swap.

EXAMPLE 17

Equity Swap Cash Flows

Suppose we entered a receive-equity index and pay-fixed swap. It is quarterly reset, 30/360 day count, €5,000,000 notional amount, pay-fixed (1.6% annualized, quarterly pay, or 0.4% per quarter).

1. If the equity index return was 4.0% for the quarter (not annualized), the equity swap cash flow will be *closest* to:

   A. –€220,000.

   B. –€180,000.

   C. €180,000.

Solution:

C is correct. Note that the equity index return is reported on a quarterly basis. It is not an annualized number. The fixed leg is often reported on an annual basis. Thus, one must carefully interpret the different return conventions. In this case, receive-equity index counterparty cash flows ($S_i - FS = NA_E \times AP \times (R_E - r_{FIX})$) are as follows:

€5,000,000 × (90/360) × (0.160 − 0.016) = €5,000,000 × (0.040 − 0.004)

= €180,000 (Receive 4%, pay 0.4% for the quarter).

2. If the equity index return was −6.0% for the quarter (not annualized), the equity swap cash flow will be closest to:

   A. −€320,000.

   B. −€180,000.

   C. €180,000.

Solution:

A is correct. Similar to 1, we have ($S_i - FS = NA_E \times AP \times (R_E - r_{FIX})$):

€5,000,000 × (90/360) × (−0.240 − 0.016) = €5,000,000 × (−0.060 − 0.004)

= −€320,000 (Receive −6%, pay 0.4% for the quarter).

When the equity leg of the swap is negative, then the receive-equity counterparty must pay both the equity return as well as the fixed rate (or whatever are the payment terms). Note also that equity swaps may cause liquidity problems. As seen here, if the equity return is negative, then the receive-equity return, pay-floating or pay-fixed swap may result in a large negative cash flow for the receive-equity return party.

For equity swaps, the equity position could be a wide variety of claims, including the return on a stock index with or without dividends and the return on an individual stock with or without dividends. For our objectives here, we ignore the influence of dividends with the understanding that the equity swap leg assumes all dividends are reinvested in the equity position. The arbitrage transactions for an equity swap when dividends are not included are extremely complex and beyond our objectives. The equity leg of the swap is produced by selling the equity position on a reset date and reinvesting the original equity notional amount (NA_E), leaving a remaining balance that is the cash flow required of the equity swap leg (S_i). Technically, we just sell off any equity value in excess of NA_E or purchase additional shares to return the equity value to NA_E, effectively generating S_i. Exhibit 19 shows the cash flows from an equity swap offset with an equity and bond portfolio.

Exhibit 19: Cash Flows for Receive-Fixed, Pay-Equity Swap Offset with Equity and Bond Portfolio

Position	Steps	Time 0	Time 1	Time 2	...	Time n
Equity Swap	1. Receive-fixed, pay-equity swap	$-V_{EQ}$	$+FS - S_1$	$+FS - S_2$	...	$+FS - S_n$
Offset Portfolio	2. Buy NA_E of equity	$- NA_E$	$+S_1$	$+S_2$	...	$+S_n + NA_E$
	3. Short sell fixed-rate bond	$+V_{FIX}$, (C = FS)	$-FS$	$-FS$	...	$-(FS + Par)$
	Net cash flows	$-V_{EQ} - NA_E + V_{FIX}$	0	0	0	$NA_E - Par$

Assume a portfolio manager has a large position in a stock that he/she expects to underperform in the future. Perhaps for liquidity or tax reasons, the manager prefers not to sell the stock but considers a receive-fixed, pay equity swap. Exhibit 19 shows the cash flows from such a swap as well as the offsetting portfolio (to eliminate arbitrage), which will assist us in valuing the swap. In Step 1, we enter a receive-fixed, pay equity swap. Steps 2 and 3 provide the offsetting cash flows to those of the swap, which are buy NA_E worth of equity and short sell a fixed-rate bond (with coupon equal to the fixed interest rate leg cash flows), respectively. Notice that from Time 1 to n − 1 the sum of these three transactions is always zero. Note also that the final (Time n) cash flow for the long position in the equity includes the periodic return (S_n) plus the sale proceeds of the underlying equity position (NA_E). For the terminal cash flows to equal zero, we must either set the bond par value to equal the initial equity position (NA_E = Par) or finance this difference. In this latter case, the bond par value could be different from the notional amount of equity.

As shown, the swap and pair of offsetting transactions produce 0 net cash flow from period 1 to period n − 1. In equilibrium, we require $-V_{EQ} - NA_E + V_{FIX} - PV(Par - NA_E) = 0$. That is, if the portfolio has initial value with no required cash outflow, then arbitrage will be possible. Hence, the equity swap value is:

$$V_{EQ} = V_{FIX} - NA_E - PV(Par - NA_E).$$

Assuming equilibrium ($V_{EQ} = 0$), the fixed swap rate can be expressed as the r_{FIX} rate such that $V_{FIX} = NA_E + PV(Par - NA_E)$. Note that assuming NA_E = Par = 1 and using our fixed bond pricing (Equation 13), we have the pricing equation for an equity swap:

$$r_{FIX} = \frac{1 - PV_n(1)}{\sum_{i=1}^{n} PV_i(1)} \times \frac{1}{AP}$$

You should recognize that the pricing of an equity swap is identical to Equation 11 for the pricing of a comparable interest rate swap, even though the future cash flows are dramatically different. If the swap required a floating payment, there would be no need to price the swap; the floating side effectively prices itself at par automatically at the start. If the swap involves paying one equity return against another, there would also be no need to price it. You could effectively view this arrangement as *paying equity "a" and receiving the fixed rate* as specified and *receiving equity "b" and paying the same fixed rate.* The fixed rates would cancel.

Finding the value of an equity swap after the swap is initiated, say at Time t (so, $V_{EQ,t}$), is similar to valuing an interest rate swap except that rather than adjusting the floating-rate bond for the last floating rate observed (remember, advanced set), we adjust the value of the notional amount of equity, as shown in Equation 18:

$$V_{EQ,t} = V_{FIX}(C_0) - (S_t/S_{t-1})NA_E - PV(Par - NA_E), \qquad (18)$$

where $V_{FIX}(C_0)$ denotes the value at Time t of a fixed-rate bond initiated with coupon C_0 at Time 0, S_t denotes the current equity price, S_{t-1} denotes the equity price observed at the last reset date, and PV() denotes the present value function from the swap maturity date to Time t.

EXAMPLE 18

Equity Swap Pricing

1. In Examples 13 and 14 related to interest rate swaps, we considered a five-year, annual reset, 30/360 day count, MRR-based swap. The following table provides the present values per €1, $PV_i (1)$.

Maturity (years)	Present Value Factors
1	0.990099
2	0.977876
3	0.965136
4	0.951529
5	0.937467

Assume an annual reset MRR-based floating-rate bond trading at par. The fixed rate was previously found to be 1.2968% (see Example 13). Given these same data (just shown), the fixed interest rate in the EURO STOXX 50 equity swap is *closest* to:

A. 0.0%.

B. 1.1%.

C. 1.3%.

Solution:

C is correct. The fixed rate on an equity swap is the same as that on an interest rate swap, or 1.2968% as in Example 13. That is, the fixed rate on an equity swap is simply the fixed rate on a comparable interest rate swap.

$$\sum_{i=1}^{5} PV_i(1) = 0.990099 + 0.977876 + 0.965136 + 0.951529 + 0.937467$$
$$= 4.822107.$$

Using Equation 13, the solution for the fixed swap rate is:

$$r_{FIX} = \frac{1 - 0.937467}{4.822107} \times \frac{360}{360} = 0.012968, \text{ or } 1.2968\%.$$

EXAMPLE 19

Equity Swap Valuation

Suppose six months ago we entered a receive-fixed, pay-equity five-year annual reset swap in which the fixed leg is based on a 30/360 day count. At the time the swap was entered, the fixed swap rate was 1.5%, the equity was trading at 100, and the notional amount was 10,000,000. Now all spot interest rates have fallen to 1.2% (a flat term structure), and the equity is trading for 105. Assume the Par value of the bond is equal to NA_E.

1. The current fair value of this equity swap is *closest* to:

A. −€300,000.

B. −€500,000.

C. €500,000.

Solution:

A is correct. Because we have not yet passed the first reset date, there are five remaining cash flows for this equity swap. The fair value of this swap is found by solving for the fair value of the implied fixed-rate bond. We then adjust for the equity value. The fixed rate of 1.5% results in fixed cash flows of 150,000 at each settlement. Applying the respective present value factors, which are based on the new spot rates of 1.2% (i.e., new term structure is flat), gives us the following:

Date (Years)	Present Value Factors (PV)	Fixed Cash Flow	PV (Fixed Cash Flow)
0.5	0.994036	150,000	149,105
1.5*	0.982318	150,000	147,348
2.5	0.970874	150,000	145,631
3.5	0.959693	150,000	143,954
4.5	0.948767	10,150,000	9,629,981
		Total:	10,216,019

Answers may differ due to rounding: $PV(1.5) = 1/(1 + 3 \times (0.012/2)) = 0.982318$.

Using Equation 18, we have,

$$V_{EQ,t} = V_{FIX}(C_0) - (S_t/S_{t-1})NA_E - PV(Par - NA_E).$$

Therefore, the fair value of this equity swap is:

$$V_{EQ,t} = 10,216,019 - [(105/100) \times 10,000,000] - 0 = -283,981.$$

---

2. The value of the equity swap will be *closest* to zero if the stock price is:

   A. 100.

   B. 102.

   C. 105.

Solution:

B is correct. The value of the fixed leg of the swap is 102.16% of par, = $(10,216,019/10,000,000) \times 100]$. Therefore, a stock price (S_t) of 102.1602 will result in a value of zero for the swap, as follows:

$$V_{EQ,t} = 10,216,019 - [(102.1602/100) \times 10,000,000] - 0 = 0.$$

SUMMARY

This reading on forward commitment pricing and valuation provides a foundation for understanding how forwards, futures, and swaps are both priced and valued.

Key points include the following:

- The arbitrageur would rather have more money than less and abides by two fundamental rules: Do not use your own money, and do not take any price risk.

- The no-arbitrage approach is used for the pricing and valuation of forward commitments and is built on the key concept of the law of one price, which states that if two investments have the same future cash flows, regardless of what happens in the future, these two investments should have the same current price.

- Throughout this reading, the following key assumptions are made:

  - Replicating and offsetting instruments are identifiable and investable.

  - Market frictions are nil.

  - Short selling is allowed with full use of proceeds.

  - Borrowing and lending are available at a known risk-free rate.

- Carry arbitrage models used for forward commitment pricing and valuation are based on the no-arbitrage approach.

- With forward commitments, there is a distinct difference between pricing and valuation. Pricing involves the determination of the appropriate fixed price or rate, and valuation involves the determination of the contract's current value expressed in currency units.

- Forward commitment pricing results in determining a price or rate such that the forward contract value is equal to zero.

- Using the carry arbitrage model, the forward contract price (F_0) is:

$F_0 = FV(S_0) = S_0(1 + r)^T$ (assuming annual compounding, r)

$F_0 = FV(S_0) = S_0 \exp^{r_c T}$ (assuming continuous compounding, r_c)

- The key forward commitment pricing equations with carry costs (CC) and carry benefits (CB) are:

$F_0 = FV[S_0 + CC_0 - CB_0]$ (with discrete compounding)

$F_0 = S_0 \exp^{(r_c + CC - CB)\,T}$ (with continuous compounding)

  Futures contract pricing in this reading can essentially be treated the same as forward contract pricing.

- The value of a forward commitment is a function of the price of the underlying instrument, financing costs, and other carry costs and benefits.

- The key forward commitment valuation equations are:

Long Forward: $V_t = PV[F_t - F_0] = \dfrac{[F_t - F_0]}{(1 + r)^{T-t}}$

  and

Short Forward: $-V_t = PV[F_0 - F_t] = \dfrac{[F_0 - F_t]}{(1 + r)^{T-t}}$,

  With the PV of the difference in forward prices adjusted for carry costs and benefits. Alternatively,

Long Forward: $V_t = S_t - PV[F_0] = S_t - \dfrac{F_0}{(1 + r)^{T-t}}$

  and

Short Forward: $-V_t = \text{PV}\left[F_0\right] - S_t = \dfrac{F_0}{(1+r)^{T-t}} - S_t$

- With equities and fixed-income securities, the forward price is determined such that the initial forward value is zero.

- A forward rate agreement (FRA) is a forward contract on interest rates. The FRA's fixed interest rate is determined such that the initial value of the FRA is zero.

- FRA settlements amounts at Time h are:

Pay-fixed (Long): $\text{NA} \times \{[L_m - \text{FRA}_0]\, t_m\}/[1 + D_m t_m]$ and

Receive-fixed (Short): $\text{NA} \times \{\text{FRA}_0 - L_m]\, t_m\}/[1 + D_m t_m]$.

- The FRA's fixed interest rate (annualized) at contract initiation is:

$\text{FRA}_0 = \{[1 + L_T t_T]/[1 + L_h t_h] - 1\}/t_m$.

- The Time g value of an FRA initiated at Time 0 is:

Long FRA: $V_g = \text{NA} \times \{[\text{FRA}_g - \text{FRA}_0]\, t_m\}/[1+ D_{(T-g)}\, t_{(T-g)}]$ and

Short FRA: $-V_g = \text{NA} \times \{[\text{FRA}_0 - \text{FRA}_g]\, t_m\}/[1+ D_{(T-g)}\, t_{(T-g)}]$.

- The fixed-income forward (or futures) price including conversion factor (i.e., adjusted price) is:

$F_0 = Q_0 \times \text{CF} = \text{FV}[S_0 + CC_0 - CB_0] = \text{FV}[B_0 + AI_0 - \text{PVCI}]$,

  and the conversion factor adjusted futures price (i.e., quoted futures price) is:

$Q_0 = [1/\text{CF}]\, \{\text{FV}\,[B_0 + AI_0] - AI_T - \text{FVCI}\}$.

- The general approach to pricing and valuing swaps as covered here is using a replicating portfolio or offsetting portfolio of comparable instruments, typically bonds for interest rate and currency swaps and equities plus bonds for equity swaps.

- The swap pricing equation, which sets r_{FIX} for the implied fixed bond in an interest rate swap, is:

$$r_{FIX} = \frac{1 - PV_n(1)}{\sum_{i=1}^{n} PV_i(1)} \times \frac{1}{AP}.$$

- The value of an interest rate swap at a point in Time t after initiation is the sum of the present values of the difference in fixed swap rates times the stated notional amount, or:

$$V_{SWAP,t} = \text{NA} \times \left(FS_0 - FS_t\right) \times \sum_{i=1}^{n} PV_i \quad \text{(Value of receive-fixed swap)}$$

  and

$$-V_{SWAP,t} = \text{NA} \times \left(FS_t - FS_0\right) \times \sum_{i=1}^{n} PV_i \quad \text{(Value of pay-fixed swap)}.$$

- With a basic understanding of pricing and valuing a simple interest rate swap, it is a straightforward extension to pricing and valuing currency swaps and equity swaps.

- The solution for each of the three variables, one notional amount (NA_a) and two fixed rates (one for each currency, a and b), needed to price a fixed-for-fixed currency swap are:

$$NA_a = S_0 \times NA_b; \quad r_a = \frac{1 - PV_{n,a}(1)}{\sum_{i=1}^{n} PV_{i,a}(1)} \times \frac{1}{AP} \quad \text{and} \quad r_b = \frac{1 - PV_{n,b}(1)}{\sum_{i=1}^{n} PV_{i,b}(1)} \times \frac{1}{AP}$$

- The currency swap valuation equation, for valuing the swap at time t (after initiation), can be expressed as:

$$V_{CS}$$
$$= NA_a \left[AP \times r_{Fix,a} \sum_{i=1}^{n} PV_i(1) + PV_n(1) \right] - S_t NA_b \left[AP \times r_{Fix,b} \right.$$
$$\left. \sum_{i=1}^{n} PV_i(1) + PV_n(1) \right]..$$

- For a receive-fixed, pay equity swap, the fixed rate (r_{FIX}) for the implied fixed bond that makes the swap's value (V_{EQ}) equal to "0" at initiation is:

$$r_{FIX} = \frac{1 - PV_n(1)}{\sum_{i=1}^{n} PV_i(1)} \times \frac{1}{AP}.$$

- The value of an equity swap at Time t ($V_{EQ,t}$), after initiation, is:

$$V_{EQ,t} = V_{FIX}(C_0) - (S_t/S_{t-1})NA_E - PV(Par - NA_E)$$

where $V_{FIX}(C_0)$ is the Time t value of a fixed-rate bond initiated with coupon C_0 at Time 0, S_t is the current equity price, S_{t-1} is the equity price at the last reset date, and PV() is the PV function from the swap maturity date to Time t.

PRACTICE PROBLEMS

The following information relates to questions 1-6

Tim Doyle is a portfolio manager at BestFutures Group, a hedge fund that frequently enters into derivative contracts either to hedge the risk of investments it holds or to speculate outside of those investments. Doyle works alongside Diane Kemper, a junior analyst at the hedge fund. They meet to evaluate new investment ideas and to review several of the firm's existing investments.

Carry Arbitrage Model

Doyle and Kemper discuss the carry arbitrage model and how they can take advantage of mispricing in bond markets. Specifically, they would like to execute an arbitrage transaction on a Eurodollar futures contract in which the underlying Eurodollar bond is expected to make an interest payment in two months. Doyle makes the following statements:

Statement 1   If the Eurodollar futures price is less than the price suggested by the carry arbitrage model, the futures contract should be purchased.

Statement 2   Based on the cost of carry model, the futures price would be higher if the underlying Eurodollar bond's upcoming interest payment was expected in five months instead of two.

Three-Year Treasury Note Futures Contract

Kemper then presents two investment ideas to Doyle. Kemper's first investment idea is to purchase a three-year Treasury note futures contract. The underlying 1.5%, semi-annual three-year Treasury note is quoted at a clean price of 101. It has been 60 days since the three-year Treasury note's last coupon payment, and the next coupon payment is payable in 120 days. Doyle asks Kemper to calculate the full spot price of the underlying three-year Treasury note.

10-Year Treasury Note Futures Contract

Kemper's second investment idea is to purchase a 10-year Treasury note futures contract. The underlying 2%, semi-annual 10-year Treasury note has a dirty price of 104.17. It has been 30 days since the 10-year Treasury note's last coupon payment. The futures contract expires in 90 days. The quoted futures contract price is 129. The current annualized three-month risk-free rate is 1.65%. The conversion factor is 0.7025. Doyle asks Kemper to calculate the equilibrium quoted futures contract price based on the carry arbitrage model.

Japanese Government Bonds

After discussing Kemper's new investment ideas, Doyle and Kemper evaluate one of their existing forward contract positions. Three months ago, BestFutures took a long position in eight 10-year Japanese government bond (JGB) forward contracts, with each contract having a contract notional value of 100 million yen. The contracts had a price of JPY153 (quoted as a percentage of par) when the contracts were purchased. Now, the contracts have six months left to expiration and have a price of JPY155. The annualized six-month interest rate is 0.12%. Doyle asks Kemper to value the JGB forward position.

Interest Rate Swaps

Additionally, Doyle asks Kemper to price a one-year plain vanilla swap. The spot rates and days to maturity at each payment date are presented in Exhibit 1.

Exhibit 1: Selected US Spot Rate Data

Days to Maturity	Spot Interest Rates (%)
90	1.90
180	2.00
270	2.10
360	2.20

Finally, Doyle and Kemper review one of BestFutures's pay-fixed interest rate swap positions. Two years ago, the firm entered into a JPY5 billion five-year inter-est rate swap, paying the fixed rate. The fixed rate when BestFutures entered into the swap two years ago was 0.10%. The current term structure of interest rates for JPY cash flows, which are relevant to the interest rate swap position, is presented in Exhibit 2.

Exhibit 2: Selected Japanese Interest Rate Data

Maturity (Years)	Yen Spot Interest Rates (%)	Present Value Factors
1	0.03	0.9997
2	0.06	0.9988
3	0.08	0.9976
Sum		2.9961

Doyle asks Kemper to calculate the value of the pay-fixed interest rate swap.

1. Which of Doyle's statements regarding the Eurodollar futures contract price is correct?

   A. Only Statement 1

   B. Only Statement 2

   C. Both Statement 1 and Statement 2

2. The full spot price of the three-year Treasury note is:

   A. 101.00.

   B. 101.25.

   C. 101.50.

3. The equilibrium 10-year Treasury note quoted futures contract price is *closest* to:

   A. 147.94.

   B. 148.89.

   C. 149.78.

4. The value of the JGB long forward position is *closest* to:

   A. JPY15,980,823.

   B. JPY15,990,409.

   C. JPY16,000,000.

5. Based on Exhibit 1, the fixed rate of the one-year plain vanilla swap is *closest* to:

   A. 0.48%.

   B. 2.20%.

   C. 2.88%.

6. Based on Exhibit 2, the value of the pay-fixed interest rate swap is *closest* to:

   A. −JPY6,491,550.

   B. −JPY2,980,500.

   C. −JPY994,793.

The following information relates to questions 7-11

Donald Troubadour is a derivatives trader for Southern Shores Investments. The firm seeks arbitrage opportunities in the forward and futures markets using the carry arbitrage model.

Troubadour identifies an arbitrage opportunity relating to a fixed-income futures contract and its underlying bond. Current data on the futures contract and underlying bond are presented in Exhibit 1. The current annual compounded risk-free rate is 0.30%.

Exhibit 1: Current Data for Futures and Underlying Bond

Futures Contract		Underlying Bond	
Quoted futures price	125.00	Quoted bond price	112.00
Conversion factor	0.90	Accrued interest since last coupon payment	0.08
Time remaining to contract expiration	Three months	Accrued interest at futures contract expiration	0.20
Accrued interest over life of futures contract	0.00		

Troubadour next gathers information on a Japanese equity index futures contract, the **Nikkei 225 Futures Contract**:

Troubadour holds a long position in a Nikkei 225 futures contract that has a remaining maturity of three months. The continuously compounded dividend yield on the Nikkei 225 Stock Index is 1.1%, and the current stock index level is 16,080. The continuously compounded annual interest rate is 0.2996%.

Troubadour next considers an equity forward contract for Texas Steel, Inc. (TSI).

Information regarding TSI common shares and a TSI equity forward contract is presented in Exhibit 2.

Exhibit 2: Selected Information for TSI

- The price per share of TSI's common shares is $250.
- The forward price per share for a nine-month TSI equity forward contract is $250.562289.
- Assume annual compounding.

Troubadour takes a short position in the TSI equity forward contract. His supervisor asks, "Under which scenario would our position experience a loss?"

Three months after contract initiation, Troubadour gathers information on TSI and the risk-free rate, which is presented in Exhibit 3.

Exhibit 3: Selected Data on TSI and the Risk-Free Rate (Three Months Later)

- The price per share of TSI's common shares is $245.
- The risk-free rate is 0.325% (quoted on an annual compounding basis).
- TSI recently announced its regular semiannual dividend of $1.50 per share that will be paid exactly three months before contract expiration.
- The market price of the TSI equity forward contract is equal to the no-arbitrage forward price.

7. Based on Exhibit 1 and assuming annual compounding, the arbitrage profit on the bond futures contract is *closest* to:

   A. 0.4158.

   B. 0.5356.

   C. 0.6195.

8. The current no-arbitrage futures price of the Nikkei 225 futures contract is *closest* to:

   A. 15,951.81.

   B. 16,047.86.

   C. 16,112.21.

9. Based on Exhibit 2, Troubadour should find that an arbitrage opportunity relating to TSI shares is

   A. not available.

   B. available based on carry arbitrage.

   C. available based on reverse carry arbitrage.

10. The *most appropriate* response to Troubadour's supervisor's question regarding

the TSI forward contract is:

A. a decrease in TSI's share price, all else equal.

B. an increase in the risk-free rate, all else equal

C. a decrease in the market price of the forward contract, all else equal.

11. Based on Exhibits 2 and 3, and assuming annual compounding, the per share value of Troubadour's short position in the TSI forward contract three months after contract initiation is *closest* to:

A. $1.6549.

B. $5.1561.

C. $6.6549.

The following information relates to questions 12-20

Sonal Johnson is a risk manager for a bank. She manages the bank's risks using a combination of swaps and forward rate agreements (FRAs).

Johnson prices a three-year MRR-based interest rate swap with annual resets using the present value factors presented in Exhibit 1.

Exhibit 1: Present Value Factors	
Maturity (years)	Present Value Factors
1	0.990099
2	0.977876
3	0.965136

Johnson also uses the present value factors in Exhibit 1 to value an interest rate swap that the bank entered into one year ago as the pay-fixed (receive-floating) party. Selected data for the swap are presented in Exhibit 2. Johnson notes that the current equilibrium two-year fixed swap rate is 1.12%.

Exhibit 2: Selected Data on Fixed for Floating Interest Rate Swap	
Swap notional amount	$50,000,000
Original swap term	Three years, with annual resets
Fixed swap rate (since initiation)	3.00%

One of the bank's investments is exposed to movements in the Japanese yen, and Johnson desires to hedge the currency exposure. She prices a one-year fixed-for-fixed currency swap involving yen and US dollars, with a quarterly reset. Johnson uses the interest rate data presented in Exhibit 3 to price the currency swap.

Exhibit 3: Selected Japanese and US Interest Rate Data

Days to Maturity	Yen Spot Interest Rates	US Dollar Spot Interest Rates
90	0.05%	0.20%
180	0.10%	0.40%
270	0.15%	0.55%
360	0.25%	0.70%

Johnson next reviews an equity swap with an annual reset that the bank entered into six months ago as the receive-fixed, pay-equity party. Selected data regarding the equity swap, which is linked to an equity index, are presented in Exhibit 4. At the time of initiation, the underlying equity index was trading at 100.00.

Exhibit 4: Selected Data on Equity Swap

Swap notional amount	$20,000,000
Original swap term	Five years, with annual resets
Fixed swap rate	2.00%

The equity index is currently trading at 103.00, and relevant US spot rates, along with their associated present value factors, are presented in Exhibit 5.

Exhibit 5: Selected US Spot Rates and Present Value Factors

Maturity (years)	Spot Rate	Present Value Factors
0.5	0.40%	0.998004
1.5	1.00%	0.985222
2.5	1.20%	0.970874
3.5	2.00%	0.934579
4.5	2.60%	0.895255

Johnson reviews a 6 × 9 FRA that the bank entered into 90 days ago as the pay-fixed/receive-floating party. Selected data for the FRA are presented in Exhibit 6, and current MRR data are presented in Exhibit 7. Based on her interest rate forecast, Johnson also considers whether the bank should enter into new positions in 1 × 4 and 2 × 5 FRAs.

Exhibit 6: 6 × 9 FRA Data

FRA term	6 × 9
FRA rate	0.70%

FRA notional amount	US$20,000,000
FRA settlement terms	Advanced set, advanced settle

Exhibit 7: Current MRR (Market Reference Rate)	
30-day MRR	0.75%
60-day MRR	0.82%
90-day MRR	0.90%
120-day MRR	0.92%
150-day MRR	0.94%
180-day MRR	0.95%
210-day MRR	0.97%
270-day MRR	1.00%

Three months later, the 6 × 9 FRA in Exhibit 6 reaches expiration, at which time the three-month US dollar MRR is 1.10% and the six-month US dollar MRR is 1.20%. Johnson determines that the appropriate discount rate for the FRA settlement cash flows is 1.10%.

12. Based on Exhibit 1, Johnson should price the three-year MRR-based interest rate swap at a fixed rate *closest* to:

   A. 0.34%.

   B. 1.16%.

   C. 1.19%.

13. From the bank's perspective, using data from Exhibit 1, the current value of the swap described in Exhibit 2 is *closest* to:

   A. −$2,951,963.

   B. −$1,849,897.

   C. −$1,943,000.

14. Based on Exhibit 3, Johnson should determine that the annualized equilibrium fixed swap rate for Japanese yen is *closest* to:

   A. 0.0624%.

   B. 0.1375%.

   C. 0.2496%.

15. From the bank's perspective, using data from Exhibits 4 and 5, the fair value of the equity swap is *closest* to:

   A. −$1,139,425.

   B. −$781,322.

   C. −$181,323.

16. Based on Exhibit 5, the current value of the equity swap described in Exhibit 4 would be zero if the equity index was currently trading the *closest* to:

    A. 97.30.

    B. 99.09.

    C. 100.00.

17. From the bank's perspective, based on Exhibits 6 and 7, the value of the 6 × 9 FRA 90 days after inception is *closest* to:

    A. $14,820.

    B. $19,647.

    C. $29,635.

18. Based on Exhibit 7, the no-arbitrage fixed rate on a new 1 × 4 FRA is *closest* to:

    A. 0.65%.

    B. 0.73%.

    C. 0.98%.

19. Based on Exhibit 7, the fixed rate on a new 2 × 5 FRA is *closest* to:

    A. 0.61%.

    B. 1.02%.

    C. 1.71%.

20. Based on Exhibit 6 and the three-month US dollar MRR at expiration, the payment amount that the bank will receive to settle the 6 × 9 FRA is *closest* to:

    A. $19,945.

    B. $24,925.

    C. $39,781.

SOLUTIONS

1. C is correct. Doyle's first statement is correct. Unless the Eurodollar futures contract's quoted price is equal to the no-arbitrage futures price, there is an arbitrage opportunity. Moreover, if the quoted futures price is less than the no-arbitrage futures price, then to take advantage of the arbitrage opportunity, the Eurodollar futures contract should be purchased and the underlying Eurodollar bond should be sold short. Doyle would then lend the short sale proceeds at the risk-free rate. The strategy that comprises those transactions is known as reverse carry arbitrage.

    Doyle's second statement is also correct. Based on the cost of carry model, the futures price is calculated as the future value of the sum of the underlying plus the underlying carry costs minus the future value of any ownership benefits. If the Eurodollar bond's interest payment was expected in five months instead of two, the benefit of the cash flow would occur three months later, so the future value of the benefits term would be slightly lower. Therefore, the Eurodollar futures contract price would be slightly higher if the Eurodollar bond's interest payment was expected in five months instead of two months.

    A is incorrect because Doyle's Statement 2 is correct (not incorrect). Based on the cost of carry model, the futures price would be higher if the underlying Eurodollar bond's interest payment took place in five months instead of two months.

    B is incorrect because Doyle's Statement 1 is correct (not incorrect). If the Eurodollar's futures contract price is less than the price suggested by the carry arbitrage model, the futures contract should be purchased.

2. B is correct. The full spot price of the three-year Treasury note is calculated as

    S_0 = Quoted bond price + Accrued interest = $B_0 + AI_0$.

    Accrued interest (AI) = Accrual period × Periodic coupon amount

    $= \left(\frac{NAD}{NTD}\right) \times \left(\frac{C}{n}\right)$.

    AI = (60/180) × (1.5/2) = 0.25.

    S_0 = 101 + 0.25 = 101.25.

    A is incorrect because 101 is the quoted clean (not the full spot) price of the three-year Treasury note. The clean price excludes accrued interest; the full price, also referred to as the dirty price, includes accrued interest.

    C is incorrect because the number of days until the next coupon payment (instead of the accrual period) is incorrectly used to compute accrued interest:

    AI = (120/180) × (1.5/2) = 0.50.

    S_0 = 101 + 0.50 = 101.50.

3. A is correct. The equilibrium 10-year quoted futures contract price based on the carry arbitrage model is calculated as

    $Q_0 = (1/CF) \times [FV(B_0 + AI_0) - AI_T - FVCI]$.

    CF = 0.7025.

    B_0 = 104.00.

$AI_0 = 0.17$.

$AI_T = (120/180 \times 2/2) = 0.67$.

$FVCI = 0$.

$Q_0 = (1/0.7025) \times [(1 + 0.0165)^{3/12}(104.17) - 0.67 - 0] = 147.94$.

B is incorrect because accrued interest at expiration is not subtracted in the equilibrium quoted futures contract price formula:

$Q_0 = (1/0.7025) \times [(1 + 0.0165)^{3/12}(104.17) - 0] = 148.89$.

C is incorrect because the future value is incorrectly calculated (the exponent of 3/12 is omitted):

$Q_0 = (1/0.7025) \times [(1 + 0.0165)(104.17) - 0.67 - 0] = 149.78$.

4. B is correct. The value of the JGB forward position is calculated as

$$V_t = PV[F_t - F_0] = (155 - 153)/(1 + 0.0012)^{\frac{6}{12}} = 1.9988.$$

Therefore, the value of the long forward position is 1.9988 per JPY100 par value. For the long position in eight contracts with each contract having a par value of 100 million yen, the value of the position is calculated as

$0.019988 \times (JPY100,000,000) \times 8 = JPY15,990,409$.

A is incorrect because the present value of the difference between the price when the contracts were purchased and the current price of the contracts was incorrectly computed (the exponent of 6/12 is omitted):

$V_t = F_t - F_0 = (155 - 153)/(1 + 0.0012) = 1.9980$.

$0.019980 \times (JPY100,000,000) \times 8 = JPY15,980,823$.

C is incorrect because the absolute difference (not the present value of the difference) between the price when the contracts were purchased and the current price of the contracts was computed:

$V_t = F_t - F_0 = (155 - 153) = 2$.

$0.02 \times (JPY100,000,000) \times 8 = JPY16,000,000$.

5. B is correct. The swap's fixed rate is calculated as

$$r_{FIX} = \frac{1 - PV_n(1)}{\sum_{i=1}^{n} PV_i(1)} \times \frac{1}{AP}$$

$PV_i(1) = 1/[1 + Rspot_i (NAD_i/NTD)]$.

$90 - \text{day PV factor} = 1/[1 + 0.019 \times (90/360)] = 0.9953$.

$180 - \text{day PV factor} = 1/[1 + 0.020 \times (180/360)] = 0.9901$.

$270 - \text{day PV factor} = 1/[1 + 0.021 \times (270/360)] = 0.9845$.

$360 - \text{day PV factor} = 1/[1 + 0.022 \times (360/360)] = 0.9785$.

$\sum_{i=1}^{4} PV_i(1) = 0.9953 + 0.9901 + 0.9845 + 0.9785 = 3.9483$.

$$r_{FIX} = \frac{1 - 0.9785}{[(90/360) \times 3.9483]} = 0.022 = 2.2\%$$

A is incorrect because the 90-day PV factor is incorrectly used in the numerator of the swap pricing equation instead of the final present value term:

$$r_{FIX} = \frac{1 - 0.9953}{[(90/360) \times 3.9483]} = 0.0048 = 0.48\%$$

C is incorrect because the sum of the present value terms excludes the final present value term:

$$\sum_{i=1}^{3} PV_i(1) = 0.9953 + 0.9901 + 0.9845 = 2.9699.$$

$$r_{FIX} = \frac{1 - 0.9785}{[(90/360) \times 2.9699]} = 0.0288 = 2.88\%$$

6. B is correct. The value of the pay-fixed interest rate swap is calculated as

$$-V_{SWAP,t} = NA \times (FS_t - FS_0) \times \sum_{i=1}^{n} PV_i.$$

$$FS_t = r_{FIX} = [1 - PV_n(1)] / \sum_{i=1}^{3} PV_i(1) = (1 - 0.9976)/2.9961 = 0.000801$$
$$= 0.08\%.$$

$$-V_{SWAP,t} = NA \times (FS_t - FS_0) \times \sum_{i=1}^{3} PV_i$$
$$= JPY5billion \times (0.000801 - 0.001) \times 2.9961$$
$$= -JPY2,980,500.$$

Given that rates have declined since the inception of the swap, the value of the pay-fixed, receive-floating position is currently a loss of JPY2,980,500.

A is incorrect because the arithmetic average of the yen spot rates (instead of the current fixed swap rate) was incorrectly used to calculate the value of the pay-fixed swap:

Arithmetic average of yen spot rates = (0.0003 + 0.0006 + 0.0008)/3 = 0.0006.

$$-V_{SWAP,t} = NA \times (FS_t - FS_0) \times \sum_{i=1}^{3} PV_i$$
$$= JPY5billion \times (0.0006 - 0.001) \times 2.9961$$
$$= -JPY6,491,550.$$

C is incorrect because the product of the notional amount and the difference between the initial swap fixed rate and the current swap fixed rate was not multiplied by the sum of the present values:

$$-V_{SWAP,t} = NA \times (FS_t - FS_0) = JPY5billion \times (0.0008 - 0.001)$$
$$= -JPY994,793.$$

7. B is correct.

   The no-arbitrage futures price is equal to the following:

   $F_0 = FV[B_0 + AI_0 − PVCI]$

   $F_0 = (1 + 0.003)^{0.25}(112.00 + 0.08 − 0) = 112.1640.$

   The adjusted price of the futures contract is equal to the conversion factor multiplied by the quoted futures price:

   $F_0 = CF × Q_0$

   $F_0 = (0.90)(125) = 112.50.$

   Adding the accrued interest of 0.20 in three months (futures contract expiration) to the adjusted price of the futures contract gives a total price of 112.70.

   This difference means that the futures contract is overpriced by 112.70 − 112.1640 = 0.5360. The available arbitrage profit is the present value of this difference: $0.5360/(1.003)^{0.25} = 0.5356.$

8. B is correct. The no-arbitrage futures price is

   $$F_0 = S_0 \exp^{(r_c + CC − CB)\, T}$$

   $F_0 = 16,080 \exp^{(0.002996 + 0 − 0.011)(3/12)} = 16,047.86.$

9. A is correct. The carry arbitrage model price of the forward contract is

   $FV(S_0) = S_0(1 + r)^T = \$250(1 + 0.003)^{0.75} = \$250.562289.$

   The market price of the TSI forward contract is $250.562289. A carry or reverse carry arbitrage opportunity does not exist because the market price of the forward contract is equal to the carry arbitrage model price.

10. B is correct. From the perspective of the long position, the forward value is equal to the present value of the difference in forward prices:

    $V_t = PV[F_t − F_0],$

    where

    $F_t = FV(S_t + CC_t − CB_t).$

    All else equal, an increase in the risk-free rate before contract expiration would cause the forward price, F_t, to increase. This increase in the forward price would cause the value of the TSI forward contract, from the perspective of the short, to decrease. Therefore, an increase in the risk-free rate would lead to a loss on the short position in the TSI forward contract.

11. C is correct. The no-arbitrage price of the forward contract, three months after

contract initiation, is

$$F_{0.25} = FV_{0.25}(S_{0.25} + CC_{0.25} - CB_{0.25})$$

$$F_{0.25} = [\$245 + 0 - \$1.50/(1 + 0.00325)^{(0.5 - 0.25)}](1 + 0.00325)^{(0.75 - 0.25)} = \$243.8966.$$

Therefore, from the perspective of the long, the value of the TSI forward contract is

$$V_{0.25} = PV_{0.25}[F_{0.25} - F_0]$$

$$V_{0.25} = (\$243.8966 - \$250.562289)/(1 + 0.00325)^{0.75 - 0.25} = -\$6.6549.$$

Because Troubadour is short the TSI forward contract, the value of his position is a gain of $6.6549.

12. C is correct. The swap pricing equation is

$$r_{FIX} = \frac{1 - PV_n(1)}{\sum_{i=1}^{n} PV_i(1)}.$$

That is, the fixed swap rate is equal to 1 minus the final present value factor (in this case, Year 3) divided by the sum of the present values (in this case, the sum of Years 1, 2, and 3), and AP, which in this case is (360/360) = 1. The sum of present values for Years 1, 2, and 3 is calculated as

$$\sum_{i=1}^{n} PV_i(1) = 0.990099 + 0.977876 + 0.965136 = 2.933111.$$

Thus, the fixed-swap rate is calculated as

$$r_{FIX} = \frac{1 - 0.965136}{2.933111} = 0.01189 \text{ or } 1.19\%.$$

13. B is correct. The value of a swap from the perspective of the receive-fixed (pay-floating) party is calculated as

$$V = NA \times (FS_0 - FS_t) \times \sum_{i=1}^{n} PV_i.$$

The swap has two years remaining until expiration. The sum of the present values for Years 1 and 2 is

$$\sum_{i=1}^{n} PV_i = 0.990099 + 0.977876 = 1.967975.$$

Given the current equilibrium two-year swap rate of 1.12% and the fixed swap rate at initiation of 3.00%, the swap value per dollar notional is calculated as

$$V = 1 \times (360/360)(0.03 - 0.0112) \times 1.967975 = 0.036998.$$

The current value of the swap, from the perspective of the receive-fixed party, is $50,000,000 \times 0.036998 = \$1,849,897$.

From the perspective of the bank, as the pay-fixed party, the value of the swap is −$1,849,897.

14. C is correct. The equilibrium swap periodic (quarterly) fixed rate for yen is calculated as

$$r_{JPY} = \frac{1 - PV_{n,JPY}(1)}{\sum_{i=1}^{4} PV_{i,JPY}(1)}.$$

The yen present value factors are calculated as

$$PV(1)_{i,JPY} = \frac{1}{1 + Rspo\, t_{i,JPY}\left(\frac{NAD_i}{NTD}\right)},$$

where

90-day PV factor = $1/[1 + 0.0005(90/360)]$ = 0.999875

180-day PV factor = $1/[1 + 0.0010(180/360)]$ = 0.999500

270-day PV factor = $1/[1 + 0.0015(270/360)]$ = 0.998876

360-day PV factor = $1/[1 + 0.0025(360/360)]$ = 0.997506

Sum of present value factors = 3.995757

Therefore, the yen periodic rate is calculated as

$$r_{JPY} = \frac{1 - PV_n(1)}{\sum_{i=1}^{4} PV_i(1)} = \frac{1 - 0.997506}{3.995757} = 0.000624 = 0.0624\%.$$

The annualized rate is $(360/90)$ times the periodic rate of 0.0624%, or 0.2496%.

15. B is correct. The value of an equity swap at time t is calculated as

$$V_{EQ,t} = V_{FIX}(C_0) - (S_t/S_{t-1})NA_E - PV(Par - NA_E).$$

The swap was initiated six months ago, so the first reset has not yet passed; thus, there are five remaining cash flows for this equity swap. The fair value of the swap is determined by comparing the present value of the implied fixed-rate bond with the return on the equity index. The fixed swap rate of 2.00%, the swap notional amount of $20,000,000, and the present value factors in Exhibit 5 result in a present value of the implied fixed-rate bond's cash flows of $19,818,678:

Date (in years)	PV Factors	Fixed Cash Flow	PV (fixed cash flow)
0.5	0.998004 or $1/[1 + 0.0040(180/360)]$	$400,000	$399,202
1.5	0.985222 or $1/[1 + 0.0100(540/360)]$	$400,000	$394,089
2.5	0.970874 or $1/[1 + 0.0120(900/360)]$	$400,000	$388,350
3.5	0.934579 or $1/[1 + 0.0200(1,260/360)]$	$400,000	$373,832
4.5	0.895255 or $1/[1 + 0.0260(1,620/360)]$	$20,400,000	$18,263,205
Total			$19,818,678

The value of the equity leg of the swap is calculated as $(103/100)(\$20,000,000)$ = $20,600,000.

Note the swap's notional amount and the implied fixed-rate bond's par value are both $20,000,000; therefore, the term $- PV(Par - NA_E)$ reduces to zero.

The swap was designed to profit if rates fell or equities declined. Neither happened, so the swap value will be negative for the bank. The fair value of the equity swap, from the perspective of the bank (receive-fixed, pay-equity party) is calculated as

$$V_{EQ} = \$19,818,678 - \$20,600,000 = -\$781,322.$$

16. B is correct. The equity index level at which the swap's fair value would be zero can be calculated by setting the swap valuation formula equal to zero and solving for S_t:

$$V_{EQ,t} = V_{FIX}(C_0) - (S_t/S_{t-1})NA_E = 0.$$

The value of the fixed leg of the swap has a present value of $19,818,678, or 99.0934% of par value:

Date (years)	PV Factors	Fixed Cash Flow	PV (fixed cash flow)
0.5	0.998004	$400,000	$399,202
1.5	0.985222	$400,000	$394,089
2.5	0.970874	$400,000	$388,350
3.5	0.934579	$400,000	$373,832
4.5	0.895255	$20,400,000	$18,263,205
Total			$19,818,678

Treating the swap notional value as par value and substituting the present value of the fixed leg and S_0 into the equation yields

$$0 = 99.0934 - \left(\frac{S_t}{100}\right)100$$

Solving for S_t yields

$S_t = 99.0934$.

17. A is correct. The current value of the 6×9 FRA is calculated as

$$V_g = NA \times \{[FRA_g - FRA_0]t_m\}/[1 + D_{(T-g)} t_{(T-g)}].$$

The 6×9 FRA expires six months after initiation. The bank entered into the FRA 90 days ago; thus, the FRA will expire in 90 days. To value the FRA, the first step is to compute the new FRA rate, which is the rate on Day 90 of an FRA that expires in 90 days in which the underlying is the 90-day MRR:

$FRA_g = \{[1 + L_T t_T]/[1 + L_h t_h] - 1\}/t_m$

$FRA_g = \{[1 + L_{180}(180/360)]/[1 + L_{90}(90/360)] - 1\}/(90/360)$

Exhibit 7 indicates that $L_{90} = 0.90\%$ and $L_{180} = 0.95\%$, so

$FRA_g = \{[1 + 0.0095(180/360)]/[1 + 0.0090(90/360)] - 1\}/(90/360)$

$FRA_g = \{[1.00475/1.00225] - 1]\} \times 4 = 0.009978$, or 0.9978%.

Therefore, given the FRA rate at initiation of 0.70% and notional principal of $20 million from Exhibit 1, the current value of the forward contract is calculated as

$V_g = \$20,000,000 \times [(0.009978 - 0.0070)(90/360)]/[1 + 0.0095(180/360)].$

$= \$14,890.00/1.00475 = \$14,819.61.$

18. C is correct. The no-arbitrage fixed rate on the 1×4 FRA is calculated as

$FRA_0 = \{[1 + L_T t_T]/[1 + L_h t_h] - 1\}/t_m .$

For a 1×4 FRA, the two rates needed to compute the no-arbitrage FRA fixed rate are $L_{30} = 0.75\%$ and $L_{120} = 0.92\%$. Therefore, the no-arbitrage fixed rate on the 1

$\times$ 4 FRA rate is calculated as

$\text{FRA}_0 = \{[1 + 0.0092(120/360)]/[1 + 0.0075(30/360)] - 1\}/(90/360)$.

$\text{FRA}_0 = \{[1.003066/1.000625] - 1\} \times 4 = 0.009761$, or 0.98% rounded.

19. B is correct. The fixed rate on the 2 $\times$ 5 FRA is calculated as

$\text{FRA}_0 = \{[1 + L_T t_T]/[1 + L_h t_h] - 1\}/t_m$.

For a 2 $\times$ 5 FRA, the two rates needed to compute the no-arbitrage FRA fixed rate are $L_{60} = 0.82\%$ and $L_{150} = 0.94\%$. Therefore, the no-arbitrage fixed rate on the 2 $\times$ 5 FRA rate is calculated as

$\text{FRA}_0 = \{[1 + 0.0094(150/360)]/[1 + 0.0082(60/360)] - 1\}/(90/360)$

$\text{FRA}_0 = \{[(1.003917/1.001367) - 1\} \times 4 = 0.010186$, or 1.02% rounded.

20. A is correct. Given a three-month US dollar MRR of 1.10% at expiration, the settlement amount for the bank as the pay-fixed (receive-floating) party is calculated as

Settlement amount pay-fixed (receive floating)

$= \text{NA} \times \{[L_m - \text{FRA}_0]t_m\}/[1 + D_m t_m]\}$.

Settlement amount pay-fixed (receive floating)

$= \$20,000,000 \times \{[0.011 - 0.0070] \times (90/360)]/[1 + 0.011(90/360)]\}$.

Settlement amount pay-fixed (receive floating)

$= \$20,000,000 \times (0.001)/1.00275 = \$19,945.15$.

Therefore, the bank will receive \$19,945 (rounded) as the receive-floating party.

2

Valuation of Contingent Claims

by Robert E. Brooks, PhD, CFA, and David Maurice Gentle, MEc, BSc, CFA.

Robert E. Brooks, PhD, CFA, is at the University of Alabama (USA). David Maurice Gentle, MEc, BSc, CFA, is at Omega Risk Consulting (Australia).

LEARNING OUTCOMES

Mastery	The candidate should be able to:
☐	describe and interpret the binomial option valuation model and its component terms
☐	describe how the value of a European option can be analyzed as the present value of the option's expected payoff at expiration
☐	identify an arbitrage opportunity involving options and describe the related arbitrage
☐	calculate the no-arbitrage values of European and American options using a two-period binomial model
☐	calculate and interpret the value of an interest rate option using a two-period binomial model
☐	identify assumptions of the Black–Scholes–Merton option valuation model
☐	interpret the components of the Black–Scholes–Merton model as applied to call options in terms of a leveraged position in the underlying
☐	describe how the Black–Scholes–Merton model is used to value European options on equities and currencies
☐	describe how the Black model is used to value European options on futures
☐	describe how the Black model is used to value European interest rate options and European swaptions
☐	interpret each of the option Greeks
☐	describe how a delta hedge is executed
☐	describe the role of gamma risk in options trading
☐	define implied volatility and explain how it is used in options trading

1

INTRODUCTION

A contingent claim is a derivative instrument that provides its owner a right but not an obligation to a payoff determined by an underlying asset, rate, or other derivative. Contingent claims include options, the valuation of which is the objective of this reading. Because many investments contain embedded options, understanding this material is vital for investment management.

Our primary purpose is to understand how the values of options are determined. Option values, as with the values of all financial instruments, are typically obtained using valuation models. Any financial valuation model takes certain inputs and turns them into an output that tells us the fair value or price. Option valuation models, like their counterparts in the forward, futures, and swaps markets, are based on the principle of no arbitrage, meaning that the appropriate price of an option is the one that makes it impossible for any party to earn an arbitrage profit at the expense of any other party. The price that precludes arbitrage profits is the value of the option. Using that concept, we then proceed to introduce option valuation models using two approaches. The first approach is the binomial model, which is based on discrete time, and the second is the Black–Scholes–Merton (BSM) model, which is based on continuous time.

The reading is organized as follows. Section 2 introduces the principles of the no-arbitrage approach to pricing and valuation of options. In Section 3, the binomial option valuation model is explored, and in Section 4, the BSM model is covered. In Section 5, the Black model, being a variation of the BSM model, is applied to futures options, interest rate options, and swaptions. Finally, in Section 6, the Greeks are reviewed along with implied volatility. Section 7 provides a summary.

Principles of a No-Arbitrage Approach to Valuation

Our approach is based on the concept of arbitrage. Hence, the material will be covered from an arbitrageur's perspective. Key to understanding this material is to think like an arbitrageur. Specifically, like most people, the arbitrageur would rather have more money than less. The arbitrageur, as will be detailed later, follows two fundamental rules:

Rule # 1   Do not use your own money.

Rule # 2   Do not take any price risk.

Clearly, if we can generate positive cash flows today and abide by both rules, we have a great business—such is the life of an arbitrageur. If traders could create a portfolio with no future liabilities and positive cash flow today, then it would essentially be a money machine that would be attractive to anyone who prefers more cash to less. In the pursuit of these positive cash flows today, the arbitrageur often needs to borrow to satisfy Rule #1. In effect, the arbitrageur borrows the arbitrage profit to capture it today and, if necessary, may borrow to purchase the underlying. Specifically, the arbitrageur will build portfolios using the underlying instrument to synthetically replicate the cash flows of an option. The underlying instrument is the financial instrument whose later value will be referenced to determine the option value. Examples of underlying instruments include shares, indexes, currencies, and interest rates. As we will see, with options we will often rely on a specific trading strategy that changes over time based on the underlying price behavior.

Based on the concept of comparability, the no-arbitrage valuation approach taken here is built on the concept that if two investments have the same future cash flows regardless of what happens, then these two investments should have the same current price. This principle is known as the **law of one price**. In establishing these foundations of option valuation, the following key assumptions are made: (1) Replicating instruments are identifiable and investable. (2) There are no market frictions, such as transaction costs and taxes. (3) Short selling is allowed with full use of proceeds. (4) The underlying instrument follows a known statistical distribution. (5) Borrowing and lending at a risk-free interest rate is available. When we develop the models in this reading, we will be more specific about what these assumptions mean, in particular what we mean by a known statistical distribution.

In an effort to demonstrate various valuation results based on the absence of arbitrage, we will rely heavily on cash flow tables, which are a representation of the cash flows that occur during the life of an option. For example, if an initial investment requires €100, then from an arbitrageur's perspective, we will present it as a −€100 cash flow. If an option pays off ¥1,000, we will represent it as a +¥1,000 cash flow. That is, cash outflows are treated as negative and inflows as positive.

We first demonstrate how to value options based on a two-period binomial model. The option payoffs can be replicated with a dynamic portfolio of the underlying instrument and financing. A dynamic portfolio is one whose composition changes over time. These changes are important elements of the replicating procedure. Based on the binomial framework, we then turn to exploring interest rate options using a binomial tree. Although more complex, the general approach is shown to be the same.

The multiperiod binomial model is a natural transition to the BSM option valuation model. The BSM model is based on the key assumption that the value of the underlying instrument follows a statistical process called geometric Brownian motion. This characterization is a reasonable way to capture the randomness of financial instrument prices while incorporating a pre-specified expected return and volatility of return. Geometric Brownian motion implies a lognormal distribution of the return, which implies that the continuously compounded return on the underlying is normally distributed.

We also explore the role of carry benefits, meaning the reward or cost of holding the underlying itself instead of holding the derivative on the underlying.

Next we turn to Fischer Black's futures option valuation model (Black model) and note that the model difference, versus the BSM model, is related to the underlying futures contract having no carry costs or benefits. Interest rate options and swaptions are valued based on simple modifications of the Black model.

Finally, we explore the Greeks, otherwise known as delta, gamma, theta, vega, and rho. The Greeks are representations of the sensitivity of the option value to changes in the factors that determine the option value. They provide comparative information essential in managing portfolios containing options. The Greeks are calculated based on an option valuation model, such as the binomial model, BSM model, or the Black model. This information is model dependent, so managers need to carefully select the model best suited for their particular situation. In the last section, we cover implied volatility, which is a measure derived from a market option price and can be interpreted as reflecting what investors believe is the volatility of the underlying.

The models presented here are useful first approximations for explaining observed option prices in many markets. The central theme is that options are generally priced to preclude arbitrage profits, which is not only a reasonable theoretical assumption but is sufficiently accurate in practice.

We turn now to option valuation based on the binomial option valuation model.

2   BINOMIAL OPTION VALUATION MODEL

☐ | describe and interpret the binomial option valuation model and its
  | component terms

The binomial model is a valuable tool for financial analysts. It is particularly useful as a heuristic device to understand the unique valuation approach used with options. This model is extensively used to value path-dependent options, which are options whose values depend not only on the value of the underlying at expiration but also how it got there. The path-dependency feature distinguishes this model from the Black–Scholes–Merton option valuation model (BSM model) presented in the next section. The BSM model values only path-independent options, such as European options, which depend on only the values of their respective underlyings at expiration. One particular type of path-dependent option that we are interested in is American options, which are those that can be exercised prior to expiration. In this section, we introduce the general framework for developing the binomial option valuation models for both European and American options.

The binomial option valuation model is based on the no-arbitrage approach to valuation. Hence, understanding the valuation of options improves if one can understand how an arbitrageur approaches financial markets. An arbitrageur engages in financial transactions in pursuit of an initial positive cash flow with no possibility of a negative cash flow in the future. As it appears, it is a great business if you can find it.[1]

To understand option valuation models, it is helpful to think like an arbitrageur. The arbitrageur seeks to exploit any pricing discrepancy between the option price and the underlying spot price. The arbitrageur is assumed to prefer more money compared with less money, assuming everything else is the same. As mentioned earlier, there are two fundamental rules for the arbitrageur.

Rule # 1   Do not use your own money. Specifically, the arbitrageur does not use his or her own money to acquire positions. Also, the arbitrageur does not spend proceeds from short selling transactions on activities unrelated to the transaction at hand.

Rule # 2   Do not take any price risk. The focus here is only on market price risk related to the underlying and the derivatives used. We do not consider other risks, such as liquidity risk and counterparty credit risk.

We will rely heavily on these two rules when developing option valuation models. Remember, these rules are general in nature, and as with many things in finance, there are nuances.

In Exhibit 1, the two key dates are the option contract initiation date (identified as Time 0) and the option contract expiration date (identified as Time T). Based on the no-arbitrage approach, the option value from the initiation date onward will be estimated with an option valuation model.

---

1 There is not a one-to-one correspondence between arbitrage and great investment opportunities. An arbitrage is certainly a great investment opportunity because it produces a risk-free profit with no investment of capital, but all great investment opportunities are not arbitrage. For example, an opportunity to invest €1 today in return for a 99% chance of receiving €1,000,000 tomorrow or a 1% chance of receiving €0 might appear to be a truly great investment opportunity, but it is not arbitrage because it is not risk free and requires the investment of capital.

Exhibit 1: Illustration of Option Contract Initiation and Expiration

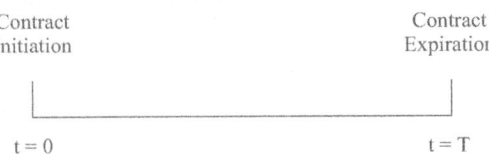

Let S_t denote the underlying instrument price observed at Time t, where t is expressed as a fraction of a year. Similarly, S_T denotes the underlying instrument price observed at the option expiration date, T. For example, suppose a call option had 90 days to expiration when purchased (T = 90/365), but now only has 35 days to expiration (t = 55/365). Further, let c_t denote a European-style call price at Time t and with expiration on Date t = T, where both t and T are expressed in years. Similarly, let C_t denote an American-style call price. At the initiation date, the subscripts are omitted, thus $c = c_0$. We follow similar notation with a put, using the letter p, in place of c. Let X denote the exercise price.[2]

For example, suppose on 15 April a 90-day European-style call option contract with a 14 July expiration is initiated with a call price of c = €2.50 and T = 90/365 = 0.246575.

At expiration, the call and put values will be equal to their intrinsic value or exercise value. These **exercise values** can be expressed as

$$c_T = Max(0, S_T - X) \text{ and}$$

$$p_T = Max(0, X - S_T),$$

respectively. If the option values deviate from these expressions, then there will be arbitrage profits available. The option is expiring, there is no uncertainty remaining, and the price must equal the market value obtained from exercising it or letting it expire.

Technically, European options do not have exercise values prior to expiration because they cannot be exercised until expiration. Nonetheless, the notion of the value of the option if it could be exercised, $Max(0, S_t - X)$ for a call and $Max(0, X - S_t)$ for a put, forms a basis for understanding the notion that the value of an option declines with the passage of time. Specifically, option values contain an element known as time value, which is just the market valuation of the potential for higher exercise value relative to the potential for lower exercise value. The time value is always non-negative because of the asymmetry of option payoffs at expiration. For example, for a call, the upside is unlimited, whereas the downside is limited to zero. At expiration, time value is zero.

Although option prices are influenced by a variety of factors, the underlying instrument has a particularly significant influence. At this point, the underlying is assumed to be the only uncertain factor affecting the option price. We now look in detail at the one-period binomial option valuation model. The one-period binomial model is foundational for the material that follows.

---

2 In financial markets, the exercise price is also commonly called the strike price.

3

ONE-PERIOD BINOMIAL MODEL

<table>
<tr><td>☐</td><td>describe and interpret the binomial option valuation model and its component terms</td></tr>
<tr><td>☐</td><td>describe how the value of a European option can be analyzed as the present value of the option's expected payoff at expiration</td></tr>
</table>

Exhibit 2 illustrates the one-period binomial process for an asset priced at S. In the figure on the left, each dot represents a particular outcome at a particular point in time in the binomial lattice. The dots are termed nodes. At the Time 0 node, there are only two possible future paths in the binomial process, an up move and a down move, termed arcs. The figure on the right illustrates the underlying price at each node. At Time 1, there are only two possible outcomes: S^+ denotes the outcome when the underlying goes up, and S^- denotes the outcome when the underlying goes down.

Exhibit 2: One-Period Binomial Lattice with Underlying Distribution Illustrated

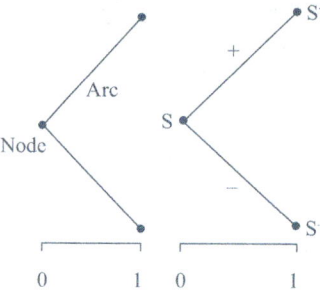

At Time 1, there are only two possible outcomes and two resulting values of the underlying, S^+ (up occurs) and S^- (down occurs). Although the one-period binomial model is clearly unrealistic, it will provide key insights into the more realistic multiperiod binomial as well as the BSM model.

We further define the total returns implied by the underlying movements as

$$u = \frac{S^+}{S} \text{ (up factor) and}$$

$$d = \frac{S^-}{S} \text{ (down factor).}$$

The up factors and down factors are the total returns; that is, one plus the rate of return. The magnitudes of the up and down factors are based on the volatility of the underlying. In general, higher volatility will result in higher up values and lower down values.

We briefly review option valuation within a one-period binomial tree. With this review, we can move quickly to option valuation within a two-period binomial lattice by performing the one-period exercise three times.

We consider the fair value of a two-period call option value measured at Time 1 when an up move occurs, that is c^+. Based on arbitrage forces, we know this option value at expiration is either

$$c^{++} = Max(0, S^{++} - X) = Max(0, u^2 S - X), \text{ or}$$

$$c^{+-} = Max(0, S^{+-} - X) = Max(0, udS - X).$$

At this point, we assume that there are no costs or benefits from owning the underlying instrument. Now consider the transactions illustrated in Exhibit 3. These transactions are presented as cash flows. Thus, if we write a call option, we receive money at Time Step 0 and may have to pay out money at Time Step 1. Suppose the first trade is to write or sell one call option within the single-period binomial model. The value of a call option is positively related to the value of the underlying. That is, they both move up or down together. Hence, by writing a call option, the trader will lose money if the underlying goes up and make money if the underlying falls. Therefore, to execute a hedge, the trader will need a position that will make money if the underlying goes up. Thus, the second trade needs to be a long position in the underlying. Specifically, the trader buys a certain number of units, h, of the underlying. The symbol h is used because it represents a hedge ratio.

Note that with these first two trades, neither arbitrage rule is satisfied. The future cash flow could be either $-c^- + hS^-$ or $-c^+ + hS^+$ and can be positive or negative. Thus, the cash flows at the Time Step 1 could result in the arbitrageur having to pay out money if one of these values is less than zero. To resolve both of these issues, we set the Time Step 1 cash flows equal to each other—that is, $-c^+ + hS^+ = -c^- + hS^-$—and solve for the appropriate hedge ratio:

$$h = \frac{c^+ - c^-}{S^+ - S^-} \geq 0 \tag{1}$$

We determine the hedge ratio such that we are indifferent to the underlying going up or down. Thus, we are hedged against moves in the underlying. A simple rule for remembering this formula is that the hedge ratio is the value of the call if the underlying goes up minus the value of the call if the underlying goes down divided by the value of the underlying if it goes up minus the value of the underlying if it goes down. The up and down patterns are the same in the numerator and denominator, but the numerator contains the option and the denominator contains the underlying.

Because call prices are positively related to changes in the underlying price, we know that h is non-negative. As shown in Exhibit 3, we will buy h underlying units as depicted in the second trade, and we will finance the present value of the net cash flows as depicted in the third trade. If we assume r denotes the per period risk-free interest rate, then the present value calculation, denoted as PV, is equal to $1/(1 + r)$. We need to borrow or lend an amount such that the future net cash flows are equal to zero. Therefore, we finance today the present value of $-hS^- + c^-$ which also equals $-hS^+ + c^+$. At this point we do not know if the finance term is positive or negative, thus we may be either borrowing or lending, which will depend on c, h, and S.

Exhibit 3: Writing One Call Hedge with h Units of the Underlying and Finance

Strategy	Time Step 0	Time Step 1 Down Occurs	Time Step 1 Up Occurs
1) Write one call option	+c	$-c^-$	$-c^+$
2) Buy h underlying units	$-hS$	$+hS^-$	$+hS^+$

Strategy	Time Step 0	Time Step 1 Down Occurs	Time Step 1 Up Occurs
3) Borrow or lend	$-PV(-hS^- + c^-)$ $= -PV(-hS^+ + c^+)$	$-hS^- + c^-$	$-hS^+ + c^+$
Net Cash Flow	$+c - hS$ $-PV(-hS^- + c^-)$	0	0

The value of the net portfolio at Time Step 0 should be zero or there is an arbitrage opportunity. If the net portfolio has positive value, then arbitrageurs will engage in this strategy, which will push the call price down and the underlying price up until the net is no longer positive. We assume the size of the borrowing will not influence interest rates. If the net portfolio has negative value, then arbitrageurs will engage in the opposite strategy—buy calls, short sell the underlying, and lend—pushing the call price up and the underlying price down until the net cash flow at Time 0 is no longer positive. Therefore, within the single-period binomial model, we have

$$+c - hS - PV(-hS^- + c^-) = 0$$

or, equivalently,

$$+c - hS - PV(-hS^+ + c^+) = 0.$$

Therefore, the **no-arbitrage approach** leads to the following single-period call option valuation equation:

$$c = hS + PV(-hS^- + c^-) \tag{2}$$

or, equivalently, $c = hS + PV(-hS^+ + c^+)$. In words, long a call option is equal to owning h shares of stock partially financed, where the financed amount is $PV(-hS^- + c^-)$, or using the per period rate, $(-hS^- + c^-)/(1 + r)$.[3]

We will refer to Equation 2 as the no-arbitrage single-period binomial option valuation model. This equation is foundational to understanding the two-period binomial as well as other option valuation models. The option can be replicated with the underlying and financing, a point illustrated in the following example.

EXAMPLE 1

Long Call Option Replicated with Underlying and Financing

---

1. Identify the trading strategy that will generate the payoffs of taking a long position in a call option within a single-period binomial framework.

   A. Buy $h = (c^+ + c^-)/(S^+ + S^-)$ units of the underlying and financing of $-PV(-hS^- + c^-)$

   B. Buy $h = (c^+ - c^-)/(S^+ - S^-)$ units of the underlying and financing of $-PV(-hS^- + c^-)$

   C. Short sell $h = (c^+ - c^-)/(S^+ - S^-)$ units of the underlying and financing of $+PV(-hS^- + c^-)$

Solution:

B is correct. The following table shows the terminal payoffs to be identical between a call option and buying the underlying with financing.

---

3 Or, by the same logic, $PV(-hS^+ + c^+)$, which is $(-hS^+ + c^+)/(1 + r)$.

Strategy	Time Step 0	Time Step 1 Down Occurs	Time Step 1 Up Occurs
Buy 1 call option	$-c$	$+c^-$	$+c^+$
OR A REPLICATING PORTFOLIO			
Buy h underlying units	$-hS$	$+hS^-$	$+hS^+$
Borrow or lend	$-PV(-hS^- + c^-)$ $= -PV(-hS^+ + c^+)$	$-hS^- + c^-$	$-hS^+ + c^+$
Net	$-hS - PV(-hS^- + c^-)$	$+c^-$	$+c^+$

Recall that by design, h is selected such that $-hS^- + c^- = -hS^+ + c^+$ or $h = (c^+ - c^-)/(S^+ - S^-)$. Therefore, a call option can be replicated with the underlying and financing. Specifically, the call option is equivalent to a leveraged position in the underlying.

Thus, the no-arbitrage approach is a replicating strategy: A call option is synthetically replicated with the underlying and financing. Following a similar strategy with puts, the no-arbitrage approach leads to the following no-arbitrage single-period put option valuation equation:

$$p = hS + PV(-hS^- + p^-) \tag{3}$$

or, equivalently, $p = hS + PV(-hS^+ + p^+)$ where

$$h = \frac{p^+ - p^-}{S^+ - S^-} \leq 0 \tag{4}$$

Because p^+ is less than p^-, the hedge ratio is negative. Hence, to replicate a long put position, the arbitrageur will short sell the underlying and lend a portion of the proceeds. Note that a long put position would be replicated by trading h units of the underlying. With h negative, this trade is a short sale, and because $-h$ is positive, the value $-hS$ results in a positive cash flow at Time Step 0.

EXAMPLE 2

Long Put Option Replicated with Underlying and Financing

1. Identify the trading strategy that will generate the payoffs of taking a long position in a put option within a single-period binomial framework.

   A. Short sell $-h = -(p^+ - p^-)/(S^+ - S^-)$ units of the underlying and financing of $-PV(-hS^- + p^-)$

   B. Buy $-h = (p^+ - p^-)/(S^+ - S^-)$ units of the underlying and financing of $-PV(-hS^- + p^-)$

   C. Short sell $h = (p^+ - p^-)/(S^+ - S^-)$ units of the underlying and financing of $+PV(-hS^- + p^-)$

Solution:

A is correct. Before illustrating the replicating portfolio, we make a few observations regarding the hedge ratio. Note that by design, h is selected such that $-hS^- + p^- = -hS^+ + p^+$ or $h = (p^+ - p^-)/(S^+ - S^-)$. Unlike calls, the put hedge ratio is not positive (note that $p^+ < p^-$ but $S^+ > S^-$). Remember that taking a position in $-h$ units of the underlying is actually short selling the underlying rather than buying it. The following table shows the terminal payoffs to be identical between a put option and a position in the underlying with financing.

Strategy	Time Step 0	Time Step 1 Down Occurs	Time Step 1 Up Occurs
Buy 1 Put Option	$-p$	$+p^-$	$+p^+$
OR A REPLICATING PORTFOLIO			
Short sell $-h$ Underlying Units	$-hS$	$+hS^-$	$+hS^+$
Borrow or Lend	$-PV(-hS^- + p^-)$ $= -PV(-hS^+ + p^+)$	$-hS^- + p^-$	$-hS^+ + p^+$
Net	$-hS - PV(-hS^- + p^-)$	$+p^-$	$+p^+$

Therefore, a put option can be replicated with the underlying and financing. Specifically, the put option is simply equivalent to a short position in the underlying with financing in the form of lending.

What we have shown to this point is the no-arbitrage approach. Before turning to the expectations approach, we mention, for the sake of completeness, that the transactions for replicating the payoffs for writing options are the reverse for those of buying them. Thus, for writing a call option, the writer will be selling stock short and investing proceeds (i.e. lending), whereas for a put, the writer will be purchasing stock on margin (i.e. borrowing). Once again, we see the powerful result that the same basic conceptual structure is used for puts and calls, whether written or purchased. Only the exercise and expiration conditions vary.

The no-arbitrage results that have been presented can be expressed as the present value of a unique expectation of the option payoffs.[4] Specifically, the **expectations approach** results in an identical value as the no-arbitrage approach, but it is usually easier to compute. The formulas are viewed as follows:

$$c = PV[\pi c^+ + (1 - \pi)c^-] \text{ and} \tag{5}$$

$$p = PV[\pi p^+ + (1 - \pi)p^-] \tag{6}$$

where the probability of an up move is

$$\pi = [FV(1) - d]/(u - d)$$

Recall the future value is simply the reciprocal of the present value or $FV(1) = 1/PV(1)$. Thus, if $PV(1) = 1/(1 + r)$, then $FV(1) = (1 + r)$. Note that the option values are simply the present value of the expected terminal option payoffs. The expected terminal option payoffs can be expressed as

$$E(c_1) = \pi c^+ + (1 - \pi)c^- \text{ and}$$

$$E(p_1) = \pi p^+ + (1 - \pi)p^-$$

where c_1 and p_1 are the values of the options at Time 1. The present value and future value calculations are based on the risk-free rate, denoted r.[5] Thus, the option values based on the expectations approach can be written and remembered concisely as

$$c = PV_r[E(c_1)] \text{ and}$$

$$p = PV_r[E(p_1)]$$

---

4 It takes a bit of algebra to move from the no-arbitrage expression to the present value of the expected future payoffs, but the important point is that both expressions yield exactly the same result.
5 We will suppress "r" most of the time and simply denote the calculation as PV. The "r" will be used at times to reinforce that the present value calculation is based on the risk-free interest rate.

The expectations approach to option valuation differs in two significant ways from the discounted cash flow approach to securities valuation. First, the expectation is not based on the investor's beliefs regarding the future course of the underlying. That is, the probability, π, is objectively determined and not based on the investor's personal view. This probability has taken several different names, including risk-neutral (RN) probability. Importantly, we did not make any assumption regarding the arbitrageur's risk preferences: The expectations approach is a result of this arbitrage process, not an assumption regarding risk preferences. Hence, they are called risk-neutral probabilities. Although we called them probabilities from the very start, they are not the true probabilities of up and down moves.

Second, the discount rate is *not* risk adjusted. The discount rate is simply based on the estimated risk-free interest rate. The expectations approach here is often viewed as superior to the discounted cash flow approach because both the subjective future expectation as well as the subjective risk-adjusted discount rate have been replaced with more objective measures.

EXAMPLE 3

Single-Period Binomial Call Value

A non-dividend-paying stock is currently trading at €100. A call option has one year to mature, the periodically compounded risk-free interest rate is 5.15%, and the exercise price is €100. Assume a single-period binomial option valuation model, where u = 1.35 and d = 0.74.

1. The optimal hedge ratio will be *closest* to:

    A. 0.57.

    B. 0.60.

    C. 0.65.

Solution:

A is correct. Given the information provided, we know the following:

$S^+ = uS = 1.35(100) = 135$

$S^- = dS = 0.74(100) = 74$

$c^+ = Max(0,uS - X) = Max(0,135 - 100) = 35$

$c^- = Max(0,dS - X) = Max(0,74 - 100) = 0$

With this information, we can compute both the hedge ratio as well as the call option value. The hedge ratio is:

$$h = \frac{c^+ - c^-}{S^+ - S^-} = \frac{35 - 0}{135 - 74} = 0.573770$$

---

2. The call option value will be *closest* to:

    A. €13.

    B. €15.

    C. €17.

Solution:

C is correct. The risk-neutral probability of an up move is

$\pi = [FV(1) - d]/(u - d) = (1.0515 - 0.74)/(1.35 - 0.74) = 0.510656,$

where $FV(1) = (1 + r) = 1.0515$.

Thus the call value by the expectations approach is

$c = PV[\pi c^+ + (1 - \pi)c^-] = 0.951022[(0.510656)35 + (1 - 0.510656)0]$

$= €16.998,$

where $PV(1) = 1/(1 + r) = 1/(1.0515) = 0.951022$.

Note that the call value by the no-arbitrage approach yields the same answer:

$c = hS + PV(-hS^- + c^-) = 0.573770(100) + 0.951022[-0.573770(74) + 0] =$
$€16.998.$

The value of a put option can also be found based on put–call parity. Put–call parity can be remembered as simply two versions of portfolio insurance, long stock and long put or lend and long call, where the exercise prices for the put and call are identical. Put–call parity with symbols is

$$S + p = PV(X) + c \qquad (7)$$

Put–call parity holds regardless of the particular valuation model being used. Depending on the context, this equation can be rearranged. For example, a call option can be expressed as a position in a stock, financing, and a put, or

$$c = S - PV(X) + p$$

EXAMPLE 4

Single-Period Binomial Put Value

1. You again observe a €100 price for a non-dividend-paying stock with the same inputs as the previous box. That is, the call option has one year to mature, the periodically compounded risk-free interest rate is 5.15%, the exercise price is €100, u = 1.35, and d = 0.74. The put option value will be *closest* to:

   A. €12.00.

   B. €12.10.

   C. €12.20.

Solution:

B is correct. For puts, we know the following:

$p^+ = Max(0,100 - uS) = Max(0,100 - 135) = 0$

$p^- = Max(0,100 - dS) = Max(0,100 - 74) = 26$

With this information, we can compute the put option value based on risk-neutral probability from the previous example or [recall that PV(1) = 0.951022]

$p = PV[\pi p^+ + (1 - \pi)p^-] = 0.951022[(0.510656)0 + (1 - 0.510656)26] = €12.10$

Therefore, in summary, option values can be expressed either in terms of replicating portfolios or as the present value of the expected future cash flows. Both expressions yield the same valuations.

TWO-PERIOD BINOMIAL MODEL: CALL OPTIONS 4

The two-period binomial lattice can be viewed as three one-period binomial lattices, as illustrated in Exhibit 4. Clearly, if we understand the one-period model, then the process can be repeated three times. First, we analyze Box 1 and Box 2. Finally, based on the results of Box 1 and Box 2, we analyze Box 3.

Exhibit 4: Two-Period Binomial Lattice as Three One-Period Binomial Lattices

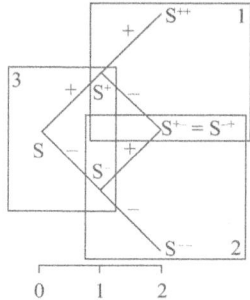

At Time 2, there are only three values of the underlying, S^{++} (an up move occurs twice), S^{--} (a down move occurs twice), and $S^{+-} = S^{-+}$ (either an up move occurs and then a down move or a down move occurs and then an up move). For computational reasons, it is extremely helpful that the lattice recombines—that is, $S^{+-} = S^{-+}$, meaning that if the underlying goes up and then down, it ends up at the same price as if it goes down and then up. A recombining binomial lattice will always have just one more ending node in the final period than the number of time steps. In contrast, a non-recombining lattice of n time steps will have 2^n ending nodes, which poses a tremendous computational challenge even for powerful computers.

For our purposes here, we assume the up and down factors are constant throughout the lattice, ensuring that the lattice recombines—that is $S^{+-} = S^{-+}$. For example, assume u = 1.25, d = 0.8, and S_0 = 100. Note that S^{+-} = 1.25(0.8)100 = 100 and S^{-+} = 0.8(1.25)100 = 100. So the middle node at Time 2 is 100 and can be reached from either of two paths.

The two-period binomial option valuation model illustrates two important concepts, self-financing and dynamic replication. Self-financing implies that the replicating portfolio will not require any additional funds from the arbitrageur during the life of this dynamically rebalanced portfolio. If additional funds are needed, then they are financed externally. Dynamic replication means that the payoffs from the option can be exactly replicated through a planned trading strategy. Option valuation relies on self-financing, dynamic replication.

Mathematically, the no-arbitrage approach for the two-period binomial model is best understood as working backward through the binomial tree. At Time 2, the payoffs are driven by the option's exercise value.

For calls:

$$c^{++} = Max(0, S^{++} - X) = Max(0, u^2 S - X),$$

$$c^{+-} = Max(0, S^{+-} - X) = Max(0, udS - X), \text{ and}$$

$$c^{--} = Max(0, S^{--} - X) = Max(0, d^2 S - X)$$

For puts:

$$p^{++} = Max(0, X - S^{++}) = Max(0, X - u^2 S),$$

$$p^{+-} = Max(0, X - S^{+-}) = Max(0, X - udS), \text{ and}$$

$$p^{--} = Max(0, X - S^{--}) = Max(0, X - d^2 S)$$

At Time 1, the option values are driven by the arbitrage transactions that synthetically replicate the payoffs at Time 2. We can compute the option values at Time 1 based on the option values at Time 2 using the no-arbitrage approach based on Equations 1 and 2. At Time 0, the option values are driven by the arbitrage transactions that synthetically replicate the value of the options at Time 1 (again based on Equations 1 and 2).

We illustrate the no-arbitrage approach for solving the two-period binomial call value. Suppose the annual interest rate is 3%, the underlying stock is S = 72, u = 1.356, d = 0.541, and the exercise price is X = 75. The stock does not pay dividends. Exhibit 5 illustrates the results.

Exhibit 5: Two-Period Binomial Tree with Call Values and Hedge Ratios

Item	Value
Underlying	132.389
Call	57.389

Item	Value
Underlying	97.632
Call	33.43048
Hedge Ratio	0.72124

Item	Value
Underlying	52.81891
Call	0

Item	Value
Underlying	72
Call	19.47407
Hedge Ratio	0.56971

Item	Value
Underlying	38.952
Call	0
Hedge Ratio	0

Item	Value
Underlying	21.07303
Call	0

We now verify selected values reported in Exhibit 5. At Time Step 2 and assuming up occurs twice, the underlying stock value is $u^2 S = (1.356)^2 72 = 132.389$, and hence, the call value is 57.389 [= Max(0,132.389 − 75)]. The hedge ratio at Time Step 1, assuming up occurs once, is

$$h^+ = \frac{c^{++} - c^{+-}}{S^{++} - S^{+-}} = \frac{57.389 - 0}{132.389 - 52.819} = 0.72124$$

The RN probability of an up move throughout this tree is

$$\pi = [FV(1) - d]/(u - d) = (1.03 - 0.541)/(1.356 - 0.541) = 0.6$$

With this information, we can compute the call price at Time 1 when an up move occurs as

$$c = PV[\pi c^{++} + (1 - \pi)c^{+-}] = (1/1.03)[(0.6)57.389 + (1 - 0.6)0] = 33.43048$$

and at Time Step 0,

$$h = \frac{c^+ - c^-}{S^+ - S^-} = \frac{33.43048 - 0}{97.632 - 38.952} = 0.56971$$

Thus, the call price at the start is

$$c = PV[\pi c^+ + (1 - \pi)c^-] = (1/1.03)[(0.6)33.43048 + (1 - 0.6)0] = 19.47$$

From the no-arbitrage approach, the call payoffs can be replicated by purchasing h shares of the underlying and financing $-PV(-hS^- + c^-)$. Therefore, we purchase 0.56971 shares of stock for 41.019 [= 0.56971(72)] and borrow 21.545 {or in cash flow terms, $-21.545 = (1/1.03)[-0.56971(38.952) + 0]$}, replicating the call values at Time 0. We then illustrate Time 1 assuming that an up move occurs. The stock position will now be worth 55.622 [= 0.56971(97.632)], and the borrowing must be repaid with interest or 22.191 [= 1.03(21.545)]. Note that the portfolio is worth 33.431 (55.622 – 22.191), the same value as the call except for a small rounding error. Therefore, the portfolio of stock and the financing dynamically replicates the value of the call option.

The final task is to demonstrate that the portfolio is self-financing. Self-financing can be shown by observing that the new portfolio at Time 1, assuming an up move occurs, is equal to the old portfolio that was formed at Time 0 and liquidated at Time 1. Notice that the hedge ratio rose from 0.56971 to 0.72124 as we moved from Time 0 to Time 1, assuming an up move occurs, requiring the purchase of additional shares. These additional shares will be financed with additional borrowing. The total borrowing is 36.98554 {= $-PV(-hS^{+-} + c^{+-}) = -(1/1.03)[-0.72124(52.81891) + 0]$}. The borrowing at Time 0 that is due at Time 1 is 22.191. The funds borrowed at Time 1 grew to 36.98554. Therefore, the strategy is self-financing.

The two-period binomial model can also be represented as the present value of an expectation of future cash flows. Based on the one-period results, it follows by repeated substitutions that

$$c = PV[\pi^2 c^{++} + 2\pi(1 - \pi)c^{+-} + (1 - \pi)^2 c^{--}] \tag{8}$$

and

$$p = PV[\pi^2 p^{++} + 2\pi(1 - \pi)p^{+-} + (1 - \pi)^2 p^{--}] \tag{9}$$

Therefore, the two-period binomial model is again simply the present value of the expected future cash flows based on the RN probability. Again, the option values are simply the present value of the expected terminal option payoffs. The expected terminal option payoffs can be expressed as

$$E(c_2) = \pi^2 c^{++} + 2\pi(1 - \pi)c^{+-} + (1 - \pi)^2 c^{--}$$

and

$$E(p_2) = \pi^2 p^{++} + 2\pi(1 - \pi)p^{+-} + (1 - \pi)^2 p^{--}$$

Thus, the two-period binomial option values based on the expectations approach can be written and remembered concisely as

$$c = PV_r[E\pi(c_2)] \text{ and}$$

$$p = PV_r[E\pi(p_2)]$$

It is vital to remember that this present value is over two periods, so the discount factor with discrete rates is $PV = [1/(1 + r)^2]$. Recall the subscript "r" just emphasizes the present value calculation and is based on the risk-free interest rate.

EXAMPLE 5

Two-Period Binomial Model Call Valuation

You observe a €50 price for a non-dividend-paying stock. The call option has two years to mature, the periodically compounded risk-free interest rate is 5%, the exercise price is €50, u = 1.356, and d = 0.744. Assume the call option is European-style.

1. The probability of an up move based on the risk-neutral probability is *closest* to:

    A. 30%.

    B. 40%.

    C. 50%.

Solution:

C is correct. Based on the RN probability equation, we have:

$\pi = [FV(1) - d]/(u - d) = [(1 + 0.05) - 0.744]/(1.356 - 0.744) = 0.5$ or 50%

2. The current call option value is *closest* to:

    A. €9.53.

    B. €9.71.

    C. €9.87.

Solution:

B is correct. The current call option value calculations are as follows:

$c^{++} = Max(0, u^2S - X) = Max[0, 1.356^2(50) - 50] = 41.9368$

$c^{-+} = c^{+-} = Max(0, udS - X) = Max[0, 1.356(0.744)(50) - 50] = 0.44320$

$c^{--} = Max(0, d^2S - X) = Max[0, 0.744^2(50) - 50] = 0.0$

With this information, we can compute the call option value:

$c = PV[E(c_2)] = PV[\pi^2c^{++} + 2\pi(1 - \pi)c^{+-} + (1 - \pi)^2c^{--}]$

$= [1/(1 + 0.05)]^2[0.5^241.9368 + 2(0.5)(1 - 0.5)0.44320 + (1 - 0.5)^20.0]$

$= 9.71$

It is vital to remember that the present value is over two periods, hence the single-period PV is squared. Thus, the current call price is €9.71.

3. The current put option value is *closest* to:

    A. €5.06.

    B. €5.33.

    C. €5.94.

> **Solution:**
>
> A is correct. The put option value can be computed simply by applying put–call parity or $p = c + PV(X) - S = 9.71 + [1/(1 + 0.05)]^2 50 - 50 = 5.06$. Thus, the current put price is €5.06.

TWO-PERIOD BINOMIAL MODEL: PUT OPTIONS

5

☐ | describe and interpret the binomial option valuation model and its component terms
☐ | calculate the no-arbitrage values of European and American options using a two-period binomial model

We now turn to consider American-style options. It is well-known that call options on non-dividend-paying stock will not be exercised early because the minimum price of the option exceeds its exercise value. To illustrate by example, consider a call on a US$100 stock, with an exercise price of US$10 (that is, very deep in the money). Suppose the call is worth its exercise value of only US$90. To get stock exposure, one could fund and pay US$100 to buy the stock, or fund and pay only US$90 for the call and pay the last US$10 at expiration only if the stock is at or above US$100 at that time. Because the latter choice is preferable, the call must be worth more than the US$90 exercise value. Another way of looking at it is that it would make no sense to exercise this call because you do not believe the stock can go any higher and you would thus simply be obtaining a stock that you believe would go no higher. Moreover, the stock would require that you pay far more money than you have tied up in the call. It is always better to just sell the call in this situation because it will be trading for more than the exercise value.

The same is not true for put options. By early exercise of a put, particularly a deep in-the-money put, the sale proceeds can be invested at the risk-free rate and earn interest worth more than the time value of the put. Thus, we will examine how early exercise influences the value of an American-style put option. As we will see, when early exercise has value, the no-arbitrage approach is the only way to value American-style options.

Suppose the periodically compounded interest rate is 3%, the non-dividend-paying underlying stock is currently trading at 72, the exercise price is 75, $u = 1.356$, $d = 0.541$, and the put option expires in two years. Exhibit 6 shows the results for a European-style put option.

Exhibit 6: Two-Period Binomial Model for a European-Style Put Option

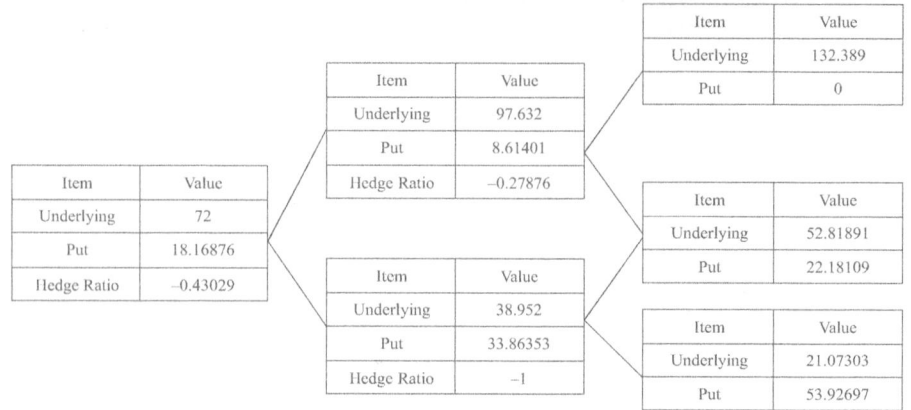

The Time 1 down move is of particular interest. The exercise value for this put option is 36.048 [= Max(0,75 − 38.952)]. Therefore, the exercise value is higher than the put value. So, if this same option were American-style, then the option would be worth more exercised than not exercised. Thus, the put option should be exercised. Exhibit 7 illustrates how the analysis changes if this put option were American-style. Clearly, the right to exercise early translates into a higher value.

Exhibit 7: Two-Period Binomial Model for an American-Style Put Option

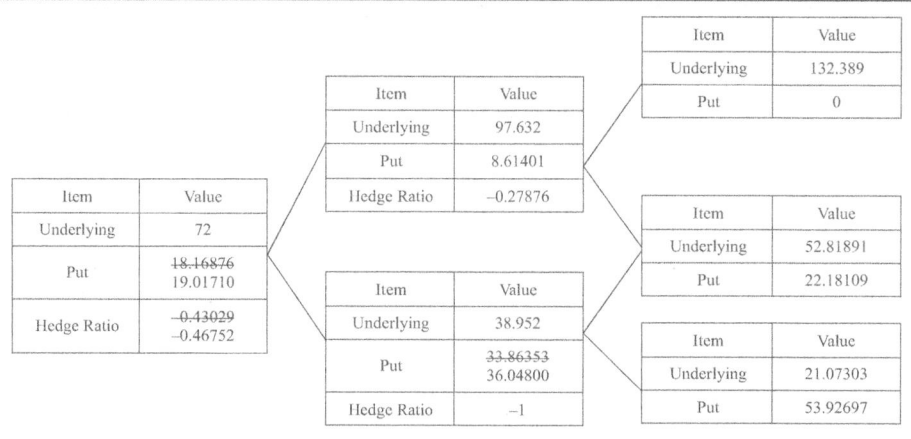

American-style option valuation requires that one work backward through the binomial tree and address whether early exercise is optimal at each step. In Exhibit 7, the early exercise premium at Time 1 when a down move occurs is 2.18447 (36.048 − 33.86353). Also, if we replace 33.86353 with 36.048—in bold below for emphasis—in the Time 0 calculation, we obtain a put value of

$$p = PV[\pi p^+ + (1 − \pi)p^-] = (1/1.03)[(0.6)8.61401 + (1 − 0.6)\mathbf{36.048}] = 19.02$$

Thus, the early exercise premium at Time 0 is 0.85 (19.02 − 18.17). From this illustration, we see clearly that in a multiperiod setting, American-style put options cannot be valued simply as the present value of the expected future option payouts, as shown in Equation 9. American-style put options can be valued as the present value of the expected future option payout in a single-period setting. Hence, when early exercise is a consideration, we must address the possibility of early exercise as we work backward through the binomial tree.

EXAMPLE 6

Two-Period Binomial American-Style Put Option Valuation

1. Suppose you are given the following information: $S_0 = 26$, $X = 25$, $u = 1.466$, $d = 0.656$, $n = 2$ (time steps), $r = 2.05\%$ (per period), and no dividends. The tree is provided in Exhibit 8.

Exhibit 8: Two-Period Binomial American-Style Put Option

Item	Value
Underlying	55.87806
Put	0

Item	Value
Underlying	38.116
Put	0
Hedge Ratio	0

Item	Value
Underlying	26
Put	4.01174
Hedge Ratio	-0.35345

Item	Value
Underlying	25.00410
Put	0

Item	Value
Underlying	17.056
Put	7.44360
Hedge Ratio	-0.99970

Item	Value
Underlying	11.18874
Put	13.81126

The early exercise premium of the above American-style put option is *closest* to:

A. 0.27.

B. 0.30.

C. 0.35.

Solution:

A is correct. The exercise value at Time 1 with a down move is 7.944 [= Max(0,25 − 17.056)]. Thus, we replace this value in the binomial tree and compute the hedge ratio at Time 0. The resulting put option value at Time 0 is thus 4.28143 (see Exhibit 9).

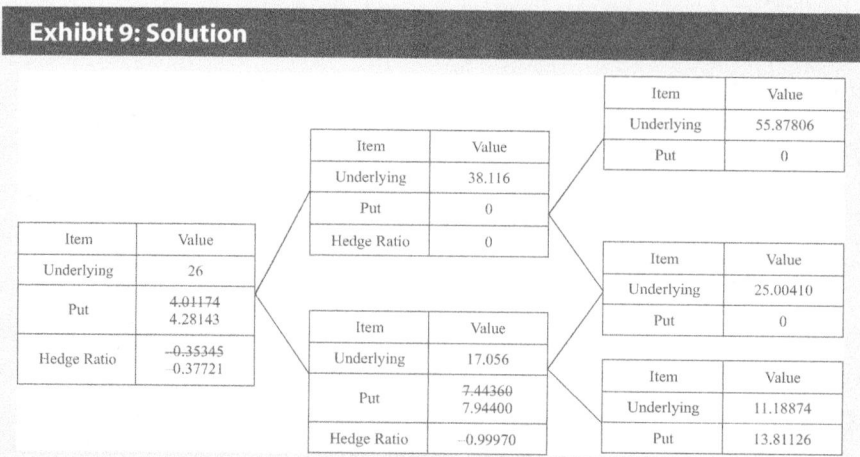

Exhibit 9: Solution

In Exhibit 9, the early exercise premium at Time 1 when a down move occurs is 0.5004 (7.944 − 7.44360). Thus, if we replace 7.44360 with 7.944—in bold below for emphasis—in the Time 0 calculation, we have the put value of

$$p = PV[\pi p^+ + (1 - \pi)p^-] = (1/1.0205)[(0.45)0 + (1 - 0.45)\mathbf{7.944}] = 4.28$$

Thus, the early exercise premium at Time 0 when a down move occurs 0.27 (= 4.28 − 4.01).

6   TWO-PERIOD BINOMIAL MODEL: ROLE OF DIVIDENDS

☐ | describe and interpret the binomial option valuation model and its component terms

We now briefly introduce the role of dividend payments within the binomial model. Our approach here is known as the escrow method. Because dividends lower the value of the stock, a call option holder is hurt. Although it is possible to adjust the option terms to offset this effect, most option contracts do not provide protection against dividends. Thus, dividends affect the value of an option. We assume dividends are perfectly predictable; hence, we split the underlying instrument into two components: the underlying instrument without the known dividends and the known dividends.[6] For example, the current value of the underlying instrument without dividends can be expressed as

$$\hat{S} = S - \gamma$$

where γ denotes the present value of dividend payments. We use the ^ symbol to denote the underlying instrument without dividends. In this case, we model the uncertainty of the stock based on $\hat{S}$ and not S. At expiration, the underlying instrument value is the same, $\hat{S}_T = S_T$, because we assume any dividends have already been paid. The value of an investment in the stock, however, would be $S_T + \gamma_T$, which assumes the dividend payments are reinvested at the risk-free rate.

---

6 The reading focuses on regular, "known" dividends. In the case of large, special dividends, option exchanges may adjust the exercise price.

To illustrate by example, consider a call on a US$100 stock with exercise price of US$95. The periodically compounded interest rate is 1.0%, the stock will pay a US$3 dividend at Time Step 1, u = 1.224, d = 0.796, and the call option expires in two years. Exhibit 10 shows some results for an American-style call option. The computations in Exhibit 10 involve several technical nuances that are beyond the scope of our objectives. The key objective here is to see how dividend-motivated early exercise influences American options.

The Time 1 up move is particularly interesting. At Time 0, the present value of the US$3 dividend payment is US$2.970297 (= 3/1.01). Therefore, 118.7644 = (100 − 2.970297)1.224 is the stock value without dividends at Time 1, assuming an up move occurs. The exercise value for this call option, including dividends, is 26.7644 [= Max(0,118.7644 + 3 − 95)], whereas the value of the call option per the binomial model is 24.9344. In other words, the stock price just before it goes ex-dividend is 118.7644 + 3 = 121.7644, so the option can be exercised for 121.7644 − 95 = 26.7644. If not exercised, the stock drops as it goes ex-dividend and the option becomes worth 24.9344 at the ex-dividend price. Thus, by exercising early, the call buyer acquires the stock just before it goes ex-dividend and thus is able to capture the dividend. If the call is not exercised, the call buyer will not receive this dividend. The American-style call option is worth more than the European-style call option because at Time Step 1 when an up move occurs, the call is exercised early, capturing additional value.

Exhibit 10: Two-Period Binomial Model for an American-Style Call Option with Dividends

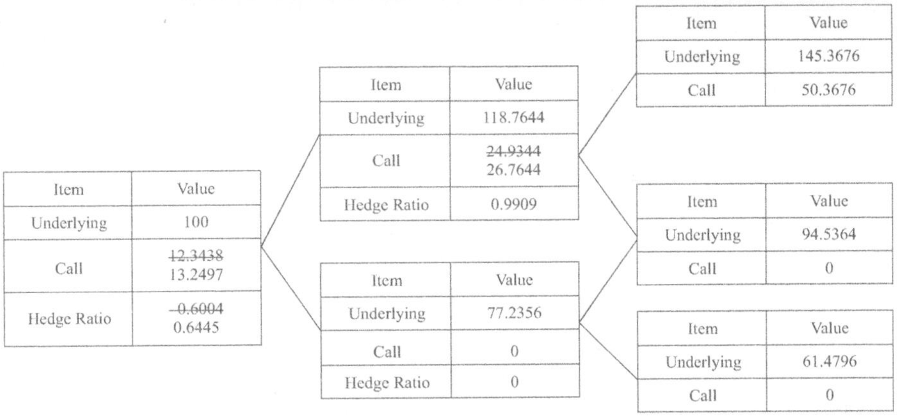

We now provide a comprehensive binomial option valuation example. In this example, we contrast European-style exercise with American-style exercise.

EXAMPLE 7

Comprehensive Two-Period Binomial Option Valuation Model Exercise

Suppose you observe a non-dividend-paying Australian equity trading for A$7.35. The call and put options have two years to mature, the periodically compounded risk-free interest rate is 4.35%, and the exercise price is A$8.0. Based on an analysis of this equity, the estimates for the up and down moves are u = 1.445 and d = 0.715, respectively.

1. Calculate the European-style call and put option values at Time Step 0 and Time Step 1. Describe and interpret your results.

Solution:

The expectations approach requires the following preliminary calculations:

RN probability: $\pi = [FV(1) - d]/(u - d)$

$= [(1 + 0.0435) - 0.715]/(1.445 - 0.715) = 0.45$

$c^{++} = Max(0, u^2 S - X)$

$= Max[0, 1.445^2(7.35) - 8.0] = 7.347$

$c^{+-} = Max(0, udS - X)$

$= Max[0, 1.445(0.715)7.35 - 8.0] = 0$

$c^{--} = Max(0, d^2 S - X)$

$= Max[0, 0.715^2(7.35) - 8.0] = 0$

$p^{++} = Max(0, X - u^2 S)$

$= Max[0, 8.0 - 1.445^2(7.35)] = 0$

$p^{+-} = Max(0, X - udS)$

$= Max[0, 8.0 - 1.445(0.715)7.35] = 0.406$

$p^{--} = Max(0, X - d^2 S)$

$= Max[0, 8.0 - 0.715^2(7.35)] = 4.24$

Therefore, at Time Step 1, we have (note that $c_2 \big|_1^+$ is read as the call value expiring at Time Step 2 observed at Time Step 1, assuming an up move occurs)

$E\left(c_2 \big|_1^+\right) = \pi c^{++} + (1 - \pi)c^{+-} = 0.45(7.347) + (1 - 0.45)0 = 3.31$

$E\left(c_2 \big|_1^-\right) = \pi c^{-+} + (1 - \pi)c^{--} = 0.45(0.0) + (1 - 0.45)0.0 = 0.0$

$E\left(p_2 \big|_1^+\right) = \pi p^{++} + (1 - \pi)p^{+-} = 0.45(0.0) + (1 - 0.45)0.406 = 0.2233$

$E\left(p_2 \big|_1^-\right) = \pi p^{-+} + (1 - \pi)p^{--} = 0.45(0.406) + (1 - 0.45)4.24 = 2.51$

Thus, because $PV_{1,2}(1) = 1/(1 + 0.0435) = 0.958313$, we have the Time Step 1 option values of

$c^+ = PV_{1,2}\left[E\left(c_2 \big|_1^+\right)\right] = 0.958313(3.31) = 3.17$

$c^- = PV_{1,2}\left[E\left(c_2 \big|_1^-\right)\right] = 0.958313(0.0) = 0.0$

$p^+ = PV_{1,2}\left[E\left(p_2 \big|_1^+\right)\right] = 0.958313(0.2233) = 0.214$

$p^- = PV_{1,2}\left[E\left(p_2 \big|_1^-\right)\right] = 0.958313(2.51) = 2.41$

At Time Step 0, we have

$E\left(c_2 \big|_0\right) = \pi^2 c^{++} + 2\pi(1 - \pi)c^{+-} + (1 - \pi)^2 c^{--}$

$= 0.45^2(7.347) + 2(0.45)(1 - 0.45)0 + (1 - 0.45)^2 0 = 1.488$

$$E\left(p_2\big|_0\right) = \pi^2 p^{++} + 2\pi(1-\pi)p^{+-} + (1-\pi)^2 p^{--}$$

$$= 0.45^2(0) + 2(0.45)(1-0.45)0.406 + (1-0.45)^2 4.24 = 1.484$$

Thus,

$$c = PV_{rf,0,2}\left[E\left(c_2\big|_0\right)\right] = 0.91836(1.488) = 1.37 \text{ and}$$

$$p = PV_{rf,0,2}\left[E\left(p_2\big|_0\right)\right] = 0.91836(1.484) = 1.36$$

With the two-period binomial model, the call and put values based on the expectations approach are simply the present values of the expected payoffs. The present value of the expected payoffs is based on the risk-free interest rate and the expectations approach is based on the risk-neutral probability. The parameters in this example were selected so that the European-style put and call would have approximately the same value. Notice that the stock price is less than the exercise price by roughly the present value factor or $7.35 = 8.0/1.0435^2$. One intuitive explanation is put–call parity, which can be expressed as $c - p = S - PV(X)$. Thus, if $S = PV(X)$, then $c = p$.

2. Calculate the European-style call and put option hedge ratios at Time Step 0 and Time Step 1. Based on these hedge ratios, interpret the component terms of the binomial option valuation model.

Solution:

The computation of the hedge ratios at Time Step 1 and Time Step 0 will require the option values at Time Step 1 and Time Step 2. The terminal values of the options are given in Solution 1.

$$S^{++} = u^2 S = 1.445^2(7.35) = 15.347$$

$$S^{+-} = udS = 1.445(0.715)7.35 = 7.594$$

$$S^{--} = d^2 S = 0.715^2(7.35) = 3.758$$

$$S^{+} = uS = 1.445(7.35) = 10.621$$

$$S^{-} = dS = 0.715(7.35) = 5.255$$

Therefore, the hedge ratios at Time 1 are

$$h_c^{+} = \frac{c^{++} - c^{+-}}{S^{++} - S^{+-}} = \frac{7.347 - 0.0}{15.347 - 7.594} = 0.9476$$

$$h_c^{-} = \frac{c^{-+} - c^{--}}{S^{-+} - S^{--}} = \frac{0.0 - 0.0}{7.594 - 3.758} = 0.0$$

$$h_p^{+} = \frac{p^{++} - p^{+-}}{S^{++} - S^{+-}} = \frac{0.0 - 0.406}{15.347 - 7.594} = -0.05237$$

$$h_p^{-} = \frac{p^{-+} - p^{--}}{S^{-+} - S^{--}} = \frac{0.406 - 4.24}{7.594 - 3.758} = -1.0$$

In the last hedge ratio calculation, both put options are in the money (p^{-+} and p^{--}). In this case, the hedge ratio will be −1, subject to a rounding error. We now turn to interpreting the model's component terms. Based on the no-arbitrage approach, we have for the call price, assuming an up move has occurred, at Time Step 1,

$$c^+ = h_c^+ S^+ + PV_{1,2}\left(-h_c^+ S^{+-} + c^{+-}\right)$$
$$= 0.9476(10.621) + (1/1.0435)[-0.9476(7.594) + 0.0] = 3.1684$$

Thus, the call option can be interpreted as a leveraged position in the stock. Specifically, long 0.9476 shares for a cost of 10.0645 [= 0.9476(10.621)] partially financed with a 6.8961 {= (1/1.0435)[−0.9476(7.594) + 0.0]} loan. Note that the loan amount can be found simply as the cost of the position in shares less the option value [6.8961 = 0.9476(10.621) − 3.1684]. Similarly, we have

$$c^- = h_c^- S^- + PV_{1,2}\left(-h_c^- S^{--} + c^{--}\right)$$
$$= 0.0(5.255) + (1/1.0435)[-0.0(3.758) + 0.0] = 0.0$$

Specifically, long 0.0 shares for a cost of 0.0 [= 0.0(5.255)] with no financing. For put options, the interpretation is different. Specifically, we have

$$p^+ = PV_{1,2}\left(-h_p^+ S^{++} + p^{++}\right) + h_p^+ S^+$$
$$= (1/1.0435)[-(-0.05237)15.347 + 0.0] + (-0.05237)10.621 = 0.2140$$

Thus, the put option can be interpreted as lending that is partially financed with a short position in shares. Specifically, short 0.05237 shares for a cost of 0.55622 [= (−0.05237)10.621] with financing of 0.77022 {= (1/1.0435)[−(−0.05237)15.347 + 0.0]}. Note that the lending amount can be found simply as the proceeds from the short sale of shares plus the option value [0.77022 = (0.05237)10.621 + 0.2140]. Again, we have

$$p^- = PV_{1,2}\left(-h_p^- S^{-+} + p^{-+}\right) + h_p^- S^-$$
$$= (1/1.0435)[-(-1.0)7.594 + 0.406] + (-1.0)5.255 = 2.4115$$

Here, we short 1.0 shares for a cost of 5.255 [= (−1.0)5.255] with financing of 7.6665 {= (1/1.0435)[−(−1.0)7.594 + 0.406]}. Again, the lending amount can be found simply as the proceeds from the short sale of shares plus the option value [7.6665 = (1.0)5.255 + 2.4115].

Finally, we have at Time Step 0

$$h_c = \frac{c^+ - c^-}{S^+ - S^-} = \frac{3.1684 - 0}{10.621 - 5.255} = 0.5905$$

$$h_p = \frac{p^+ - p^-}{S^+ - S^-} = \frac{0.2140 - 2.4115}{10.621 - 5.255} = -0.4095$$

The interpretations remain the same at Time Step 0:

$$c = h_c S + PV_{0,1}(-h_c S^- + c^-)$$

$$= 0.5905(7.35) + (1/1.0435)[-0.5905(5.255) + 0.0] = 1.37$$

Here, we are long 0.5905 shares for a cost of 4.3402 [=0.5905(7.35)] partially financed with a 2.97 {= (1/1.0435)[-0.5905(5.255) + 0.0] or = 0.5905(7.35) - 1.37} loan.

$$p = PV_{0,1}(-h_p S^+ + p^+) + h_p S$$

$$= (1/1.0435)\{-[-0.4095(10.621)] + 0.214\} + (-0.4095)7.35 = 1.36$$

Here, we short 0.4095 shares for a cost of 3.01 [= (-0.4095)7.35] with financing of 4.37 (= (1/1.0435){-[-0.4095(10.621)] + 0.214} or = (0.4095)7.35 + 1.36).

3. Calculate the American-style call and put option values and hedge ratios at Time Step 0 and Time Step 1. Explain how your results differ from the European-style results.

Solution:

We know that American-style call options on non-dividend-paying stock are worth the same as European-style call options because early exercise will not occur. Thus, as previously computed, $c^+ = 3.17$, $c^- = 0.0$, and $c = 1.37$. Recall that the call exercise value (denoted with EV) is simply the maximum of zero or the stock price minus the exercise price. We note that the EVs are less than or equal to the call model values; that is,

$$c_{EV}^+ = Max(0, S^+ - X) = Max(0, 10.621 - 8.0) = 2.621 \; (< 3.1684)$$

$$c_{EV}^- = Max(0, S^- - X) = Max(0, 5.255 - 8.0) = 0.0 \; (= 0.0)$$

$$c_{EV} = Max(0, S - X) = Max(0, 7.35 - 8.0) = 0.0 \; (< 1.37)$$

Therefore, the American-style feature for non-dividend-paying stocks has no effect on either the hedge ratio or the option value. The binomial model for American-style calls on non-dividend-paying stocks can be described and interpreted the same as a similar European-style call. This point is consistent with what we said earlier. If there are no dividends, an American-style call will not be exercised early.

This result is not true for puts. We know that American-style put options on non-dividend-paying stock may be worth more than the analogous European-style put options. The hedge ratios at Time Step 1 will be the same as European-style puts because there is only one period left. Therefore, as previously shown, $p^+ = 0.214$ and $p^- = 2.41$.

The put exercise values are

$$p_{EV}^+ = Max(0, X - S^+) = Max(0, 8.0 - 10.621) = 0 \; (< 0.214)$$

$$p_{EV}^- = Max(0, X - S^-) = Max(0, 8.0 - 5.255) = 2.745 \; (> 2.41)$$

Because the exercise value for the put at Time Step 1, assuming a down move occurred, is greater than the model value, we replace the model value with the exercise value. Hence,

$p^- = 2.745$

and the hedge ratio at Time Step 0 will be affected. Specifically, we now have

$$h_p = \frac{p^+ - p^-}{S^+ - S^-} = \frac{0.2140 - 2.745}{10.621 - 5.255} = -0.4717$$

and thus the put model value is

$$p = (1/1.0435)[0.45(0.214) + 0.55(2.745)] = 1.54$$

Clearly, the early exercise feature has a significant impact on both the hedge ratio and the put option value in this case. The hedge ratio goes from −0.4095 to −0.4717. The put value is raised from 1.36 to 1.54.

We see through the simple two-period binomial model that an option can be viewed as a position in the underlying with financing. Furthermore, this valuation model can be expressed as the present value of the expected future cash flows, where the expectation is taken under the RN probability and the discounting is at the risk-free rate.

Up to this point, we have focused on equity options. The binomial model can be applied to any underlying instrument though often requiring some modifications. For example, currency options would require incorporating the foreign interest rate. Futures options would require a binomial lattice of the futures prices. Interest rate options, however, require somewhat different tools that we now examine.

7   INTEREST RATE OPTIONS AND MULTIPERIOD MODEL

☐ | calculate and interpret the value of an interest rate option using a two-period binomial model

In this section, we will briefly illustrate how to value interest rate options. There are a wide variety of approaches to valuing interest rate options. We do not delve into how arbitrage-free interest rate trees are generated. The particular approach used here assumes the RN probability of an up move at each node is 50%.

Exhibit 11 presents a binomial lattice of interest rates covering two years along with the corresponding zero-coupon bond values. The rates are expressed in annual compounding. Therefore, at Time 0, the spot rate is (1.0/0.970446) − 1 or 3.04540%.[7] Note that at Time 1, the value in the column labeled "Maturity" reflects time to maturity not calendar time. The lattice shows the rates on one-period bonds, so all bonds have a maturity of 1. The column labeled "Value" is the value of a zero-coupon bond with the stated maturity based on the rates provided.

---

7 The values in the first box from the left are observed at t = 0. The values in the remainder of the lattice are derived by using a technique that is outside the scope of this reading.

Exhibit 11: Two-Year Binomial Interest Rate Lattice by Year

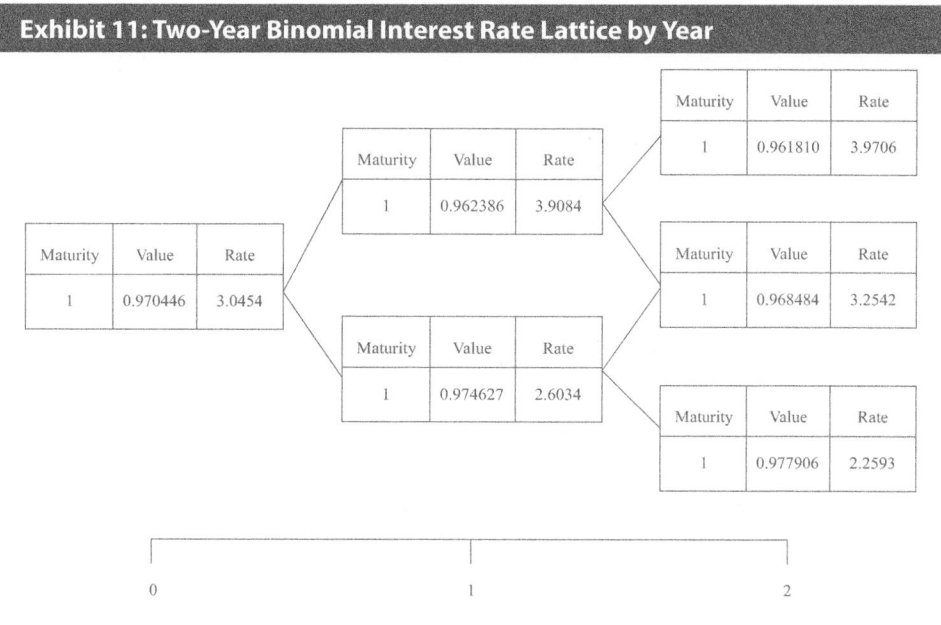

The underlying instrument for interest rate options here is the spot rate. A call option on interest rates will be in the money when the current spot rate is above the exercise rate. A put option on interest rates will be in the money when the current spot rate is below the exercise rate. Thus, based on the notation in the previous section, the current spot rate is denoted S. Option valuation follows the expectations approach discussed in the previous section but taken only one period at a time. The procedure is illustrated with an example.

EXAMPLE 8

Option on Interest Rates

1. This example is based on Exhibit 11. Suppose we seek to value two-year European-style call and put options on the periodically compounded one-year spot interest rate (the underlying). Assume the notional amount of the options is US$1,000,000 and the call and put exercise rate is 3.25% of par.

Assume the RN probability is 50% and these option cash settle at Time 2 based on the observed rates.[8]

Solution:

Using the expectations approach introduced in the last section, we have (per US$1) at Time Step 2

$$c^{++} = Max(0, S^{++} - X) = Max[0, 0.039706 - 0.0325] = 0.007206$$

$$c^{+-} = Max(0, S^{+-} - X) = Max[0, 0.032542 - 0.0325] = 0.000042$$

$$c^{--} = Max(0, S^{--} - X) = Max[0, 0.022593 - 0.0325] = 0.0$$

$$p^{++} = Max(0, X - S^{++}) = Max[0, 0.0325 - 0.039706] = 0.0$$

$$p^{+-} = Max(0, X - S^{+-}) = Max[0, 0.0325 - 0.032542] = 0.0$$

$$p^{--} = Max(0, X - S^{--}) = Max[0, 0.0325 - 0.022593] = 0.009907$$

At Time Step 1, we have

$$c^{+} = PV_{1,2}[\pi c^{++} + (1 - \pi)c^{+-}]$$

$$= 0.962386[0.5(0.007206) + (1 - 0.5)0.000042]$$

$$= 0.003488$$

$$c^{-} = PV_{1,2}[\pi c^{+-} + (1 - \pi)c^{--}]$$

$$= 0.974627[0.5(0.000042) + (1 - 0.5)0.0]$$

$$= 0.00002$$

$$p^{+} = PV_{1,2}[\pi p^{++} + (1 - \pi)p^{+-}]$$

$$= 0.962386[0.5(0.0) + (1 - 0.5)0.0]$$

$$= 0.0$$

$$p^{-} = PV_{1,2}[\pi p^{+-} + (1 - \pi)p^{--}]$$

$$= 0.974627[0.5(0.0) + (1 - 0.5)0.009907]$$

$$= 0.004828$$

Notice how the present value factors are different for the up and down moves. At Time Step 1 in the + outcome, we discount by a factor of 0.962386, and in the − outcome, we discount by the factor 0.974627. Because this is an option on interest rates, it should not be surprising that we have to allow the interest rate to vary.

---

8 In practice, interest rate options usually have a settlement procedure that results in a deferred payoff. The deferred payoff arises from the fact that the underlying interest rate is based on an instrument that pays interest at the end of its life. For the instrument underlying the interest rate, the interest payment occurs after the interest has accrued. To accommodate this reality in this problem, we would have to introduce an instrument that matures at time three. The purpose of this example is merely to illustrate the procedure for rolling backward through an interest rate tree when the underlying is the interest rate. We simplify this example by omitting this deferred settlement. In Section 5.2, we discuss in detail the deferred settlement procedure and incorporate it into the pricing model.

Therefore, at Time Step 0, we have

$c = PV_{rf,0,1}[\pi c^+ + (1 - \pi)c^-]$

$= 0.970446[0.5(0.003488) + (1 - 0.5)0.00002]$

$= 0.00170216$

$p = PV_{rf,0,1}[\pi p^+ + (1 - \pi)p^-]$

$= 0.970446[0.5(0.0) + (1 - 0.5)0.004828]$

$= 0.00234266$

Because the notional amount is US$1,000,000, the call value is US$1,702.16 [= US$1,000,000(0.00170216)] and the put value is US$2,342.66 [= US$1,000,000(0.00234266)]. The key insight is to just work a two-period binomial model as three one-period binomial models.

We turn now to briefly generalize the binomial model as it leads naturally to the Black–Scholes–Merton option valuation model.

Multiperiod Model

The multiperiod binomial model provides a natural bridge to the Black–Scholes–Merton option valuation model presented in the next section. The idea is to take the option's expiration and slice it up into smaller and smaller periods. The two-period model divides the expiration into two periods. The three-period model divides expiration into three periods and so forth. The process continues until you have a large number of time steps. The key feature is that each time step is of equal length. Thus, with a maturity of T, if there are n time steps, then each time step is T/n in length.

For American-style options, we must also test at each node whether the option is worth more exercised or not exercised. As in the two-period case, we work backward through the binomial tree testing the model value against the exercise value and always choosing the higher one.

The binomial model is an important and useful methodology for valuing options. The expectations approach can be applied to European-style options and will lead naturally to the BSM model in the next section. This approach simply values the option as the present value of the expected future payoffs, where the expectation is taken under the risk-neutral probability and the discounting is based on the risk-free rate. The no-arbitrage approach can be applied to either European-style or American-style options because it provides the intuition for the fair value of options.

BLACK-SCHOLES-MERTON (BSM) OPTION VALUATION MODEL

8

☐ | identify assumptions of the Black–Scholes–Merton option valuation model

The BSM model, although very complex in its derivation, is rather simple to use and interpret. The objective here is to illustrate several facets of the BSM model with the objective of highlighting its practical usefulness. After a brief introduction, we examine the assumptions of the BSM model and then delve into the model itself.

Introductory Material

Louis Bachelier published the first known mathematically rigorous option valuation model in 1900. By the late 1960s, there were several published quantitative option models. Fischer Black, Myron Scholes, and Robert Merton introduced the BSM model in 1973 in two published papers, one by Black and Scholes and the other by Merton. The innovation of the BSM model is essentially the no-arbitrage approach introduced in the previous section but applied with a continuous time process, which is equivalent to a binomial model in which the length of the time step essentially approaches zero. It is also consistent with the basic statistical fact that the binomial process with a "large" number of steps converges to the standard normal distribution. Myron Scholes and Robert Merton won the 1997 Nobel Prize in Economics based, in part, on their work related to the BSM model.[9] Let us now examine the BSM model assumptions.

Assumptions of the BSM Model

The key assumption for option valuation models is how to model the random nature of the underlying instrument. This characteristic of how an asset evolves randomly is called a stochastic process. Many financial instruments enjoy limited liability; hence, the values of instruments cannot be negative, but they certainly can be zero. In 1900, Bachelier proposed the normal distribution. The key advantages of the normal distribution are that zero is possible, meaning that bankruptcy is allowable, it is symmetric, it is relatively easy to manipulate, and it is additive (which means that sums of normal distributions are normally distributed). The key disadvantage is that negative stock values are theoretically possible, which violates the limited liability principal of stock ownership. Based on research on stock prices in the 1950s and 1960s, a preference emerged for the lognormal distribution, which means that log returns are distributed normally. Black, Scholes, and Merton chose to use the lognormal distribution.

Recall that the no-arbitrage approach requires self-financing and dynamic replication; we need more than just an assumption regarding the terminal distribution of the underlying instrument. We need to model the value of the instrument as it evolves over time, which is what we mean by a stochastic process. The stochastic process chosen by Black, Scholes, and Merton is called geometric Brownian motion (GBM).

Exhibit 12 illustrates GBM, assuming the initial stock price is S = 50. We assume the stock will grow at 3% (μ = 3% annually, geometrically compounded rate). This GBM process also reflects a random component that is determined by a volatility (σ) of 45%. This volatility is the annualized standard deviation of continuously compounded percentage change in the underlying, or in other words, the log return. Note that as a particular sample path drifts upward, we observe more variability on an absolute basis, whereas when the particular sample path drifts downward, we observe less variability on an absolute basis. For example, examine the highest and lowest lines shown in Exhibit 12. The highest line is much more erratic than the lowest line. Recall that a 10% move in a stock with a price of 100 is 10 whereas a 10% move in a stock with a price of 10 is only 1. Thus, GBM can never hit zero nor go below it. This property is

---

9 Fischer Black passed away in 1995 and the Nobel Prize is not awarded posthumously.

appealing because many financial instruments enjoy limited liability and cannot be negative. Finally, note that although the stock movements are rather erratic, there are no large jumps—a common feature with marketable financial instruments.

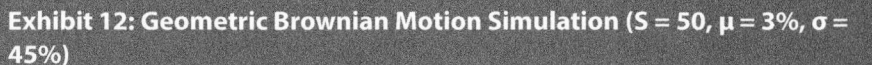

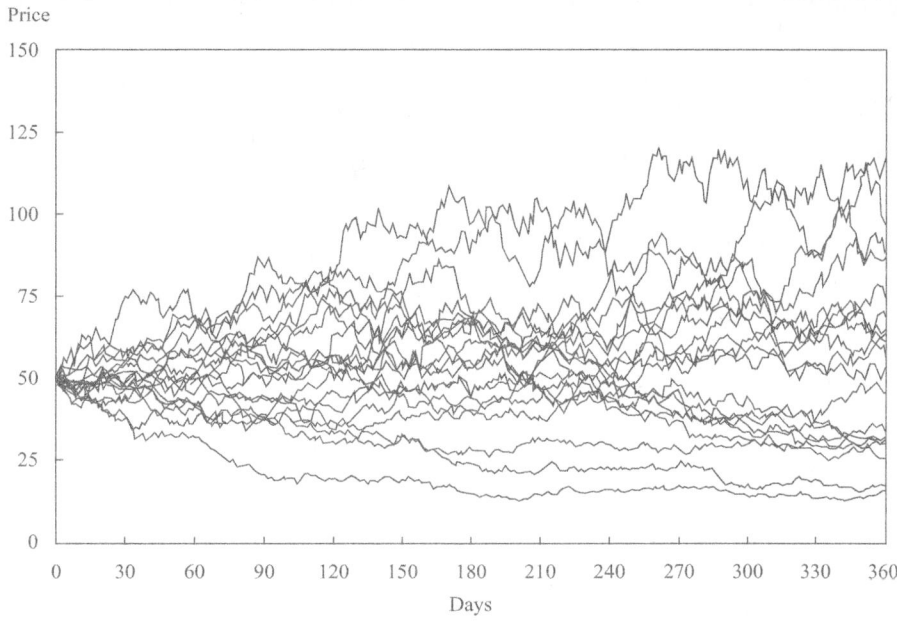

Exhibit 12: Geometric Brownian Motion Simulation (S = 50, μ = 3%, σ = 45%)

Within the BSM model framework, it is assumed that all investors agree on the distributional characteristics of GBM except the assumed growth rate of the underlying. This growth rate depends on a number of factors, including other instruments and time. The standard BSM model assumes a constant growth rate and constant volatility.

The specific assumptions of the BSM model are as follows:

- The underlying follows a statistical process called geometric Brownian motion, which implies that the continuously compounded return is normally distributed.

- Geometric Brownian motion implies continuous prices, meaning that the price of underlying instrument does not jump from one value to another; rather, it moves smoothly from value to value.

- The underlying instrument is liquid, meaning that it can be easily bought and sold.

- Continuous trading is available, meaning that in the strictest sense one must be able to trade at every instant.

- Short selling of the underlying instrument with full use of the proceeds is permitted.

- There are no market frictions, such as transaction costs, regulatory constraints, or taxes.

- No arbitrage opportunities are available in the marketplace.

- The options are European-style, meaning that early exercise is not allowed.

- The continuously compounded risk-free interest rate is known and constant; borrowing and lending is allowed at the risk-free rate.
- The volatility of the return on the underlying is known and constant.
- If the underlying instrument pays a yield, it is expressed as a continuous known and constant yield at an annualized rate.

Naturally, the foregoing assumptions are not absolutely consistent with real financial markets, but, as in all financial models, the question is whether they produce models that are tractable and useful in practice, which they do.

EXAMPLE 9

BSM Model Assumptions

1. Which is the *correct* pair of statements? The BSM model assumes:

   A. the return on the underlying has a normal distribution. The price of the underlying can jump abruptly to another price.

   B. brokerage costs are factored into the BSM model. It is impossible to trade continuously.

   C. volatility can be predicted with certainty. Arbitrage is non-existent in the marketplace.

Solution:

C is correct. All four of the statements in A and B are incorrect within the BSM model paradigm.

---

9   BSM MODEL: COMPONENTS

☐ | interpret the components of the Black–Scholes–Merton model as applied to call options in terms of a leveraged position in the underlying

We turn now to a careful examination of the BSM model.

The BSM model is a continuous time version of the discrete time binomial model. Given that the BSM model is based on continuous time, it is customary to use a continuously compounded interest rate rather than some discretely compounded alternative. Thus, when an interest rate is used here, denoted simply as r, we mean solely the annualized continuously compounded rate.[10] The volatility, denoted as σ, is also expressed in annualized percentage terms. Initially, we focus on a non-dividend-paying stock. The BSM model, with some adjustments, applies to other underlying instruments, which will be examined later.

The BSM model for stocks can be expressed as

$$c = SN(d_1) - e^{-rT}XN(d_2) \tag{10}$$

and

$$p = e^{-rT}XN(-d_2) - SN(-d_1) \tag{11}$$

---

10 Note $e^r = 1 + r_d$, where r_d is the annually compounded rate.

where

$$d_1 = \frac{\ln(S/X) + (r + \sigma^2/2)T}{\sigma\sqrt{T}}$$

$$d_2 = d_1 - \sigma\sqrt{T}$$

N(x) denotes the standard normal cumulative distribution function, which is the probability of obtaining a value of less than x based on a standard normal distribution. In our context, x will have the value of d_1 or d_2. N(x) reflects the likelihood of observing values less than x from a random sample of observations taken from the standard normal distribution.

Although the BSM model appears very complicated, it has straightforward interpretations that will be explained. N(x) can be estimated by a computer program or a spreadsheet or approximated from a lookup table. The normal distribution is a symmetric distribution with two parameters, the mean and standard deviation. The standard normal distribution is a normal distribution with a mean of 0 and a standard deviation of 1.

Exhibit 13 illustrates the standard normal probability density function (the standard bell curve) and the cumulative distribution function (the accumulated probability and range of 0 to 1). Note that even though GBM is lognormally distributed, the N(x) functions in the BSM model are based on the standard normal distribution. In Exhibit 13, we see that if x = −1.645, then N(x) = N(−1.645) = 0.05. Thus, if the model value of d is −1.645, the corresponding probability is 5%. Clearly, values of d that are less than 0 imply values of N(x) that are less than 0.5. As a result of the symmetry of the normal distribution, we note that N(−x) = 1 − N(x).

Exhibit 13: Standard Normal Distribution

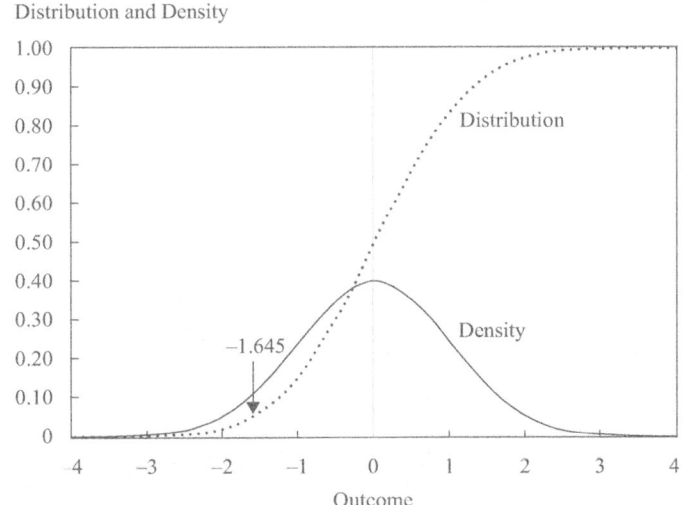

Distribution and Density

The BSM model can be described as the present value of the expected option payoff at expiration. Specifically, we can express the BSM model for calls as $c = PV_r[E(c_T)]$ and for puts as $p = PV_r[E(p_T)]$, where $E(c_T) = Se^{rT}N(d_1) - XN(d_2)$ and $E(p_T) = XN(-d_2) - Se^{rT}N(-d_1)$. The present value term in this context is simply e^{-rT}. As with most valuation tasks in finance, the value today is simply the present value of the expected future cash flows. It is important to note that the expectation is based on the risk-neutral probability measure defined in Section 3.1. The expectation is not based on the investor's subjective beliefs, which reflect an aversion to risk. Also, the present value function is based on the risk-free interest rate not on the investor's required return on invested capital, which of course is a function of risk.

Alternatively, the BSM model can be described as having two components: a stock component and a bond component. For call options, the stock component is $SN(d_1)$ and the bond component is $e^{-rT}XN(d_2)$. The BSM model call value is the stock component minus the bond component. For put options, the stock component is $SN(-d_1)$ and the bond component is $e^{-rT}XN(-d_2)$. The BSM model put value is the bond component minus the stock component.

The BSM model can be interpreted as a dynamically managed portfolio of the stock and zero-coupon bonds.[11] The goal is to replicate the option payoffs with stocks and bonds. For both call and put options, we can represent the initial cost of this replicating strategy as

Replicating strategy cost $= n_S S + n_B B$

where the equivalent number of underlying shares is $n_S = N(d_1) > 0$ for calls and $n_S = -N(-d_1) < 0$ for puts. The equivalent number of bonds is $n_B = -N(d_2) < 0$ for calls and $n_B = N(-d_2) > 0$ for puts. The price of the zero-coupon bond is $B = e^{-rT}X$. Note, if n is positive, we are buying the underlying and if n is negative we are selling (short selling) the underlying. The cost of the portfolio will exactly equal either the BSM model call value or the BSM model put value.

For calls, we are simply buying stock with borrowed money because $n_S > 0$ and $n_B < 0$. Again the cost of this portfolio will equal the BSM model call value, and if appropriately rebalanced, then this portfolio will replicate the payoff of the call option. Therefore, a call option can be viewed as a leveraged position in the stock.

Similarly, for put options, we are simply buying bonds with the proceeds from short selling the underlying because $n_S < 0$ and $n_B > 0$. The cost of this portfolio will equal the BSM model put value, and if appropriately rebalanced, then this portfolio will replicate the payoff of the put option. Note that a short position in a put will result in receiving money today and $n_S > 0$ and $n_B < 0$. Therefore, a short put can be viewed as an over-leveraged or over-geared position in the stock because the borrowing exceeds 100% of the cost of the underlying.

Exhibit 14 illustrates the direct comparison between the no-arbitrage approach to the single-period binomial option valuation model and the BSM option valuation model. The parallel between the h term in the binomial model and $N(d_1)$ is easy to see. Recall that the term hedge ratio was used with the binomial model because we were creating a no-arbitrage portfolio. Note for call options, $-N(d_2)$ implies borrowing money or short selling $N(d_2)$ shares of a zero-coupon bond trading at $e^{-rT}X$. For put options, $N(-d_2)$ implies lending money or buying $N(-d_2)$ shares of a zero-coupon bond trading at $e^{-rT}X$.

Exhibit 14: BSM and Binomial Option Valuation Model Comparison

Option Valuation Model Terms	Call Option		Put Option	
	Underlying	Financing	Underlying	Financing
Binomial Model	hS	$PV(-hS^- + c^-)$	hS	$PV(-hS^- + p^-)$
BSM Model	$N(d_1)S$	$-N(d_2)e^{-rT}X$	$-N(-d_1)S$	$N(-d_2)e^{-rT}X$

---

11 When covering the binomial model, the bond component was generically termed financing. This component is typically handled with bank borrowing or lending. With the BSM model, it is easier to understand as either buying or short selling a risk-free zero-coupon bond.

If the value of the underlying, S, increases, then the value of $N(d_1)$ also increases because S has a positive effect on d_1. Thus, the replicating strategy for calls requires continually buying shares in a rising market and selling shares in a falling market.

Within the BSM model theory, the aggregate losses from this "buy high/sell low" strategy, over the life of the option, adds up exactly to the BSM model option premium received for the option at inception.[12] This result must be the case; otherwise there would be arbitrage profits available. Because transaction costs are not, in fact, zero, the frequent rebalancing by buying and selling the underlying adds significant costs for the hedger. Also, markets can often move discontinuously, contrary to the BSM model's assumption that prices move continuously, thus allowing for continuous hedging adjustments. Hence, in reality, hedges are imperfect. For example, if a company announces a merger, then the company's stock price may jump substantially higher, contrary to the BSM model's assumption.

In addition, volatility cannot be known in advance. For these reasons, options are typically more expensive than they would be as predicted by the BSM model theory. In order to continue using the BSM model, the volatility parameter used in the formula is usually higher (by, say, 1% or 2%, but this can vary a lot) than the volatility of the stock actually expected by market participants. We will ignore this point for now, however, as we focus on the mechanics of the model.

EXAMPLE 10

Illustration of BSM Model Component Interpretation

Suppose we are given the following information on call and put options on a stock: S = 100, X = 100, r = 5%, T = 1.0, and σ = 30%. Thus, based on the BSM model, it can be demonstrated that PV(X) = 95.123, d_1 = 0.317, d_2 = 0.017, $N(d_1)$ = 0.624, $N(d_2)$ = 0.507, $N(-d_1)$ = 0.376, $N(-d_2)$ = 0.493, c = 14.23, and p = 9.35.

---

1. The initial trading strategy required by the no-arbitrage approach to replicate the call option payoffs for a buyer of the option is:

    A. buy 0.317 shares of stock and short sell −0.017 shares of zero-coupon bonds.

    B. buy 0.624 shares of stock and short sell 0.507 shares of zero-coupon bonds.

    C. short sell 0.317 shares of stock and buy 0.017 shares of zero-coupon bonds.

Solution:

B is correct. The no-arbitrage approach to replicating the call option involves purchasing $n_S = N(d_1) = 0.624$ shares of stock partially financed with $n_B = -N(d_2) = -0.507$ shares of zero-coupon bonds priced at $B = Xe^{-rT} = 95.123$ per bond. Note that by definition the cost of this replicating strategy is the BSM call model value or $n_S S + n_B B = 0.624(100) + (-0.507)95.123 = 14.17$. Without rounding errors, the option value is 14.23.

---

2. Identify the initial trading strategy required by the no-arbitrage approach to replicate the put option payoffs for a buyer of the put.

    A. Buy 0.317 shares of stock and short sell −0.017 shares of zero-coupon bonds.

---

12 The validity of this claim does not rest on the validity of the BSM model assumptions; rather the validity depends only on whether the BSM model accurately predicts the replication cost.

B. Buy 0.624 shares of stock and short sell 0.507 shares of zero-coupon bonds.

C. Short sell 0.376 shares of stock and buy 0.493 shares of zero-coupon bonds.

Solution:

C is correct. The no-arbitrage approach to replicating the put option is similar. In this case, we trade $n_S = -N(-d_1) = -0.376$ shares of stock—specifically, short sell 0.376 shares—and buy $n_B = N(-d_2) = 0.493$ shares of zero-coupon bonds. Again, the cost of the replicating strategy is $n_S S + n_B B$ $= -0.376(100) + (0.493)95.123 = 9.30$. Without rounding errors, the option value is 9.35. Thus, to replicate a call option based on the BSM model, we buy stock on margin. To replicate a put option, we short the stock and buy zero-coupon bonds.

Note that the $N(d_2)$ term has an additional important interpretation. It is a unique measure of the probability that the call option expires in the money, and correspondingly, $1 - N(d_2) = N(-d_2)$ is the probability that the put option expires in the money. Specifically, the probability based on the RN probability of being in the money, not one's own estimate of the probability of being in the money nor the market's estimate. That is, $N(d_2) = \text{Prob}(S_T > X)$ based on the unique RN probability.

10 BSM MODEL: CARRY BENEFITS AND APPLICATIONS

☐ | describe how the Black–Scholes–Merton model is used to value European options on equities and currencies

We now turn to incorporating various carry benefits into the BSM model. Carry benefits include dividends for stock options, foreign interest rates for currency options, and coupon payments for bond options. For other underlying instruments, there are carry costs that can easily be treated as negative carry benefits, such as storage and insurance costs for agricultural products. Because the BSM model is established in continuous time, it is common to model these carry benefits as a continuous yield, denoted generically here as γ^c or simply γ.

The BSM model requires a few adjustments to accommodate carry benefits. The carry benefit-adjusted BSM model is

$$c = Se^{-\gamma T}N(d_1) - e^{-rT}XN(d_2) \tag{12}$$

and

$$p = e^{-rT}XN(-d_2) - Se^{-\gamma T}N(-d_1) \tag{13}$$

where

$$d_1 = \frac{\ln(S/X) + (r - \gamma + \sigma^2/2)T}{\sigma\sqrt{T}}$$

Note that d_2 can be expressed again simply as $d_2 = d_1 - \sigma\sqrt{T}$. The value of a put option can also be found based on the carry benefit-adjusted put–call parity:

$$p + Se^{-\gamma T} = c + e^{-rT}X \tag{14}$$

The carry benefit-adjusted BSM model can again be described as the present value of the expected option payoff at expiration. Now, however, $E(c_T) = Se^{(r-\gamma)T}N(d_1) - XN(d_2)$ and $E(p_T) = XN(-d_2) - Se^{(r-\gamma)T}N(-d_1)$. The present value term remains simply e^{-rT}. Carry benefits will have the effect of lowering the expected future value of the underlying

Again, the carry benefit adjusted BSM model can be described as having two components, a stock component and a bond component. For call options, the stock component is $Se^{-\gamma T}N(d_1)$ and the bond component is again $e^{-rT}XN(d_2)$. For put options, the stock component is $Se^{-\gamma T}N(-d_1)$ and the bond component is again $e^{-rT}XN(-d_2)$. Although both d_1 and d_2 are reduced by carry benefits, the general approach to valuation remains the same. An increase in carry benefits will lower the value of the call option and raise the value of the put option.

Note that $N(d_2)$ term continues to be interpreted as the RN probability of a call option being in the money. The existence of carry benefits has the effect of lowering d_1 and d_2, hence the probability of being in the money with call options declines as the carry benefit rises. This RN probability is an important element to describing how the BSM model is used in various valuation tasks.

For stock options, $\gamma = \delta$, which is the continuously compounded dividend yield. The dividend-yield BSM model can again be interpreted as a dynamically managed portfolio of the stock and zero coupon bonds. Based on the call model above applied to a dividend yielding stock, the equivalent number of units of stock is now $n_S = e^{-\delta T}N(d_1) > 0$ and the equivalent number of units of bonds remains $n_B = -N(d_2) < 0$. Similarly with puts, the equivalent number of units of stock is now $n_S = -e^{-\delta T}N(-d_1) < 0$ and the equivalent number of units of bonds again remains $n_B = N(-d_2) > 0$.

With dividend paying stocks, the arbitrageur is able to receive the benefits of dividend payments when long the stock and has to pay dividends when short the stock. Thus, the burden of carrying the stock is diminished for a long position. The key insight is that dividends influence the dynamically managed portfolio by lowering the number of shares to buy for calls and raising the number of shares to short sell for puts. Higher dividends will lower the value of d_1, thus lowering $N(d_1)$. Also, higher dividends will lower the number of bonds to short sell for calls and raise the number of bonds to buy for puts.

EXAMPLE 11

BSM Model Applied to Equities

Suppose we are given the following information on an underlying stock and options: $S = 60$, $X = 60$, $r = 2\%$, $T = 0.5$, $\delta = 2\%$, and $\sigma = 45\%$. Assume we are examining European-style options.

---

1. Which answer *best* describes how the BSM model is used to value a call option with the parameters given?

    A. The BSM model call value is the exercise price times $N(d_1)$ less the present value of the stock price times $N(d_2)$.

    B. The BSM model call value is the stock price times $e^{-\delta T}N(d_1)$ less the exercise price times $e^{-rT}N(d_2)$.

    C. The BSM model call value is the stock price times $e^{-\delta T}N(-d_1)$ less the present value of the exercise price times $e^{-rT}N(-d_2)$.

Solution:

B is correct. The BSM call model for a dividend-paying stock can be expressed as $Se^{-\delta T}N(d_1) - Xe^{-rT}N(d_2)$.

2. Which answer *best* describes how the BSM model is used to value a put option with the parameters given?

   A. The BSM model put value is the exercise price times $N(d_1)$ less the present value of the stock price times $N(d_2)$.

   B. The BSM model put value is the exercise price times $e^{-\delta T}N(-d_2)$ less the stock price times $e^{-rT}N(-d_2)$.

   C. The BSM model put value is the exercise price times $e^{-rT}N(-d_2)$ less the stock price times $e^{-\delta T}N(-d_1)$.

Solution:

C is correct. The BSM put model for a dividend-paying stock can be expressed as $Xe^{-rT}N(-d_2) - Se^{-\delta T}N(-d_1)$.

3. Suppose now that the stock does not pay a dividend—that is, $\delta = 0\%$. Identify the correct statement.

   A. The BSM model option value is the same as the previous problems because options are not dividend adjusted.

   B. The BSM model option values will be different because there is an adjustment term applied to the exercise price, that is $e^{-\delta T}$, which will influence the option values.

   C. The BSM model option value will be different because d_1, d_2, and the stock component are all adjusted for dividends.

Solution:

C is correct. The BSM model option value will be different because d_1, d_2, and the stock component are all adjusted for dividends.

EXAMPLE 12

How the BSM Model Is Used to Value Stock Options

1. Suppose that we have some Bank of China shares that are currently trading on the Hong Kong Stock Exchange at HKD4.41. Our view is that the Bank of China's stock price will be steady for the next three months, so we decide to sell some three-month out-of-the-money calls with exercise price at 4.60 in order to enhance our returns by receiving the option premium. Risk-free government securities are paying 1.60% and the stock is yielding HKD 0.24%. The stock volatility is 28%. We use the BSM model to value the calls.

   Which statement is correct? The BSM model inputs (underlying, exercise, expiration, risk-free rate, dividend yield, and volatility) are:

   A. 4.60, 4.41, 3, 0.0160, 0.0024, and 0.28.

   B. 4.41, 4.60, 0.25, 0.0160, 0.0024, and 0.28.

   C. 4.41, 4.41, 0.3, 0.0160, 0.0024, and 0.28.

Solution:

B is correct. The spot price of the underlying is HKD4.41. The exercise price is HKD4.60. The expiration is 0.25 years (three months). The risk-free rate is 0.016. The dividend yield is 0.0024. The volatility is 0.28.

For foreign exchange options, $\gamma = r^f$, which is the continuously compounded foreign risk-free interest rate. When quoting an exchange rate, we will give the value of the domestic currency per unit of the foreign currency. For example, Japanese yen (¥) per unit of the euro (€) will be expressed as the euro trading for ¥135 or succinctly 135¥/€. This is called the foreign exchange spot rate. Thus, the foreign currency, the euro, is expressed in terms of the Japanese yen, which is in this case the domestic currency. This is logical, for example, when a Japanese firm would want to express its foreign euro holdings in terms of its domestic currency, Japanese yen.

With currency options, the underlying instrument is the foreign exchange spot rate. Again, the carry benefit is the interest rate in the foreign country because the foreign currency could be invested in the foreign country's risk-free instrument. Also, with currency options, the underlying and the exercise price must be quoted in the same currency unit. Lastly, the volatility in the model is the volatility of the log return of the spot exchange rate. Each currency option is for a certain quantity of foreign currency, termed the notional amount, a concept analogous to the number of shares of stock covered in an option contract. The total cost of the option would be obtained by multiplying the formula value by the notional amount in the same way that one would multiply the formula value of an option on a stock by the number of shares the option contract covers.

The BSM model applied to currencies can be described as having two components, a foreign exchange component and a bond component. For call options, the foreign exchange component is $Se^{-r^f T}N(d_1)$ and the bond component is $e^{-rT}XN(d_2)$, where r is the domestic risk-free rate. The BSM call model applied to currencies is simply the foreign exchange component minus the bond component. For put options, the foreign exchange component is $Se^{-r^f T}N(-d_1)$ and the bond component is $e^{-rT}XN(-d_2)$. The BSM put model applied to currencies is simply the bond component minus the foreign exchange component. Remember that the underlying is expressed in terms of the domestic currency.

EXAMPLE 13

BSM Model Applied to Value Options on Currency

A Japanese camera exporter to Europe has contracted to receive fixed euro (€) amounts each quarter for his goods. The spot price of the currency pair is 135¥/€. If the exchange rate falls to, say, 130¥/€, then the yen will have strengthened because it will take fewer yen to buy one euro. The exporter is concerned that the yen will strengthen because in this case, his forthcoming fixed euro will buy fewer yen. Hence, the exporter is considering buying an at-the-money spot euro put option to protect against this fall; this in essence is a call on yen. The Japanese risk-free rate is 0.25% and the European risk-free rate is 1.00%.

1. What are the underlying and exercise prices to use in the BSM model to get the euro put option value?

   A. 1/135; 1/135

   B. 135; 135

   C. 135; 130

Solution:

B is correct. The underlying is the spot FX price of 135 ¥/€. Because the put is at-the-money spot, the exercise price equals the spot price.

2. What are the risk-free rate and the carry rate to use in the BSM model to get the euro put option value?

   A. 0.25%; 1.00%

   B. 0.25%; 0.00%

   C. 1.00%; 0.25%

Solution:

A is correct. The risk-free rate to use is the Japanese rate because the Japanese yen is the domestic currency unit per the exchange rate quoting convention. The carry rate is the foreign currency's risk-free rate, which is the European rate.

11   BLACK OPTION VALUATION MODEL AND EUROPEAN OPTIONS ON FUTURES

☐ | describe how the Black model is used to value European options on futures

We turn now to examine a modification of the BSM model when the underlying is a forward or futures contract.

In 1976, Fischer Black introduced a modified version of the BSM model approach that is applicable to options on underlying instruments that are costless to carry, such as options on futures contracts—for example, equity index futures—and options on forward contracts. The latter include interest rate-based options, such as caps, floors, and swaptions.

European Options on Futures

We assume that the futures price also follows geometric Brownian motion. We ignore issues like margin requirements and marking to market. Black proposed the following model for European-style futures options:

$$c = e^{-rT}[F_0(T)N(d_1) - XN(d_2)] \tag{15}$$

and

$$p = e^{-rT}[XN(-d_2) - F_0(T)N(-d_1)] \tag{16}$$

where

$$d_1 = \frac{\ln[F_0(T)/X] + (\sigma^2/2)T}{\sigma\sqrt{T}} \text{ and}$$

$$d_2 = d_1 - \sigma\sqrt{T}$$

Note that $F_0(T)$ denotes the futures price at Time 0 that expires at Time T, and σ denotes the volatility related to the futures price. The other terms are as previously defined. Black's model is simply the BSM model in which the futures contract is assumed to reflect the carry arbitrage model. Futures option put–call parity can be expressed as

$$c = e^{-rT}[F_0(T) - X] + p \tag{17}$$

As we have seen before, put–call parity is a useful tool for describing the valuation relationship between call and put values within various option valuation models.

The Black model can be described in a similar way to the BSM model. The Black model has two components, a futures component and a bond component. For call options, the futures component is $F_0(T)e^{-rT}N(d_1)$ and the bond component is again $e^{-rT}XN(d_2)$. The Black call model is simply the futures component minus the bond component. For put options, the futures component is $F_0(T)e^{-rT}N(-d_1)$ and the bond component is again $e^{-rT}XN(-d_2)$. The Black put model is simply the bond component minus the futures component.

Alternatively, futures option valuation, based on the Black model, is simply computing the present value of the difference between the futures price and the exercise price. The futures price and exercise price are appropriately adjusted by the N(d) functions. For call options, the futures price is adjusted by $N(d_1)$ and the exercise price is adjusted by $-N(d_2)$ to arrive at difference. For put options, the futures price is adjusted by $-N(-d_1)$ and the exercise price is adjusted by $+N(-d_2)$.

EXAMPLE 14

European Options on Futures Index

The S&P 500 Index (a spot index) is presently at 1,860 and the 0.25 expiration futures contract is trading at 1,851.65. Suppose further that the exercise price is 1,860, the continuously compounded risk-free rate is 0.2%, time to expiration is 0.25, volatility is 15%, and the dividend yield is 2.0%. Based on this information, the following results are obtained for options on the futures contract.[13]

Options on Futures	
Calls	**Puts**
$N(d_1) = 0.491$	$N(-d_1) = 0.509$
$N(d_2) = 0.461$	$N(-d_2) = 0.539$
c = US$51.41	p = US$59.76

---

1. Identify the statement that *best* describes how the Black model is used to value a European call option on the futures contract just described.

   A. The call value is the present value of the difference between the exercise price times 0.461 and the current futures price times 0.539.

   B. The call value is the present value of the difference between the current futures price times 0.491 and the exercise price times 0.461.

   C. The call value is the present value of the difference between the current spot price times 0.491 and the exercise price times 0.461.

Solution:

B is correct. Recall Black's model for call options can be expressed as $c = e^{-rT}[F_0(T)N(d_1) - XN(d_2)]$.

---

[13] We ignore the effect of the multiplier. As of this writing, the S&P 500 futures option contract has a multiplier of 250. The prices reported here have not been scaled up by this amount. In practice, the option cost would by 250 times the option value.

2. Which statement *best* describes how the Black model is used to value a European put options on the futures contract just described?

   A. The put value is the present value of the difference between the exercise price times 0.539 and the current futures price times 0.509.

   B. The put value is the present value of the difference between the current futures price times 0.491 and the exercise price times 0.461.

   C. The put value is the present value of the difference between the current spot price times 0.491 and the exercise price times 0.461.

Solution:

A is correct. Recall Black's model for put options can be expressed as $p = e^{-rT}[XN(-d_2) - F_0(T)N(-d_1)]$.

3. What are the underlying and exercise prices to use in the Black futures option model?

   A. 1,851.65; 1,860

   B. 1,860; 1,860

   C. 1,860; 1,851.65

Solution:

A is correct. The underlying is the futures price of 1,851.65 and the exercise price was given as 1,860.

---

12   INTEREST RATE OPTIONS

☐   describe how the Black model is used to value European interest rate options and European swaptions

With interest rate options, the underlying instrument is a reference interest rate, such as three-month MRR. An interest rate call option gains when the reference interest rate rises and an interest rate put option gains when the reference interest rate falls. Interest rate options are the building blocks of many other instruments.

For an interest rate call option on three-month MRR with one year to expiration, the underlying interest rate is a forward rate agreement (FRA) rate that expires in one year. This FRA is observed today and is the underlying rate used in the Black model. The underlying rate of the FRA is a 3-month MRR deposit that is investable in 12 months and matures in 15 months. Thus, in one year, the FRA rate typically converges to the three-month spot MRR.

Interest rates are typically set in advance, but interest payments are made in arrears, which is referred to as advanced set, settled in arrears. For example, with a bank deposit, the interest rate is usually set when the deposit is made, say t_{j-1}, but the interest payment is made when the deposit is withdrawn, say t_j. The deposit, therefore, has $t_m = t_j - t_{j-1}$ time until maturity. Thus, the rate is advanced set, but the payment is settled in arrears. Likewise with a floating rate loan, the rate is usually set and the interest accrues at this known rate, but the payment is made later. Similarly, with some interest rate options, the time to option expiration (t_{j-1}) when the interest rate is set does not correspond to the option settlement (t_j) when the cash payment is made, if any. For example, if an interest rate option payment based on three-month MRR is US$5,000 determined on January 15th, the actual payment of the US$5,000 would occur on April 15.

Interest rates are quoted on an annual basis, but the underlying implied deposit is often less than a year. Thus, the annual rates must be adjusted for the accrual period. Recall that the accrual period for a quarterly reset 30/360 day count FRA is 0.25 (= 90/360). If the day count is on an actual (ACT) number of days divided by 360 (ACT/360), then the accrual period may be something like 0.252778 (= 91/360), assuming 91 days in the period. Typically, the accrual period in FRAs is based on 30/360 whereas the accrual period based on the option is actual number of days in the contract divided by the actual number of days in the year (identified as ACT/ACT or ACT/365).

The model presented here is known as the standard market model and is a variation of Black's futures option valuation model. Again, let t_{j-1} denote the time to option expiration (ACT/365), whereas let t_j denote the time to the maturity date of the underlying FRA. Note that the interest accrual on the underlying begins at the option expiration (Time t_{j-1}). Let $FRA(0,t_{j-1},t_m)$ denote the fixed rate on a FRA at Time 0 that expires at Time t_{j-1}, where the underlying matures at Time t_j (= $t_{j-1} + t_m$), with all times expressed on an annual basis. We assume the FRA is 30/360 day count. For example, $FRA(0,0.25,0.5) = 2\%$ denotes the 2% fixed rate on a forward rate agreement that expires in 0.25 years with settlement amount being paid in 0.75 (= 0.25 + 0.5) years.[14] Let R_X denote the exercise rate expressed on an annual basis. Finally, let σ denote the interest rate volatility. Specifically, σ is the annualized standard deviation of the continuously compounded percentage change in the underlying FRA rate.

Interest rate options give option buyers the right to certain cash payments based on observed interest rates. For example, an interest rate call option gives the call buyer the right to a certain cash payment when the underlying interest rate exceeds the exercise rate. An interest rate put option gives the put buyer the right to a certain cash payment when the underlying interest rate is below the exercise rate.

With the standard market model, the prices of interest rate call and put options can be expressed as

$$c = (AP) e^{-r\left(t_{j-1}+t_m\right)} \left[FRA\left(0, t_{j-1}, t_m\right) N(d_1) - R_X N(d_2) \right] \tag{18}$$

and

$$p = (AP) e^{-r\left(t_{j-1}+t_m\right)} \left[R_X N(-d_2) - FRA\left(0, t_{j-1}, t_m\right) N(-d_1) \right] \tag{19}$$

where

AP denotes the accrual period in years

$$d_1 = \frac{\ln\left[FRA\left(0, t_{j-1}, t_m\right) / R_X\right] + (\sigma^2/2)t_{j-1}}{\sigma\sqrt{t_{j-1}}}$$

$$d_2 = d_1 - \sigma\sqrt{t_{j-1}}$$

The formulas here give the value of the option for a notional amount of 1. In practice, the notional would be more than one, so the full cost of the option is obtained by multiplying these formula amounts by the notional amount. Of course, this point is just the same as finding the value of an option on a single share of stock and then multiplying that value by the number of shares covered by the option contract.

---

14 Note that in other contexts the time periods are expressed in months. For example with months, this FRA would be expressed as FRA(0,3,6). Note that the third term in parentheses denotes the maturity of the underlying deposit from the expiration of the FRA.

Immediately, we note that the standard market model requires an adjustment when compared with the Black model for the accrual period. In other words, a value such as $FRA(0, t_{j-1}, t_m)$ or the strike rate, R_X, as appearing in the formula given earlier, is stated on an annual basis, as are interest rates in general. The actual option premium would have to be adjusted for the accrual period. After accounting for this adjustment, this model looks very similar to the Black model, but there are important but subtle differences. First, the discount factor, $e^{-r(t_{j-1}+t_m)}$, does not apply to the option expiration, t_{j-1}. Rather, the discount factor is applied to the maturity date of the FRA or $t_j (= t_{j-1} + t_m)$. We express this maturity as $(t_{j-1} + t_m)$ rather than t_j to emphasize the settlement in arrears nature of this option. Second, rather than the underlying being a futures price, the underlying is an interest rate, specifically a forward rate based on a forward rate agreement or $FRA(0, t_{j-1}, t_m)$. Third, the exercise price is really a rate and reflects an interest rate, not a price. Fourth, the time to the option expiration, t_{j-1}, is used in the calculation of d_1 and d_2. Finally, both the forward rate and the exercise rate should be expressed in decimal form and not as percent (for example, 0.02 and not 2.0). Alternatively, if expressed as a percent, then the notional amount adjustment could be divided by 100.

As with other option models, the standard market model can be described as simply the present value of the expected option payoff at expiration. Specifically, we can express the standard market model for calls as $c = PV[E(c_{tj})]$ and for puts as $p = PV[E(p_{tj})]$, where $E(c_{tj}) = (AP)[FRA(0, t_{j-1}, t_m)N(d_1) - R_X N(d_2)]$ and $E(p_{tj}) = (AP)[R_X N(-d_2) - FRA(0, t_{j-1}, t_m)N(-d_1)]$. The present value term in this context is simply $e^{-rt_j} = e^{-r(t_{j-1}+t_m)}$. Again, note we discount from Time t_j, the time when the cash flows are settled on the FRA.

There are several interesting and useful combinations that can be created with interest rate options. We focus on a few that will prove useful for understanding swaptions in the next section. First, if the exercise rate is selected so as to equal the current FRA rate, then long an interest rate call option and short an interest rate put option is equivalent to a receive-floating, pay-fixed FRA.

Second, if the exercise rate is again selected so it is equal to the current FRA rate, then long an interest rate put option and short an interest rate call option is equivalent to a receive-fixed, pay-floating FRA. Note that FRAs are the building blocks of interest rate swaps.

Third, an interest rate cap is a portfolio or strip of interest rate call options in which the expiration of the first underlying corresponds to the expiration of the second option and so forth. The underlying interest rate call options are termed caplets. Thus, a set of floating-rate loan payments can be hedged with a long position in an interest rate cap encompassing a series of interest rate call options.

Fourth, an interest rate floor is a portfolio or strip of interest rate put options in which the expiration of the first underlying corresponds with the expiration of the second option and so forth. The underlying interest rate put options are termed floorlets. Thus, a floating-rate bond investment or any other floating-rate lending situation can be hedged with an interest rate floor encompassing a series of interest rate put options.

Fifth, applying put–call parity as discussed earlier, long an interest rate cap and short an interest rate floor with the exercise prices set at the swap rate is equivalent to a receive-floating, pay-fixed swap. On a settlement date, when the underlying rate is above the strike, both the cap and the swap pay off to the party. When the underlying rate is below the strike on a settlement date, the party must make a payment on the short floor, just as the case with a swap. For the opposite position, long an interest rate floor and short an interest rate cap result in the party making a payment when the underlying rate is above the strike and receiving one when the underlying rate is below the strike, just as is the case for a pay-floating, receive-fixed swap.

Finally, if the exercise rate is set equal to the swap rate, then the value of the cap must be equal to the value of the floor at the start. When an interest rate swap is initiated, its current value is zero and is known as an at-market swap. When an exercise rate is selected such that the cap value equals the floor value, then the initial cost of being long a cap and short the floor is also zero. This occurs when the cap and floor strike are equal to the swap rate.

EXAMPLE 15

European Interest Rate Options

Suppose you are a speculative investor in Singapore. On 15 May, you anticipate that some regulatory changes will be enacted, and you want to profit from this forecast. On 15 June, you intend to borrow 10,000,000 Singapore dollars to fund the purchase of an asset, which you expect to resell at a profit three months after purchase, say on 15 September. The current three-month SORA (that is, Singapore MRR) is 0.55%. The appropriate FRA rate over the period of 15 June to 15 September is currently 0.68%. You are concerned that rates will rise, so you want to hedge your borrowing risk by purchasing an interest rate call option with an exercise rate of 0.60%.

1. In using the Black model to value this interest rate call option, what would the underlying rate be?

   A. 0.55%

   B. 0.68%

   C. 0.60%

Solution:

B is correct. In using the Black model, a forward or futures price is used as the underlying. This approach is unlike the BSM model in which a spot price is used as the underlying.

---

2. The discount factor used in pricing this option would be over what period of time?

   A. 15 May–15 June

   B. 15 June–15 September

   C. 15 May–15 September

Solution:

C is correct. You are pricing the option on 15 May. An option expiring 15 June when the underlying is three-month Sibor will have its payoff determined on 15 June, but the payment will be made on 15 September. Thus, the expected payment must be discounted back from 15 September to 15 May.

Interest rate option values are linked in an important way with interest rate swap values through caps and floors. As we will see in the next section, an interest rate swap serves as the underlying for swaptions. Thus, once again, we see that important links exist between interest rate options, swaps, and swaptions.

13   SWAPTIONS

<table><tr><td>☐</td><td>describe how the Black model is used to value European interest rate options and European swaptions</td></tr></table>

A swap option or swaption is simply an option on a swap. It gives the holder the right, but not the obligation, to enter a swap at the pre-agreed swap rate—the exercise rate. Interest rate swaps can be either receive fixed, pay floating or receive floating, pay fixed. A payer swaption is an option on a swap to pay fixed, receive floating. A receiver swaption is an option on a swap to receive fixed, pay floating. Note that the terms "call" and "put" are often avoided because of potential confusion over the nature of the underlying. Notice also that the terminology focuses on the fixed swap rate.

A payer swaption buyer hopes the fixed rate goes up before the swaption expires. When exercised, the payer swaption buyer is able to enter into a pay-fixed, receive-floating swap at the predetermined exercise rate, R_X. The buyer can then immediately enter an offsetting at-market receive-fixed, pay-floating swap at the current fixed swap rate. The floating legs of both swaps will offset, leaving the payer swaption buyer with an annuity of the difference between the current fixed swap rate and the swaption exercise rate. Thus, swaption valuation will reflect an annuity.

Swap payments are advanced set, settled in arrears. Let the swap reset dates be expressed as t_0, t_1, t_2, ..., t_n. Let R_{FIX} denote the fixed swap rate starting when the swaption expires, denoted as before with T, quoted on an annual basis, and R_X denote the exercise rate starting at Time T, again quoted on an annual basis. As before, we will assume a notional amount of 1.

Because swap rates are quoted on an annual basis, let AP denote the accrual period. Finally, we need some measure of uncertainty. Let σ denote the volatility of the forward swap rate. More precisely, σ denotes annualized, standard deviation of the continuously compounded percentage changes in the forward swap rate.

The swaption model presented here is a modification of the Black model. Let the present value of an annuity matching the forward swap payment be expressed as

$$\text{PVA} = \sum_{j=1}^{n} PV_{0,t_j}(1)$$

This term is equivalent to what is sometimes referred to as an annuity discount factor. It applies here because a swaption creates a series of equal payments of the difference in the market swap rate at expiration and the chosen exercise rate. Therefore, the payer swaption valuation model is

$$\text{PAY}_{\text{SWN}} = (\text{AP})\text{PVA}[R_{FIX}N(d_1) - R_X N(d_2)] \tag{20}$$

and the receiver swaption valuation model

$$\text{REC}_{\text{SWN}} = (\text{AP})\text{PVA}[R_X N(-d_2) - R_{FIX}N(-d_1)] \tag{21}$$

where

$$d_1 = \frac{\ln\left(R_{FIX}/R_X\right) + (\sigma^2/2)\,T}{\sigma\sqrt{T}}, \text{ and as always,}$$

$$d_2 = d_1 - \sigma\sqrt{T}$$

As noted with interest rate options, the actual premium would need to be scaled by the notional amount. Once again, we can see the similarities to the Black model. We note that the swaption model requires two adjustments, one for the accrual period and one for the present value of an annuity. After accounting for these adjustments, this model looks very similar to the Black model but there are important subtle differences.

First, the discount factor is absent. The payoff is not a single payment but a series of payments. Thus, the present value of an annuity used here embeds the option-related discount factor. Second, rather than the underlying being a futures price, the underlying is the fixed rate on a forward interest rate swap. Third, the exercise price is really expressed as an interest rate. Finally, both the forward swap rate and the exercise rate should be expressed in decimal form and not as percent (for example, 0.02 and not 2.0).

As with other option models, the swaption model can be described as simply the present value of the expected option payoff at expiration. Specifically, we can express the payer swaption model value as

$$PAY_{SWN} = PV[E(PAY_{SWN,T})]$$

and the receiver swaption model value as

$$REC_{SWN} = PV[E(REC_{SWN,T})],$$

where

$$E(PAY_{SWN,T}) = e^{rT}PAY_{SWN} \text{ and}$$

$$E(REC_{SWN,T}) = e^{rT}REC_{SWN}.$$

The present value term in this context is simply e^{-rT}. Because the annuity term embedded the discounting over the swaption life, the expected swaption values are the current swaption values grossed up by the current risk-free interest rate.

Alternatively, the swaption model can be described as having two components, a swap component and a bond component. For payer swaptions, the swap component is $(AP)PVA(R_{FIX})N(d_1)$ and the bond component is $(AP)PVA(R_X)N(d_2)$. The payer swaption model value is simply the swap component minus the bond component. For receiver swaptions, the swap component is $(AP)PVA(R_{FIX})N(-d_1)$ and the bond component is $(AP)PVA(R_X)N(-d_2)$. The receiver swaption model value is simply the bond component minus the swap component.

As with nearly all derivative instruments, there are many useful equivalence relationships. Recall that long an interest rate cap and short an interest rate floor with the same exercise rate is equal to a receive-floating, pay-fixed interest rate swap. Also, short an interest rate cap and long an interest rate floor with the same exercise rate is equal to a pay-floating, receive-fixed interest rate swap. There are also equivalence relationships with swaptions. In a similar way, long a receiver swaption and short a payer swaption with the same exercise rate is equivalent to entering a receive-fixed, pay-floating forward swap. Long a payer swaption and short a receiver swaption with the same exercise rate is equivalent to entering a receive-floating, pay-fixed forward swap. Note that if the exercise rate is selected such that the receiver and payer swaptions have the same value, then the exercise rate is equal to the at-market forward swap rate. Thus, there is again a put–call parity relationship important for valuation.

In addition, being long a callable fixed-rate bond can be viewed as being long a straight fixed-rate bond and short a receiver swaption. A receiver swaption gives the buyer the right to receive a fixed rate. Hence, the seller will have to pay the fixed rate when this right is exercised in a lower rate environment. Recall that the bond issuer has the right to call the bonds. If the bond issuer sells a receiver swaption with similar terms, then the bond issuer has essentially converted the callable bond into a straight bond. The bond issuer will now pay the fixed rate on the underlying swap and the floating rate received will be offset by the floating-rate loan created when the bond was refinanced. Specifically, the receiver swaption buyer will benefit when rates fall and the swaption is exercised. Thus, the embedded call feature is similar to a receiver swaption.

EXAMPLE 16

European Swaptions

1. Suppose you are an Australian company and have ongoing floating-rate debt. You have profited for some time by paying at a floating rate because rates have been falling steadily for the last few years. Now, however, you are concerned that within three months the Australian central bank may tighten its monetary policy and your debt costs will thus increase. Rather than lock in your borrowing via a swap, you prefer to hedge by buying a swaption expiring in three months, whereby you will have the choice, but not the obligation, to enter a five-year swap locking in your borrowing costs. The current three-month forward, five-year swap rate is 2.65%. The current five-year swap rate is 2.55%. The current three-month risk-free rate is 2.25%.

   With reference to the Black model to value the swaption, which statement is correct?

   A. The underlying is the three-month forward, five-year swap rate.

   B. The discount rate to use is 2.55%.

   C. The swaption time to expiration, T, is five years.

Solution:

A is correct. The current five-year swap rate is not used as a discount rate with swaptions. The swaption time to expiration is 0.25, not the life of the swap.

---

14   OPTION GREEKS AND IMPLIED VOLATILITY: DELTA

☐ interpret each of the option Greeks

☐ describe how a delta hedge is executed

With option valuation models, such as the binomial model, BSM model, and Black's model, we are able to estimate a wide array of comparative information, such as how much the option value will change for a small change in a particular parameter.[15] We will explore this derived information as well as implied volatility in this section. These topics are essential for those managing option positions and in general in obtaining a solid understanding of how option prices change. Our discussion will be based on stock options, though the material covered in this section applies to all types of options.

The measures examined here are known as the Greeks and include, delta, gamma, theta, vega, and rho. With these calculations, we seek to address how much a particular portfolio will change for a given small change in the appropriate parameter. These measures are sometimes referred to as static risk measures in that they capture movements in the option value for a movement in one of the factors that affect the option value, while holding all other factors constant.

---

15 Parameters in the BSM model, for example, include the stock price, exercise price, volatility, time to expiration, and the risk-free interest rate.

Our focus here is on European stock options in which the underlying stock is assumed to pay a dividend yield (denoted δ). Note that for non-dividend-paying stocks, $\delta = 0$.

Delta

Delta is defined as the change in a given instrument for a given small change in the value of the stock, holding everything else constant. Thus, the delta of long one share of stock is by definition $+1.0$, and the delta of short one share of stock is by definition -1.0. The concept of the option delta is similarly the change in an option value for a given small change in the value of the underlying stock, holding everything else constant. The option deltas for calls and puts are, respectively,

$$\text{Delta}_c = e^{-\delta T}N(d_1) \tag{22}$$

and

$$\text{Delta}_p = -e^{-\delta T}N(-d_1) \tag{23}$$

Note that the deltas are a simple function of $N(d_1)$. The delta of an option answers the question of how much the option will change for a given change in the stock, holding everything else constant. Therefore, delta is a static risk measure. It does not address how likely this particular change would be. Recall that $N(d_1)$ is a value taken from the cumulative distribution function of a standard normal distribution. As such, the range of values is between 0 and 1. Thus, the range of call delta is 0 and $e^{-\delta T}$ and the range of put delta is $-e^{-\delta T}$ and 0. As the stock price increases, the call option goes deeper in the money and the value of $N(d_1)$ is moving toward 1. As the stock price decreases, the call option goes deeper out of the money and the value of $N(d_1)$ is moving toward zero. When the option gets closer to maturity, the delta will drift either toward 0 if it is out of the money or drift toward 1 if it is in the money. Clearly, as the stock price changes and as time to maturity changes, the deltas are also changing.

Delta hedging an option is the process of establishing a position in the underlying stock of a quantity that is prescribed by the option delta so as to have no exposure to very small moves up or down in the stock price. Hence, to execute a single option delta hedge, we first calculate the option delta and then buy or sell delta units of stock. In practice, rarely does one have only one option position to manage. Thus, in general, delta hedging refers to manipulating the underlying portfolio delta by appropriately changing the positions in the portfolio. A delta neutral portfolio refers to setting the portfolio delta all the way to zero. In theory, the delta neutral portfolio will not change in value for small changes in the stock instrument. Let N_H denote the number of units of the hedging instrument and Delta_H denote the delta of the hedging instrument, which could be the underlying stock, call options, or put options. Delta neutral implies the portfolio delta plus $N_H \text{Delta}_H$ is equal to zero. The optimal number of hedging units, N_H, is

$$N_H = -\frac{\text{Portfolio delta}}{\text{Delta}_H}$$

Note that if N_H is negative, then one must short the hedging instrument, and if N_H is positive, then one must go long the hedging instrument. Clearly, if the portfolio is options and the hedging instrument is stock, then we will buy or sell shares to offset the portfolio position. For example, if the portfolio consists of 100,000 shares of stock at US$10 per share, then the portfolio delta is 100,000. The delta of the hedging instrument, stock, is $+1$. Thus, the optimal number of hedging units, N_H, is $-100,000$ ($= -100,000/1$) or short 100,000 shares. Alternatively, if the portfolio delta is 5,000 and a particular call option with delta of 0.5 is used as the hedging instrument, then to arrive at a delta neutral portfolio, one must sell 10,000 call options ($= -5,000/0.5$).

Alternatively, if a portfolio of options has a delta of −1,500, then one must buy 1,500 shares of stock to be delta neutral [= −(−1,500)/1]. If the hedging instrument is stock, then the delta is +1 per share.

EXAMPLE 17

Delta Hedging

1. Apple stock is trading at US$125. We write calls (that is, we sell calls) on 1,000 Apple shares and now are exposed to an increase in the price of the Apple stock. That is, if Apple rises, we will lose money because the calls we sold will go up in value, so our liability will increase. Correspondingly, if Apple falls, we will make money. We want to neutralize our exposure to Apple. Say the call delta is 0.50, which means that if Apple goes up by US$0.10, a call on one Apple share will go up US$0.05. We need to trade in such a way as to make money if Apple goes up, to offset our exposure. Hence, we buy 500 Apple shares to hedge. Now, if Apple goes up US$0.10, the sold calls will go up US$50 (our liability goes up), but our long 500 Apple hedge will profit by US$50. Hence, we are delta hedged.

   Identify the *incorrect* statement:

   A. If we sell Apple puts, we need to buy Apple stock to delta hedge.

   B. Call delta is non-negative (≥ 0); put delta is non-positive (≤ 0).

   C. Delta hedging is the process of neutralizing exposure to the underlying.

Solution:

   A is the correct answer because statement A is incorrect. If we sell puts, we need to short sell stock to delta hedge.

One final interpretation of option delta is related to forecasting changes in option prices. Let $\hat{c}$, $\hat{p}$, and $\hat{S}$ denote some new value for the call, put, and stock. Based on an approximation method, the change in the option price can be estimated with a concept known as a delta approximation or

$$\hat{c} - c \cong Delta_c \left(\hat{S} - S \right) \text{ for calls and}$$

$$\hat{p} - p \cong Delta_p \left(\hat{S} - S \right) \text{ for puts.}^{[16]}$$

We can now illustrate the actual call values as well as the estimated call values based on delta. Exhibit 15 illustrates the call value based on the BSM model and the call value based on the delta approximation,

$$\hat{c} = c + Delta_c \left(\hat{S} - S \right).$$

Notice for very small changes in the stock, the delta approximation is fairly accurate. For example, if the stock value rises from 100 to 101, notice that both the call line and the call (delta) estimated line are almost the same value. If, however, the stock value rises from 100 to 150, the call line is now significantly above the call (delta) estimated line. Thus, we see that as the change in the stock increases, the estimation error also increases. The delta approximation is biased low for both a down move and an up move.

---

16 The symbol $\cong$ denotes approximately. The approximation method is known as a Taylor series. Also note that the put delta is non-positive (≤ 0).

Exhibit 15: Call Values and Delta Estimated Call Values (S = 100 = X, r = 5%, σ = 30%, δ = 0)

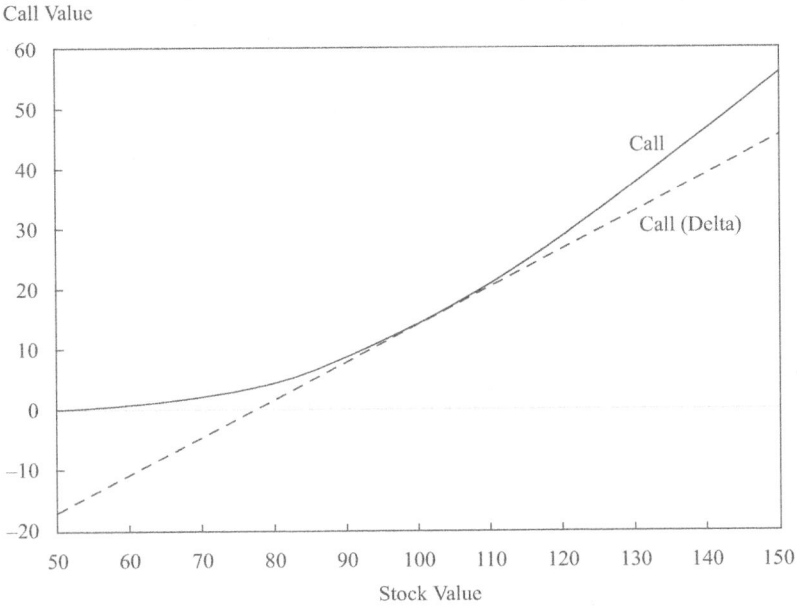

We see that delta hedging is imperfect and gets worse as the underlying moves further away from its original value of 100. Based on the graph, the BSM model assumption of continuous trading is essential to avoid hedging risk. This hedging risk is related to the difference between these two lines and the degree to which the underlying price experiences large changes.

EXAMPLE 18

Delta Hedging

Suppose we know S = 100, X = 100, r = 5%, T = 1.0, σ = 30%, and δ = 5%. We have a short position in put options on 10,000 shares of stock. Based on this information, we note $Delta_c$ = 0.532, and $Delta_p$ = −0.419. Assume each stock option contract is for one share of stock.

1. The appropriate delta hedge, assuming the hedging instrument is stock, is executed by which of the following transactions? Select the *closest* answer.

   A. Buy 5,320 shares of stock.

   B. Short sell 4,190 shares of stock.

   C. Buy 4,190 shares of stock.

Solution:

B is correct. Recall that $N_H = -\dfrac{\text{Portfolio delta}}{\text{Delta}_H}$. The put delta is given as −0.419, thus the short put delta is 0.419. In this case, Portfolio delta = 10,000(0.419) = 4,190 and $Delta_H$ = 1.0. Thus, the number of number of hedging units is −4,190 [= −(4,190/1)] or short sell 4,190 shares of stock.

2. The appropriate delta hedge, assuming the hedging instrument is calls, is executed by which of the following transactions? Select the *closest* answer.

A. Sell 7,876 call options.

B. Sell 4,190 call options.

C. Buy 4,190 call options.

Solution:

A is correct. Again the Portfolio delta = 4,190 but now Delta_H = 0.532. Thus, the number of hedging units is −7,875.9 [= −(4,190/0.532)] or sell 7,876 call options.

3. Identify the correct interpretation of an option delta.

A. Option delta measures the curvature in the option price with respect to the stock price.

B. Option delta is the change in an option value for a given small change in the stock's value, holding everything else constant.

C. Option delta is the probability of the option expiring in the money.

Solution:

B is correct. Delta is defined as the change in a given portfolio for a given small change in the stock's value, holding everything else constant. Option delta is defined as the change in an option value for a given small change in the stock's value, holding everything else constant.

15   GAMMA

☐   interpret each of the option Greeks

☐   describe the role of gamma risk in options trading

Recall that delta is a good approximation of how an option price will change for a small change in the stock. For larger changes in the stock, we need better accuracy. **Gamma** is defined as the change in a given instrument's delta for a given small change in the stock's value, holding everything else constant. Option gamma is similarly defined as the change in a given option delta for a given small change in the stock's value, holding everything else constant. Option gamma is a measure of the curvature in the option price in relationship to the stock price. Thus, the gamma of a long or short position in one share of stock is zero because the delta of a share of stock never changes. A stock always moves one-for-one with itself. Thus, its delta is always +1 and, of course, −1 for a short position in the stock. The gamma for a call and put option are the same and can be expressed as

$$\text{Gamma}_c = \text{Gamma}_p = \frac{e^{-\delta T}}{S\sigma\sqrt{T}} n\left(d_1\right) \tag{24}$$

where $n(d_1)$ is the standard normal probability density function. The lowercase "n" is distinguished from the cumulative normal distribution—which the density function generates—and that we have used elsewhere in this reading denoted by uppercase "N". The gamma of a call equals the gamma of a similar put based on put–call parity or $c - p = S_0 - e^{-rT}X$. Note that neither S_0 nor $e^{-rT}X$ is a direct function of delta. Hence, the right-hand side of put–call parity has a delta of 1. Thus, the right-hand side delta is not sensitive to changes in the underlying. Therefore, the gamma of a call must equal the gamma of a put.

Gamma is always non-negative. Gamma takes on its largest value near at the money. Options deltas do not change much for small changes in the stock price if the option is either deep in or deep out of the money. Also, as the stock price changes and as time to expiration changes, the gamma is also changing.

Gamma measures the rate of change of delta as the stock changes. Gamma approximates the estimation error in delta for options because the option price with respect to the stock is non-linear and delta is a linear approximation. Thus, gamma is a risk measure; specifically, gamma measures the non-linearity risk or the risk that remains once the portfolio is delta neutral. A gamma neutral portfolio implies the gamma is zero. For example, gamma can be managed to an acceptable level first and then delta is neutralized as a second step. This hedging approach is feasible because options have gamma but a stock does not. Thus, in order to modify gamma, one has to include additional option trades in the portfolio. Once the revised portfolio, including any new option trades, has the desired level of gamma, then the trader can get the portfolio delta to its desired level as step two. To alter the portfolio delta, the trader simply buys or sells stock. Because stock has a positive delta, but zero gamma, the portfolio delta can be brought to its desired level with no impact on the portfolio gamma.

One final interpretation of gamma is related to improving the forecasted changes in option prices. Again, let $\hat{c}$, $\hat{p}$, and $\hat{S}$ denote new values for the call, put, and stock. Again based on an approximation method, the change in the option price can be estimated by a delta-plus-gamma approximation or

$$\hat{c} - c \approx \text{Delta}_c \left(\hat{S} - S\right) + \frac{\text{Gamma}_c}{2}\left(\hat{S} - S\right)^2 \text{ for calls and}$$

$$\hat{p} - p \approx \text{Delta}_p \left(\hat{S} - S\right) + \frac{\text{Gamma}_p}{2}\left(\hat{S} - S\right)^2 \text{ for puts.}$$

Exhibit 16 illustrates the call value based on the BSM model; the call value based on the delta approximation,

$$\hat{c} = c + \text{Delta}_c \left(\hat{S} - S\right);$$

and the call value based on the delta-plus-gamma approximation,

$$\hat{c} = c + \text{Delta}_c \left(\hat{S} - S\right) + \frac{\text{Gamma}_c}{2}\left(\hat{S} - S\right)^2.$$

Notice again that for very small changes in the stock, the delta approximation and the delta-plus-gamma approximations are fairly accurate. If the stock value rises from 100 to 150, the call line is again significantly above the delta estimated line but is below the delta-plus-gamma estimated line. Importantly, the call delta-plus-gamma estimated line is significantly closer to the BSM model call values. Thus, we see that even for fairly large changes in the stock, the delta-plus-gamma approximation is accurate. As the change in the stock increases, the estimation error also increases. From Exhibit 16, we see the delta-plus-gamma approximation is biased low for a down move but biased high for an up move. Thus, when estimating how the call price changes when the underlying changes, we see how the delta-plus-gamma approximation is an improvement when compared with using the delta approximation on its own.

Exhibit 16: Call Values, Delta Estimated Call Values, and Delta-Plus-Gamma Estimated Call Values (S = 100 = X, r = 5%, σ = 30%, δ = 0)

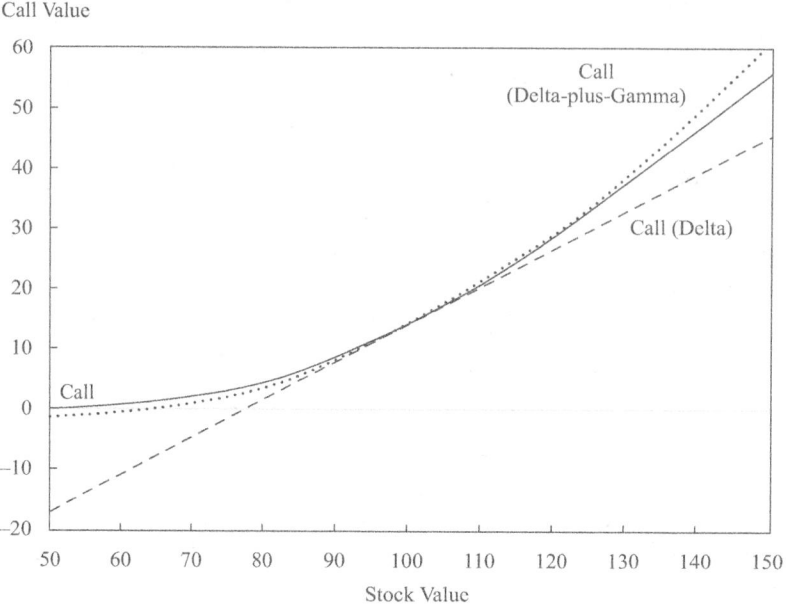

If the BSM model assumptions hold, then we would have no risk in managing option positions. In reality, however, stock prices often jump rather than move continuously and smoothly, which creates "gamma risk." Gamma risk is so-called because gamma measures the risk of stock prices jumping when hedging an option position, and thus leaving us suddenly unhedged.

EXAMPLE 19

Gamma Risk in Option Trading

1. Suppose we are options traders and have only one option position—a short call option. We also hold some stock such that we are delta hedged. Which one of the following statements is true?

    A. We are gamma neutral.

    B. Buying a call will increase our overall gamma.

    C. Our overall position is a positive gamma, which will make large moves profitable for us, whether up or down.

Solution:

B is correct. Buying options (calls or puts) will always increase net gamma. A is incorrect because we are short gamma, not gamma neutral. C is also incorrect because we are short gamma. We can only become gamma neutral from a short gamma position by purchasing options.

THETA

☐ | interpret each of the option Greeks

Theta is defined as the change in a portfolio for a given small change in calendar time, holding everything else constant. Option theta is similarly defined as the change in an option value for a given small change in calendar time, holding everything else constant. Option theta is the rate at which the option time value declines as the option approaches expiration. To understand theta, it is important to remember the "holding everything else constant" assumption. Specifically, the theta calculation assumes nothing changes except calendar time. Clearly, if calendar time passes, then time to expiration declines. Because stocks do not have an expiration date, the stock theta is zero. Like gamma, theta cannot be adjusted with stock trades.

The gain or loss of an option portfolio in response to the mere passage of calendar time is known as time decay. Particularly with long options positions, often the mere passage of time without any change in other variables, such as the stock, will result is significant losses in value. Therefore, investment managers with significant option positions carefully monitor theta and their exposure to time decay. Time decay is essentially the measure of profit and loss of an option position as time passes, holding everything else constant.

Note that theta is fundamentally different from delta and gamma in the sense that the passage of time does not involve any uncertainty. There is no chance that time will go backward. Time marches on, but it is important to understand how your investment position will change with the mere passage of time.

Typically, theta is negative for options. That is, as calendar time passes, expiration time declines and the option value also declines. Exhibit 17 illustrates the option value with respect to time to expiration. Remember, as calendar time passes, the time to expiration declines. Both the call and the put option are at the money and eventually are worthless if the stock does not change. Notice, however, how the speed of the option value decline increases as time to expiration decreases.

Exhibit 17: Option Values and Time to Expiration (S = 100 = X, r = 5%, σ = 30%, δ = 0)

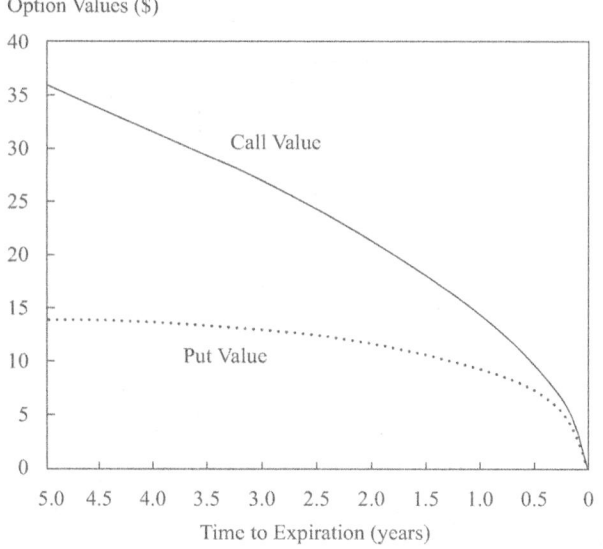

Option Values ($)

Call Value

Put Value

Time to Expiration (years)

---

17 VEGA

☐ | interpret each of the option Greeks

Vega is defined as the change in a given portfolio for a given small change in volatility, holding everything else constant. Vega measures the sensitivity of a given portfolio to volatility. The vega of an option is positive. An increase in volatility results in an increase in the option value for both calls and puts.

The vega of a call equals the vega of a similar put based on put–call parity or $c - p = S_0 - e^{-rT}X$. Note that neither S_0 nor $e^{-rT}X$ is a direct function of volatility. Therefore, the vega of a call must offset the vega of a put so that the vega of the right-hand side is zero.

Unlike the Greeks we have already discussed, vega is based on an unobservable parameter, future volatility. Although historical volatility can be calculated, there is no objective measure of future volatility. Similar to the concept of expected value, future volatility is subjective. Thus, vega measures the sensitivity of a portfolio to changes in the volatility used in the option valuation model. Option values are generally quite sensitive to volatility. In fact, of the five variables in the BSM, an option's value is most sensitive to volatility changes.

At extremely low volatility, the option values tend toward their lower bounds. The lower bound of a European-style call option is zero or the stock less the present value of the exercise price, whichever is greater. The lower bound of a European-style put option is zero or the present value of the exercise price less the stock, whichever is greater. Exhibit 18 illustrates the option values with respect to volatility. In this case, the call lower bound is 4.88 and the put lower bound is 0. The difference between the call and put can be explained by put–call parity.

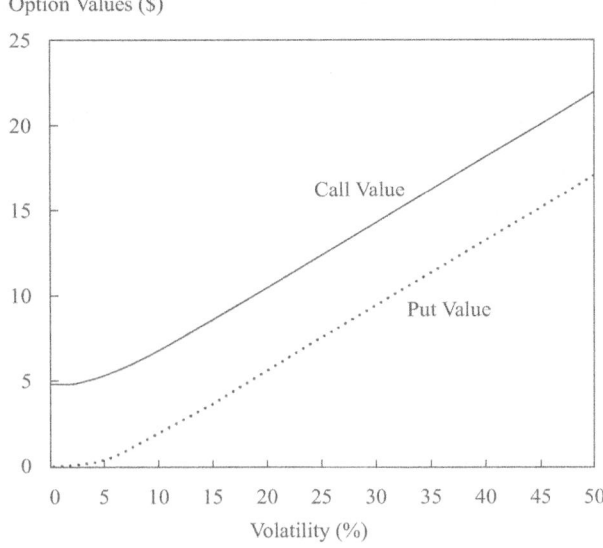

Exhibit 18: Option Values and Volatility (S = 100 = X, r = 5%, T = 1, δ = 0)

Vega is very important in managing an options portfolio because option values can be very sensitive to volatility changes. Vega is high when options are at or near the money. Volatility is usually only hedged with other options and volatility itself can be quite volatile. Volatility is sometimes considered a separate asset class or a separate risk factor. Because it is rather exotic and potentially dangerous, exposure to volatility needs to be managed, bearing in mind that risk managers, board members, and clients may not understand or appreciate losses if volatility is the source.

RHO

18

☐ | interpret each of the option Greeks

Rho is defined as the change in a given portfolio for a given small change in the risk-free interest rate, holding everything else constant. Thus, rho measures the sensitivity of the portfolio to the risk-free interest rate.

The rho of a call is positive. Intuitively, buying an option avoids the financing costs involved with purchasing the stock. In other words, purchasing a call option allows an investor to earn interest on the money that otherwise would have gone to purchasing the stock. The higher the interest rate, the higher the call value.

The rho of a put is negative. Intuitively, the option to sell the stock delays the opportunity to earn interest on the proceeds from the sale. For example, purchasing a put option rather than selling the stock deprives an investor of the potential interest that would have been earned from the proceeds of selling the stock. The higher the interest rate, the lower the put value.

When interest rates are zero, the call and put option values are the same for at-the-money options. Recall that with put–call parity, we have $c - p = S_0 - e^{-rT}X$, and when interest rates are zero, then the present value function has no effect. As interest rates rise, the difference between call and put options increases as illustrated in Exhibit 19. The impact on option prices when interest rates change is relatively small when compared with that for volatility changes and that for changes in the stock. Hence, the influence of interest rates is generally not a major concern.[17]

Exhibit 19: Option Values and Interest Rates (S = 100 = X, r = 5%, T = 1, δ = 0)

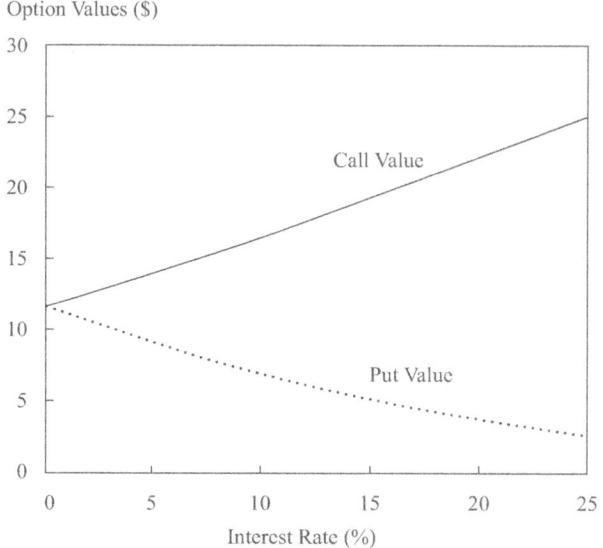

19   IMPLIED VOLATILITY

☐ │ define implied volatility and explain how it is used in options trading

As we have already touched on in Section 6.4, for most options, the value is particularly sensitive to volatility. Unlike the price of the underlying, however, volatility, is not an observable value in the marketplace. Volatility can be, and often is estimated, based on a sample of historical data. For example, for a three-month option, we might look back over the last three months and calculate the actual historical stock volatility. We can then use this figure as an estimate of volatility over the next three months. The volatility parameter in the BSM model, however, is the *future* volatility. As we know, history is a very frail guide of the future, so the option may appear to be "mispriced" with respect to the actual future volatility experienced. Different investors will have different views of the future volatility. The one with the most accurate forecast will have the most accurate assessment of the option value.

Much like yield to maturity with bonds, volatility can be inferred from option prices. This inferred volatility is called the **implied volatility**. Thus, one important use of the BSM model is to invert the model and estimate implied volatility. The key advantage

---

17 An exception to this rule is that with interest rate options, the interest rate is not constant and serves as the underlying. The relationship between the option value and the underlying interest rate is, therefore, captured by the delta, not the rho. Rho is really more generally the relationship between the option value and the rate used to discount cash flows.

is that implied volatility provides information regarding the perceived uncertainty going forward and thereby allows us to gain an understanding of the collective opinions of investors on the volatility of the underlying and the demand for options. If the demand for options increases and the no-arbitrage approach is not perfectly reflected in market prices—for example, because of transaction costs—then the preference for buying options will drive option prices up, and hence, the observed implied volatility. This kind of information is of great value to traders in options.

Recall that one assumption of the BSM model is that all investors agree on the value of volatility and that this volatility is non-stochastic. Note that the original BSM model assumes the underlying instrument volatility is constant in our context. That is, when we calculate option values, we have assumed a single volatility number, like 30%. In practice, it is very common to observe different implied volatilities for different exercise prices and observe different implied volatilities for calls and puts with the same terms. Implied volatility also varies across time to expiration as well as across exercise prices. The implied volatility with respect to time to expiration is known as the term structure of volatility, whereas the implied volatility with respect to the exercise price is known as the volatility smile or sometimes skew depending on the particular shape. It is common to construct a three dimensional plot of the implied volatility with respect to both expiration time and exercise prices, a visualization known as the volatility surface. If the BSM model assumptions were true, then one would expect to find the volatility surface flat.

Implied volatility is also not constant through calendar time. As implied volatility increases, market participants are communicating an increased market price of risk. For example, if the implied volatility of a put increases, it is more expensive to buy downside protection with a put. Hence, the market price of hedging is rising. With index options, various volatility indexes have been created, and these indexes measure the collective opinions of investors on the volatility in the market. Investors can now trade futures and options on various volatility indexes in an effort to manage their vega exposure in other options.

Exhibit 20 provides a look at a couple of decades of one such volatility index, the Chicago Board Options Exchange S&P 500 Volatility Index, known as the VIX. The VIX is quoted as a percent and is intended to approximate the implied volatility of the S&P 500 over the next 30 days. VIX is often termed the fear index because it is viewed as a measure of market uncertainty. Thus, an increase in the VIX index is regarded as greater investor uncertainty. From this figure, we see that the implied volatility of the S&P 500 is not constant and goes through periods when the VIX is low and periods when the VIX is high. In the 2008 global financial crisis, the VIX was extremely high, indicating great fear and uncertainty in the equity market. Remember that implied volatility reflects both beliefs regarding future volatility as well as a preference for risk mitigating products like options. Thus, during the crisis, the higher implied volatility reflected both higher expected future volatility as well as increased preference for buying rather than selling options.

Exhibit 20: VIX Daily Values, 2 January 1990–18 July 2014

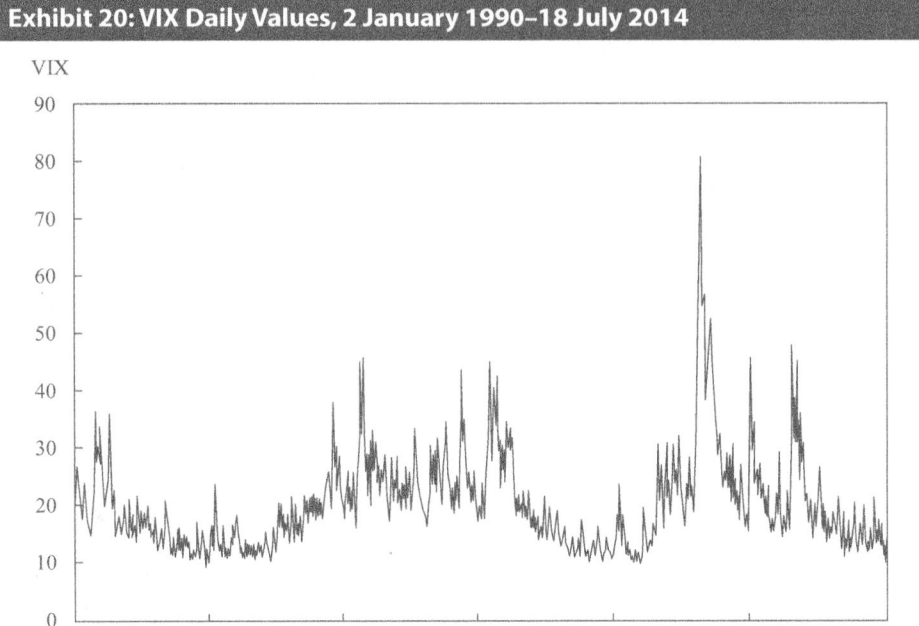

Implied volatility has several uses in option trading. An understanding of implied volatility is essential in managing an options portfolio. This reading explains the valuation of options as a function of the value of the underlying, the exercise price, the expiration date, the risk-free rate, dividends or other benefits paid by the underlying, and the volatility of the underlying. Note that each of these parameters is observable except the volatility of the underlying over the option term looking ahead. This volatility has to be estimated in some manner, such as by calculating historical volatility. But as noted, historical volatility involves looking back in time. There are, however, a vast number of liquid options traded on exchanges around the world so that a wide variety of option prices are observable. Because we know the price and all the parameters except the volatility, we can back out the volatility needed by the option valuation model to get the known price. This volatility is the implied volatility.

Hence, implied volatility can be interpreted as the market's view of how to value options. In the option markets, participants use volatility as the medium in which to quote options. The price is simply calculated by the use of an agreed model with the quoted volatility. For example, rather than quote a particular call option as trading for €14.23, it may be quoted as 30.00, where 30.00 denotes in percentage points the implied volatility based on a €14.23 option price. Note that there is a one-to-one relationship between the implied volatility and the option price, ignoring rounding errors.

The benefit of quoting via implied volatility (or simply volatility), rather than price, is that it allows volatility to be traded in its own right. Volatility is the "guess factor" in option pricing. All other inputs—value of the underlying, exercise price, expiration, risk-free rate, and dividend yield—are agreed.[18] Volatility is often the same order of magnitude across exercise prices and expiration dates. This means that traders can compare the values of two options, which may have markedly different exercise prices and expiration dates, and therefore, markedly different prices in a common unit of measure, specifically implied volatility.

---

18 The risk-free rate and dividend yield may not be entirely agreed, but the impact of variations to these parameters is generally very small compared with the other inputs.

EXAMPLE 20

Implied Volatility in Option Trading within One Market

1. Suppose we hold portfolio of options all tied to FTSE 100 futures contracts. Let the current futures price be 6,850. A client calls to request our offer prices on out-of-the-money puts and at-the-money puts, both with the same agreed expiration date. We calculate the prices to be respectively, 190 and 280 futures points. The client wants these prices quoted in implied volatility as well as in futures points because she wants to compare prices by comparing the quoted implied volatilities. The implied volatilities are 16% for the out-of-the-money puts and 15.2% for the at-the-money puts. Why does the client want the quotes in implied volatility?

   A. Because she can better compare the two options for value—that is, she can better decide which is cheap and which is expensive.

   B. Because she can assess where implied volatility is trading at that time, and thus consider revaluing her options portfolio at the current market implied volatilities for the FTSE 100.

   C. Both A and B are valid reasons for quoting options in volatility units.

Solution:

C is correct. Implied volatility can be used to assess the relative value of different options, neutralizing the moneyness and time to expiration effects. Also, implied volatility is useful for revaluing existing positions over time.

EXAMPLE 21

Implied Volatility in Option Trading Across Markets

1. Suppose an options dealer offers to sell a three-month at-the-money call on the FTSE index option at 19% implied volatility and a one-month in-the-money put on Vodaphone (VOD) at 24%. An option trader believes that based on the current outlook, FTSE volatility should be closer to 25% and VOD volatility should be closer to 20%. What actions might the trader take to benefit from her views?

   A. Buy the FTSE call and the VOD put.

   B. Buy the FTSE call and sell the VOD put.

   C. Sell the FTSE call and sell the VOD puts.

Solution:

B is correct. The trader believes that the FTSE call volatility is understated by the dealer and that the VOD put volatility is overstated. Thus, the trader would expect FTSE volatility to rise and VOD volatility to fall. As a result, the FTSE call would be expected to increase in value and the VOD put would be expected to decrease in value. The trader would take the positions as indicated in B.

Regulators, banks, compliance officers, and most option traders use implied volatilities to communicate information related to options portfolios. This is because implied volatilities, together with standard pricing models, give the "market consensus" valuation, in the same way that other assets are valued using market prices.

In summary, as long as all market participants agree on the underlying option model and how other parameters are calculated, then implied volatility can be used as a quoting mechanism. Recall that there are calls and puts, various exercise prices, various maturities, American and European, and exchange-traded and OTC options. Thus, it is difficult to conceptualize all these different prices. For example, if two call options on the same stock had different prices, but one had a longer expiration and lower exercise price and the other had a shorter expiration and higher exercise, which should be the higher priced option? It is impossible to tell on the surface. But if one option implied a higher volatility than the other, we know that after taking into account the effects of time and exercise, one option is more expensive than the other. Thus, by converting the quoted price to implied volatility, it is easier to understand the current market price of various risk exposures.

SUMMARY

This reading on the valuation of contingent claims provides a foundation for understanding how a variety of different options are valued. Key points include the following:

- The arbitrageur would rather have more money than less and abides by two fundamental rules: Do not use your own money and do not take any price risk.

- The no-arbitrage approach is used for option valuation and is built on the key concept of the law of one price, which says that if two investments have the same future cash flows regardless of what happens in the future, then these two investments should have the same current price.

- Throughout this reading, the following key assumptions are made:

  - Replicating instruments are identifiable and investable.
  - Market frictions are nil.
  - Short selling is allowed with full use of proceeds.
  - The underlying instrument price follows a known distribution.
  - Borrowing and lending is available at a known risk-free rate.

- The two-period binomial model can be viewed as three one-period binomial models, one positioned at Time 0 and two positioned at Time 1.

- In general, European-style options can be valued based on the expectations approach in which the option value is determined as the present value of the expected future option payouts, where the discount rate is the risk-free rate and the expectation is taken based on the risk-neutral probability measure.

- Both American-style options and European-style options can be valued based on the no-arbitrage approach, which provides clear interpretations of the component terms; the option value is determined by working backward through the binomial tree to arrive at the correct current value.

- For American-style options, early exercise influences the option values and hedge ratios as one works backward through the binomial tree.

- Interest rate option valuation requires the specification of an entire term structure of interest rates, so valuation is often estimated via a binomial tree.

- A key assumption of the Black–Scholes–Merton option valuation model is that the return of the underlying instrument follows geometric Brownian motion, implying a lognormal distribution of the price.

- The BSM model can be interpreted as a dynamically managed portfolio of the underlying instrument and zero-coupon bonds.

- BSM model interpretations related to $N(d_1)$ are that it is the basis for the number of units of underlying instrument to replicate an option, that it is the primary determinant of delta, and that it answers the question of how much the option value will change for a small change in the underlying.

- BSM model interpretations related to $N(d_2)$ are that it is the basis for the number of zero-coupon bonds to acquire to replicate an option and that it is the basis for estimating the risk-neutral probability of an option expiring in the money.

- The Black futures option model assumes the underlying is a futures or a forward contract.

- Interest rate options can be valued based on a modified Black futures option model in which the underlying is a forward rate agreement (FRA), there is an accrual period adjustment as well as an underlying notional amount, and that care must be given to day-count conventions.

- An interest rate cap is a portfolio of interest rate call options termed caplets, each with the same exercise rate and with sequential maturities.

- An interest rate floor is a portfolio of interest rate put options termed floorlets, each with the same exercise rate and with sequential maturities.

- A swaption is an option on a swap.

- A payer swaption is an option on a swap to pay fixed and receive floating.

- A receiver swaption is an option on a swap to receive fixed and pay floating.

- Long a callable fixed-rate bond can be viewed as long a straight fixed-rate bond and short a receiver swaption.

- Delta is a static risk measure defined as the change in a given portfolio for a given small change in the value of the underlying instrument, holding everything else constant.

- Delta hedging refers to managing the portfolio delta by entering additional positions into the portfolio.

- A delta neutral portfolio is one in which the portfolio delta is set and maintained at zero.

- A change in the option price can be estimated with a delta approximation.

- Because delta is used to make a linear approximation of the non-linear relationship that exists between the option price and the underlying price, there is an error that can be estimated by gamma.

- Gamma is a static risk measure defined as the change in a given portfolio delta for a given small change in the value of the underlying instrument, holding everything else constant.

- Gamma captures the non-linearity risk or the risk—via exposure to the underlying—that remains once the portfolio is delta neutral.

- A gamma neutral portfolio is one in which the portfolio gamma is maintained at zero.

- The change in the option price can be better estimated by a delta-plus-gamma approximation compared with just a delta approximation.

- Theta is a static risk measure defined as the change in the value of an option given a small change in calendar time, holding everything else constant.

- Vega is a static risk measure defined as the change in a given portfolio for a given small change in volatility, holding everything else constant.

- Rho is a static risk measure defined as the change in a given portfolio for a given small change in the risk-free interest rate, holding everything else constant.

- Although historical volatility can be estimated, there is no objective measure of future volatility.

- Implied volatility is the BSM model volatility that yields the market option price.

- Implied volatility is a measure of future volatility, whereas historical volatility is a measure of past volatility.

- Option prices reflect the beliefs of option market participant about the future volatility of the underlying.

- The volatility smile is a two dimensional plot of the implied volatility with respect to the exercise price.

- The volatility surface is a three dimensional plot of the implied volatility with respect to both expiration time and exercise prices.

- If the BSM model assumptions were true, then one would expect to find the volatility surface flat, but in practice, the volatility surface is not flat.

PRACTICE PROBLEMS

The following information relates to questions 1-9

Bruno Sousa has been hired recently to work with senior analyst Camila Rocha. Rocha gives him three option valuation tasks.

Alpha Company

Sousa's first task is to illustrate how to value a call option on Alpha Company with a one-period binomial option pricing model. It is a non-dividend-paying stock, and the inputs are as follows.

- The current stock price is 50, and the call option exercise price is 50.
- In one period, the stock price will either rise to 56 or decline to 46.
- The risk-free rate of return is 5% per period.

Based on the model, Rocha asks Sousa to estimate the hedge ratio, the risk-neutral probability of an up move, and the price of the call option. In the illustration, Sousa is also asked to describe related arbitrage positions to use if the call option is overpriced relative to the model.

Beta Company

Next, Sousa uses the two-period binomial model to estimate the value of a European-style call option on Beta Company's common shares. The inputs are as follows.

- The current stock price is 38, and the call option exercise price is 40.
- The up factor (u) is 1.300, and the down factor (d) is 0.800.
- The risk-free rate of return is 3% per period.

Sousa then analyzes a put option on the same stock. All of the inputs, including the exercise price, are the same as for the call option. He estimates that the value of a European-style put option is 4.53. Exhibit 1 summarizes his analysis. Sousa next must determine whether an American-style put option would have the same value.

Exhibit 1: Two-Period Binomial European-Style Put Option on Beta Company

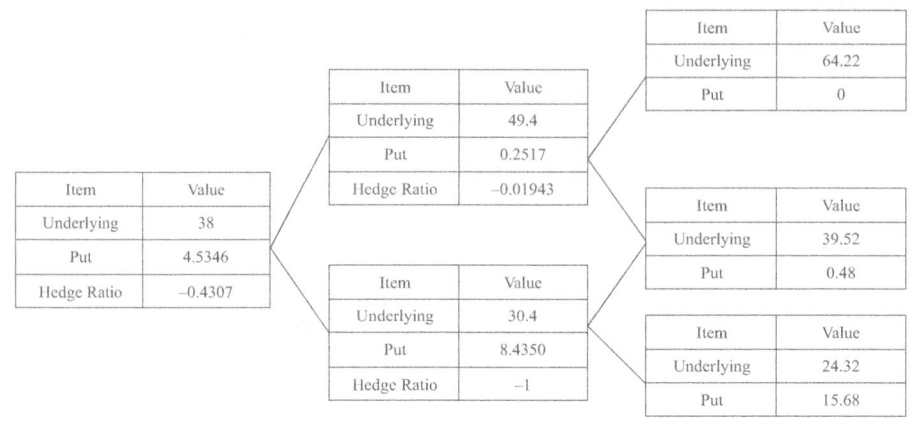

Item	Value
Underlying	38
Put	4.5346
Hedge Ratio	−0.4307

Item	Value
Underlying	49.4
Put	0.2517
Hedge Ratio	−0.01943

Item	Value
Underlying	30.4
Put	8.4350
Hedge Ratio	−1

Item	Value
Underlying	64.22
Put	0

Item	Value
Underlying	39.52
Put	0.48

Item	Value
Underlying	24.32
Put	15.68

Time = 0   Time = 1   Time = 2

Sousa makes two statements with regard to the valuation of a European-style option under the expectations approach.

Statement 1   The calculation involves discounting at the risk-free rate.

Statement 2   The calculation uses risk-neutral probabilities instead of true probabilities.

Rocha asks Sousa whether it is ever profitable to exercise American options prior to maturity. Sousa answers, "I can think of two possible cases. The first case is the early exercise of an American call option on a dividend-paying stock. The second case is the early exercise of an American put option."

Interest Rate Option

The final option valuation task involves an interest rate option. Sousa must value a two-year, European-style call option on a one-year spot rate. The notional value of the option is 1 million, and the exercise rate is 2.75%. The risk-neutral probability of an up move is 0.50. The current and expected one-year interest rates are shown in Exhibit 2, along with the values of a one-year zero-coupon bond of 1 notional value for each interest rate.

Exhibit 2: Two-Year Interest Rate Lattice for an Interest Rate Option

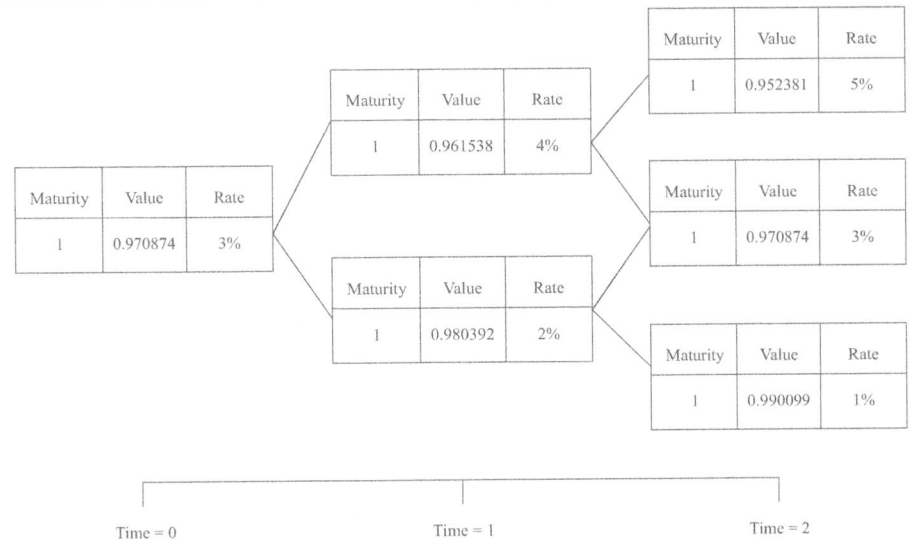

Maturity	Value	Rate
1	0.970874	3%

Maturity	Value	Rate
1	0.961538	4%

Maturity	Value	Rate
1	0.980392	2%

Maturity	Value	Rate
1	0.952381	5%

Maturity	Value	Rate
1	0.970874	3%

Maturity	Value	Rate
1	0.990099	1%

Time = 0   Time = 1   Time = 2

Rocha asks Sousa why the value of a similar in-the-money interest rate call option decreases if the exercise price is higher. Sousa provides two reasons.

Reason 1   The exercise value of the call option is lower.

Reason 2   The risk-neutral probabilities are changed.

1. The optimal hedge ratio for the Alpha Company call option using the one-period binomial model is *closest* to:

    A. 0.60.

    B. 0.67.

    C. 1.67.

2. The risk-neutral probability of the up move for the Alpha Company stock is *closest* to:

    A. 0.06.

    B. 0.40.

    C. 0.65.

3. The value of the Alpha Company call option is *closest* to:

    A. 3.71.

    B. 5.71.

    C. 6.19.

4. For the Alpha Company option, the positions to take advantage of the arbitrage opportunity are to write the call and:

    A. short shares of Alpha stock and lend.

B. buy shares of Alpha stock and borrow.

C. short shares of Alpha stock and borrow.

5. The value of the European-style call option on Beta Company shares is *closest* to:

   A. 4.83.

   B. 5.12.

   C. 7.61.

6. The value of the American-style put option on Beta Company shares is *closest* to:

   A. 4.53.

   B. 5.15.

   C. 9.32.

7. Which of Sousa's statements about binomial models is correct?

   A. Statement 1 only

   B. Statement 2 only

   C. Both Statement 1 and Statement 2

8. Based on Exhibit 2 and the parameters used by Sousa, the value of the interest rate option is *closest* to:

   A. 5,251.

   B. 6,236.

   C. 6,429.

9. Which of Sousa's reasons for the decrease in the value of the interest rate option is correct?

   A. Reason 1 only

   B. Reason 2 only

   C. Both Reason 1 and Reason 2

The following information relates to questions 10-17

Trident Advisory Group manages assets for high-net-worth individuals and family trusts.

Alice Lee, chief investment officer, is meeting with a client, Noah Solomon, to discuss risk management strategies for his portfolio. Solomon is concerned about recent volatility and has asked Lee to explain options valuation and the use of options in risk management.

Options on Stock

Lee uses the BSM model to price TCB, which is one of Solomon's holdings. Exhibit 1 provides the current stock price (S), exercise price (X), risk-free interest rate (r), volatility (σ), and time to expiration (T) in years as well as selected outputs from the BSM model. TCB does not pay a dividend.

Exhibit 1: BSM Model for European Options on TCB

BSM Inputs

S	X	r	σ	T
$57.03	55	0.22%	32%	0.25

BSM Outputs

d_1	$N(d_1)$	d_2	$N(d_2)$	BSM Call Price	BSM Put Price
0.3100	0.6217	0.1500	0.5596	$4.695	$2.634

Options on Futures

The Black model valuation and selected outputs for options on another of Solomon's holdings, the GPX 500 Index (GPX), are shown in Exhibit 2. The spot index level for the GPX is 187.95, and the index is assumed to pay a continuous dividend at a rate of 2.2% (δ) over the life of the options being valued, which expire in 0.36 years. A futures contract on the GPX also expiring in 0.36 years is currently priced at 186.73.

Exhibit 2: Black Model for European Options on the GPX Index

Black Model Inputs

GPX Index	X	r	σ	T	δ Yield
187.95	180	0.39%	24%	0.36	2.2%

Black Model Call Value	Black Model Put Value	Market Call Price	Market Put Price
$14.2089	$7.4890	$14.26	$7.20

Option Greeks

Delta (call)	Delta (put)	Gamma (call or put)	Theta (call) daily	Rho (call) per %	Vega per % (call or put)
0.6232	−0.3689	0.0139	−0.0327	0.3705	0.4231

After reviewing Exhibit 2, Solomon asks Lee which option Greek letter best describes the changes in an option's value as time to expiration declines.

Solomon observes that the market price of the put option in Exhibit 2 is $7.20. Lee responds that she used the historical volatility of the GPX of 24% as an input to the BSM model, and she explains the implications for the implied volatility for the GPX.

Options on Interest Rates

Solomon forecasts the three-month MRR will exceed 0.85% in six months and is considering using options to reduce the risk of rising rates. He asks Lee to value an interest rate call with a strike price of 0.85%. The current three-month MRR is 0.60%, and an FRA for a three-month MRR loan beginning in six months is currently 0.75%.

Hedging Strategy for the Equity Index

Solomon's portfolio currently holds 10,000 shares of an exchange-traded fund (ETF) that tracks the GPX. He is worried the index will decline. He remarks to Lee, "You have told me how the BSM model can provide useful information for reducing the risk of my GPX position." Lee suggests a delta hedge as a strategy to protect against small moves in the GPX Index.

Lee also indicates that a long position in puts could be used to hedge larger moves in the GPX. She notes that although hedging with either puts or calls can result in a delta-neutral position, they would need to consider the resulting gamma.

10. Based on Exhibit 1 and the BSM valuation approach, the initial portfolio required to replicate the long call option payoff is:

   A. long 0.3100 shares of TCB stock and short 0.5596 shares of a zero-coupon bond.

   B. long 0.6217 shares of TCB stock and short 0.1500 shares of a zero-coupon bond.

   C. long 0.6217 shares of TCB stock and short 0.5596 shares of a zero-coupon bond.

11. To determine the long put option value on TCB stock in Exhibit 1, the correct BSM valuation approach is to compute:

   A. 0.4404 times the present value of the exercise price minus 0.6217 times the price of TCB stock.

   B. 0.4404 times the present value of the exercise price minus 0.3783 times the price of TCB stock.

   C. 0.5596 times the present value of the exercise price minus 0.6217 times the price of TCB stock.

12. What are the correct spot value (S) and the risk-free rate (r) that Lee should use as inputs for the Black model?

   A. 186.73 and 0.39%, respectively

   B. 186.73 and 2.20%, respectively

   C. 187.95 and 2.20%, respectively

13. Which of the following is the correct answer to Solomon's question regarding the option Greek letter?

   A. Vega

   B. Theta

   C. Gamma

14. Based on Solomon's observation about the model price and market price for the

put option in Exhibit 2, the implied volatility for the GPX is *most likely*:

A. less than the historical volatility.

B. equal to the historical volatility.

C. greater than the historical volatility.

15. The valuation inputs used by Lee to price a call reflecting Solomon's interest rate views should include an underlying FRA rate of:

A. 0.60% with six months to expiration.

B. 0.75% with nine months to expiration.

C. 0.75% with six months to expiration.

16. The strategy suggested by Lee for hedging small moves in Solomon's ETF position would *most likely* involve:

A. selling put options.

B. selling call options.

C. buying call options.

17. Lee's put-based hedge strategy for Solomon's ETF position would *most likely* result in a portfolio gamma that is:

A. negative.

B. neutral.

C. positive.

SOLUTIONS

1. A is correct. The hedge ratio requires the underlying stock and call option values for the up move and down move. $S^+ = 56$, and $S^- = 46$. $c^+ = \text{Max}(0,S^+ - X) = \text{Max}(0,56 - 50) = 6$, and $c^- = \text{Max}(0,S^- - X) = \text{Max}(0,46 - 50) = 0$. The hedge ratio is

$$h = \frac{c^+ - c^-}{S^+ - S^-} = \frac{6 - 0}{56 - 46} = \frac{6}{10} = 0.60$$

2. C is correct. For this approach, the risk-free rate is $r = 0.05$, the up factor is $u = S^+/S = 56/50 = 1.12$, and the down factor is $d = S^-/S = 46/50 = 0.92$. The risk-neutral probability of an up move is

$$\pi = [\text{FV}(1) - d]/(u - d) = (1 + r - d)/(u - d)$$

$$\pi = (1 + 0.05 - 0.92)/(1.12 - 0.92) = 0.13/0.20 = 0.65$$

3. A is correct. The call option can be estimated using the no-arbitrage approach or the expectations approach. With the no-arbitrage approach, the value of the call option is

$$c = hS + \text{PV}(-hS^- + c^-).$$

$$h = (c^+ - c^-)/(S^+ - S^-) = (6 - 0)/(56 - 46) = 0.60.$$

$$c = (0.60 \times 50) + (1/1.05) \times [(-0.60 \times 46) + 0].$$

$$c = 30 - [(1/1.05) \times 27.6] = 30 - 26.286 = 3.714.$$

Using the expectations approach, the risk-free rate is $r = 0.05$, the up factor is $u = S^+/S = 56/50 = 1.12$, and the down factor is $d = S^-/S = 46/50 = 0.92$. The value of the call option is

$$c = \text{PV} \times [\pi c^+ + (1 - \pi)c^-].$$

$$\pi = [\text{FV}(1) - d]/(u - d) = (1.05 - 0.92)/(1.12 - 0.92) = 0.65.$$

$$c = (1/1.05) \times [0.65(6) + (1 - 0.65)(0)] = (1/1.05)(3.9) = 3.714.$$

Both approaches are logically consistent and yield identical values.

4. B is correct. You should sell (write) the overpriced call option and then go long (buy) the replicating portfolio for a call option. The replicating portfolio for a call option is to buy h shares of the stock and borrow the present value of $(hS^- - c^-)$.

$$c = hS + \text{PV}(-hS^- + c^-).$$

$$h = (c^+ - c^-)/(S^+ - S^-) = (6 - 0)/(56 - 46) = 0.60.$$

For the example in this case, the value of the call option is 3.714. If the option is overpriced at, say, 4.50, you short the option and have a cash flow at Time 0 of +4.50. You buy the replicating portfolio of 0.60 shares at 50 per share (giving you a cash flow of −30) and borrow $(1/1.05) \times [(0.60 \times 46) - 0] = (1/1.05) \times 27.6 = 26.287$. Your cash flow for buying the replicating portfolio is $-30 + 26.287 = -3.713$. Your net cash flow at Time 0 is $+ 4.50 - 3.713 = 0.787$. Your net cash flow at Time 1 for either the up move or down move is zero. You have made an arbitrage profit of 0.787.

In tabular form, the cash flows are as follows:

Transaction	Time Step 0	Time Step 1 Down Occurs	Time Step 1 Up Occurs
Sell the call option	4.50	0	−6.00
Buy h shares	$-0.6 \times 50 = -30$	$0.6 \times 46 = 27.6$	$0.6 \times 56 = 33.6$
Borrow $-PV(-hS^- + c^-)$	$-(1/1.05) \times [(-0.6 \times 46) + 0] = 26.287$	$-0.6 \times 46 = -27.6$	$-0.6 \times 46 = -27.6$
Net cash flow	0.787	0	0

5. A is correct. Using the expectations approach, the risk-neutral probability of an up move is

$$\pi = [FV(1) - d]/(u - d) = (1.03 - 0.800)/(1.300 - 0.800) = 0.46.$$

The terminal value calculations for the exercise values at Time Step 2 are

$$c^{++} = \text{Max}(0, u^2 S - X) = \text{Max}[0, 1.30^2(38) - 40] = \text{Max}(0, 24.22) = 24.22.$$

$$c^{-+} = \text{Max}(0, udS - X) = \text{Max}[0, 1.30(0.80)(38) - 40] = \text{Max}(0, -0.48) = 0.$$

$$c^{--} = \text{Max}(0, d^2 S - X) = \text{Max}[0, 0.80^2(38) - 40] = \text{Max}(0, -15.68) = 0.$$

Discounting back for two years, the value of the call option at Time Step 0 is

$$c = PV[\pi^2 c^{++} + 2\pi(1 - \pi)c^{-+} + (1 - \pi)^2 c^{--}].$$

$$c = [1/(1.03)]^2[0.46^2(24.22) + 2(0.46)(0.54)(0) + 0.54^2(0)].$$

$$c = [1/(1.03)]^2[5.1250] = 4.8308.$$

6. B is correct. Using the expectations approach, the risk-neutral probability of an up move is

$$\pi = [FV(1) - d]/(u - d) = (1.03 - 0.800)/(1.300 - 0.800) = 0.46.$$

An American-style put can be exercised early. At Time Step 1, for the up move, p^+ is 0.2517 and the put is out of the money and should not be exercised early ($X < S$, 40 < 49.4). However, at Time Step 1, p^- is 8.4350 and the put is in the money by 9.60 ($X - S = 40 - 30.40$). So, the put is exercised early, and the value of early exercise (9.60) replaces the value of not exercising early (8.4350) in the binomial tree. The value of the put at Time Step 0 is now

$$p = PV[\pi p^+ + (1 - \pi)p^-] = [1/(1.03)][0.46(0.2517) + 0.54(9.60)] = 5.145.$$

Following is a supplementary note regarding Exhibit 1: These computations refer to European-style put options.

The values in Exhibit 1 are calculated as follows.

At Time Step 2:

$p^{++} = \text{Max}(0, X - u^2 S) = \text{Max}[0, 40 - 1.300^2(38)] = \text{Max}(0, 40 - 64.22) = 0.$

$p^{-+} = \text{Max}(0, X - udS) = \text{Max}[0, 40 - 1.300(0.800)(38)] = \text{Max}(0, 40 - 39.52) = 0.48.$

$\text{p}^{--} = \text{Max}(0, X - d^2 S) = \text{Max}[0, 40 - 0.800^2(38)] = \text{Max}(0, 40 - 24.32) = 15.68.$

At Time Step 1:

$p^+ = \text{PV}[\pi p^{++} + (1 - \pi)p^{-+}] = [1/(1.03)][0.46(0) + 0.54(0.48)] = 0.2517.$

$p^- = \text{PV}[\pi p^{-+} + (1 - \pi)p^{--}] = [1/(1.03)][0.46(0.48) + 0.54(15.68)] = 8.4350.$

At Time Step 0:

$p = \text{PV}[\pi p^+ + (1 - \pi)p^-] = [1/(1.03)][0.46(0.2517) + 0.54(9.60)] = 5.145.$

7. C is correct. Both statements are correct. The expected future payoff is calculated using risk-neutral probabilities, and the expected payoff is discounted at the risk-free rate.

8. C is correct. Using the expectations approach, per 1 of notional value, the values of the call option at Time Step 2 are

$c^{++} = \text{Max}(0, S^{++} - X) = \text{Max}(0, 0.050 - 0.0275) = 0.0225.$

$c^{+-} = \text{Max}(0, S^{+-} - X) = \text{Max}(0, 0.030 - 0.0275) = 0.0025.$

$c^{--} = \text{Max}(0, S^{--} - X) = \text{Max}(0, 0.010 - 0.0275) = 0.$

At Time Step 1, the call values are

$c^+ = \text{PV}[\pi c^{++} + (1 - \pi)c^{+-}] .$

$c^+ = 0.961538[0.50(0.0225) + (1 - 0.50)(0.0025)] = 0.012019.$

$c^- = \text{PV}[\pi c^{+-} + (1 - \pi)c^{--}].$

$c^- = 0.980392[0.50(0.0025) + (1 - 0.50)(0)] = 0.001225.$

At Time Step 0, the call option value is

$c = \text{PV}[\pi c^+ + (1 - \pi)c^-].$

$c = 0.970874[0.50(0.012019) + (1 - 0.50)(0.001225)] = 0.006429.$

The value of the call option is this amount multiplied by the notional value, or $0.006429 \times 1,000,000 = 6,429.$

9. A is correct. Reason 1 is correct: A higher exercise price does lower the exercise value (payoff) at Time 2. Reason 2 is not correct because the risk-neutral probabilities are based on the paths that interest rates take, which are determined by the market and not the details of a particular option contract.

10. C is correct. The no-arbitrage approach to creating a call option involves buying Delta = $N(d_1) = 0.6217$ shares of the underlying stock and financing with $-N(d_2)$ = -0.5596 shares of a risk-free bond priced at $\exp(-rt)(X) = \exp(-0.0022 \times 0.25)$ (55) = \$54.97 per bond. Note that the value of this replicating portfolio is $n_S S + n_B B = 0.6217(57.03) - 0.5596(54.97) = \$4.6943$ (the value of the call option with slight rounding error).

11. B is correct. The formula for the BSM price of a put option is $p = e^{-rt}XN(-d_2) - SN(-d_1)$. $N(-d_1) = 1 - N(d_1) = 1 - 0.6217 = 0.3783$, and $N(-d_2) = 1 - N(d_2) = 1 - 0.5596 = 0.4404$.

    Note that the BSM model can be represented as a portfolio of the stock ($n_S S$) and zero-coupon bonds ($n_B B$). For a put, the number of shares is $n_S = -N(-d_1) < 0$ and the number of bonds is $n_B = -N(d_2) > 0$. The value of the replicating portfolio is $n_S S + n_B B = -0.3783(57.03) + 0.4404(54.97) = \$2.6343$ (the value of the put option with slight rounding error). B is a risk-free bond priced at $\exp(-rt)(X) = \exp(-0.0022 \times 0.25)(55) = \$54.97$.

12. A is correct. Black's model to value a call option on a futures contract is $c = e^{-rT}[F_0(T)N(d_1) - XN(d_2)]$. The underlying F_0 is the futures price (186.73). The correct discount rate is the risk-free rate, $r = 0.39\%$.

13. B is correct. Lee is pointing out the option price's sensitivity to small changes in time. In the BSM approach, option price sensitivity to changes in time is given by the option Greek theta.

14. A is correct. The put is priced at $7.4890 by the BSM model when using the historical volatility input of 24%. The market price is $7.20. The BSM model overpricing suggests the implied volatility of the put must be lower than 24%.

15. C is correct. Solomon's forecast is for the three-month MRR to exceed 0.85% in six months. The correct option valuation inputs use the six-month FRA rate as the underlying, which currently has a rate of 0.75%.

16. B is correct because selling call options creates a short position in the ETF that would hedge his current long position in the ETF.

    Exhibit 2 could also be used to answer the question. Solomon owns 10,000 shares of the GPX, each with a delta of +1; by definition, his portfolio delta is +10,000. A delta hedge could be implemented by selling enough calls to make the portfolio delta neutral:

    $$N_H = -\frac{\text{Portfolio delta}}{\text{Delta}_H} = -\frac{+10,000}{+0.6232} = -16,046 \text{ calls.}$$

17. C is correct. Because the gamma of the stock position is 0 and the put gamma is always non-negative, adding a long position in put options would most likely result in a positive portfolio gamma.

    Gamma is the change in delta from a small change in the stock's value. A stock position always has a delta of +1. Because the delta does not change, gamma equals 0.

    The gamma of a call equals the gamma of a similar put, which can be proven using put–call parity.

Glossary

Abnormal earnings See *residual income*.

Abnormal return The amount by which a security's actual return differs from its expected return, given the security's risk and the market's return.

Absolute convergence The idea that developing countries, regardless of their particular characteristics, will eventually catch up with the developed countries and match them in per capita output.

Absolute valuation model A model that specifies an asset's intrinsic value.

Absolute version of PPP An extension of the law of one price whereby the prices of goods and services will not differ internationally once exchange rates are considered.

Accounting estimates Estimates used in calculating the value of assets or liabilities and in the amount of revenue and expense to allocate to a period. Examples of accounting estimates include, among others, the useful lives of depreciable assets, the salvage value of depreciable assets, product returns, warranty costs, and the amount of uncollectible receivables.

Accuracy The percentage of correctly predicted classes out of total predictions. It is an overall performance metric in classification problems.

Acquisition When one company, the acquirer, purchases from the seller most or all of another company's (the target) shares to gain control of either an entire company, a segment of another company, or a specific group of assets in exchange for cash, stock, or the assumption of liabilities, alone or in combination. Once an acquisition is complete, the acquirer and target merge into a single entity and consolidate management, operations, and resources.

Activation function A functional part of a neural network's node that transforms the total net input received into the final output of the node. The activation function operates like a light dimmer switch that decreases or increases the strength of the input.

Active factor risk The contribution to active risk squared resulting from the portfolio's different-than-benchmark exposures relative to factors specified in the risk model.

Active return The return on a portfolio minus the return on the portfolio's benchmark.

Active risk The standard deviation of active returns.

Active risk squared The variance of active returns; active risk raised to the second power.

Active share A measure of how similar a portfolio is to its benchmark. A manager who precisely replicates the benchmark will have an active share of zero; a manager with no holdings in common with the benchmark will have an active share of one.

Active specific risk The contribution to active risk squared resulting from the portfolio's active weights on individual assets as those weights interact with assets' residual risk.

Activist short selling A hedge fund strategy in which the manager takes a short position in a given security and then publicly presents his/her research backing the short thesis.

Adjustable rate Interest rate for a mortgage or other loan that combines a fixed-rate period with a variable-rate period, which fluctuates based on market reference rates.

Adjusted funds from operations Funds from operations adjusted to remove any non-cash rent reported under straight-line rent accounting and to subtract maintenance-type capital expenditures and leasing costs, including leasing agents' commissions and tenants' improvement allowances.

Adjusted present value As an approach to valuing a company, the sum of the value of the company, assuming no use of debt, and the net present value of any effects of debt on company value.

Adjusted R^2 Goodness-of-fit measure that adjusts the coefficient of determination, R^2, for the number of independent variables in the model.

Advanced set An arrangement in which the reference interest rate is set at the time the money is deposited.

Advanced settled An arrangement in which a forward rate agreement (FRA) expires and settles at the same time, at the FRA expiration date.

Agglomerative clustering A bottom-up hierarchical clustering method that begins with each observation being treated as its own cluster. The algorithm finds the two closest clusters, based on some measure of distance (similarity), and combines them into one new larger cluster. This process is repeated iteratively until all observations are clumped into a single large cluster.

Akaike's information criterion (AIC) A statistic used to compare sets of independent variables for explaining a dependent variable. It is preferred for finding the model that is best suited for prediction.

Allowance for loan losses A balance sheet account; it is a contra asset account to loans.

Alpha The return on an asset in excess of the asset's required rate of return. Sometimes referred to as an *abnormal return*.

American Depositary Receipt A negotiable certificate issued by a depositary bank that represents ownership in a non-US company's deposited equity (i.e., equity held in custody by the depositary bank in the company's home market).

Analysis of variance (ANOVA) A table that presents the sums of squares, degrees of freedom, mean squares, and F-statistic for a regression model.

Application programming interface (API) A set of well-defined methods of communication between various software components and typically used for accessing external data.

Appraisals Professional estimates of current market value for a real estate property.

Arbitrage (1) The simultaneous purchase of an undervalued asset or portfolio and sale of an overvalued but equivalent asset or portfolio in order to obtain a riskless profit on the price differential. Taking advantage of a market inefficiency in a risk-free manner. (2) The condition in a financial market in which equivalent assets or combinations of assets sell for two different prices, creating an opportunity to profit at no risk with no commitment of money. In a well-functioning financial market, few arbitrage opportunities are possible. (3) A risk-free operation that earns an expected positive net profit but requires no net investment of money.

Arbitrage opportunity   An opportunity to conduct an arbitrage; an opportunity to earn an expected positive net profit without risk and with no net investment of money.

Arbitrage portfolio   The portfolio that exploits an arbitrage opportunity.

Arbitrage-free models   Term structure models that project future interest rate paths that emanate from the existing term structure. Resulting prices are based on a no-arbitrage condition.

Arbitrage-free valuation   An approach to valuation that determines security values consistent with the absence of any opportunity to earn riskless profits without any net investment of money.

Arm's-length transaction   Both buyer and seller act independently without any preexisting relationship that may sway their decision making.

Asset-based approach   Approach that values a private company based on the values of the underlying assets of the entity less the value of any related liabilities.

Asset-based valuation   An approach to valuing natural resource companies that estimates company value on the basis of the market value of the natural resources the company controls.

At market contract   When a forward contract is established, the forward price is negotiated so that the market value of the forward contract on the initiation date is zero.

Authorized participants   (APs) A special group of institutional investors who are authorized by the ETF issuer to participate in the creation/redemption process. APs are large broker/dealers, often market makers.

Autocorrelations   The correlations of a time series with its own past values.

Autoregressive model (AR)   A time series regressed on its own past values in which the independent variable is a lagged value of the dependent variable.

Back-testing   The process that approximates the real-life investment process, using historical data, to assess whether an investment strategy would have produced desirable results.

Backward propagation   The process of adjusting weights in a neural network, to reduce total error of the network, by moving backward through the network's layers.

Backwardation   A downward-sloping, or inverted, forward curve in a futures market.

Bag-of-words (BOW)   A collection of a distinct set of tokens from all the texts in a sample dataset. BOW does not capture the position or sequence of words present in the text.

Balance sheet restructuring   Altering the composition of the balance sheet by either shifting the asset composition, changing the capital structure, or both.

Bankruptcy   Legal proceedings, which vary by jurisdiction, allowing a firm whose liabilities exceed its assets to restructure existing debt obligations or liquidate assets in an orderly manner.

Barbell portfolio   Fixed-income portfolio that combines short and long maturities.

Base error   Model error due to randomness in the data.

Basic earnings per share   (EPS) Net earnings available to common shareholders (i.e., net income minus preferred dividends) divided by the weighted average number of common shares outstanding during the period.

Basis   The difference between the spot price and the futures price. As the maturity date of the futures contract nears, the basis converges toward zero.

Basis trade   A trade based on the pricing of credit in the bond market versus the price of the same credit in the CDS market. To execute a basis trade, go long the "underpriced" credit and short the "overpriced" credit. A profit is realized as the implied credit prices converge.

Bearish flattening   Term structure shift in which short-term bond yields rise more than long-term bond yields, resulting in a flatter yield curve.

Benchmark value of the multiple   In using the method of comparables, the value of a price multiple for the comparison asset; when we have comparison assets (a group), the mean or median value of the multiple for the group of assets.

Bias error   Describes the degree to which a model fits the training data. Algorithms with erroneous assumptions produce high bias error with poor approximation, causing underfitting and high in-sample error.

Bill-and-hold basis   Sales on a bill-and-hold basis involve selling products but not delivering those products until a later date.

Blockage factor   An illiquidity discount that occurs when an investor sells a large amount of stock relative to its trading volume (assuming it is not large enough to constitute a controlling ownership).

Bond indenture   A legal document between a bond issuer and investors that governs each party's rights and responsibilities.

Bond risk premium   The expected excess return of a default-free long-term bond less that of an equivalent short-term bond.

Bond yield plus risk premium (BYPRP) approach   An estimate of the cost of common equity that is produced by summing the before-tax cost of debt and a risk premium that captures the additional yield on a company's stock relative to its bonds.

Bonus issue of shares   A type of dividend in which a company distributes additional shares of its common stock to shareholders instead of cash.

Book value   Shareholders' equity (total assets minus total liabilities) minus the value of preferred stock; common shareholders' equity.

Book value of equity   Shareholders' equity (total assets minus total liabilities) minus the value of preferred stock; common shareholders' equity.

Book value per share   The amount of book value (also called carrying value) of common equity per share of common stock, calculated by dividing the book value of shareholders' equity by the number of shares of common stock outstanding.

Bootstrap aggregating (or bagging)   A technique whereby the original training dataset is used to generate n new training datasets or bags of data. Each new bag of data is generated by random sampling with replacement from the initial training set.

Bootstrapping   The use of a forward substitution process to determine zero-coupon rates by using the par yields and solving for the zero-coupon rates one by one, from the shortest to longest maturities.

Breakup value The value derived using a sum-of-the-parts valuation.

Breusch–Godfrey (BG) test A test used to detect autocorrelated residuals up to a predesignated order of the lagged residuals.

Breusch–Pagan (BP) test A test for the presence of heteroskedasticity in a regression.

Bullet portfolio A fixed-income portfolio concentrated in a single maturity.

Bullish flattening Term structure change in which the yield curve flattens in response to a greater decline in long-term rates than short-term rates.

Bullish steepening Term structure change in which short-term rates fall by more than long-term yields, resulting in a steeper term structure.

Buy-side analysts Analysts who work for investment management firms, trusts, bank trust departments, and similar institutions.

Buyback A transaction in which a company buys back its own shares. Unlike stock dividends and stock splits, share repurchases use corporate cash.

Callable bond A bond containing an embedded call option that gives the issuer the right to buy the bond back from the investor at specified prices on predetermined dates.

Canceled shares Shares that were issued, subsequently repurchased by the company, and then retired (cannot be reissued).

Capital asset pricing model (CAPM) An equation describing the expected return on any asset (or portfolio) as a linear function of its beta relative to the market portfolio.

Capital charge The company's total cost of capital in money terms.

Capital deepening An increase in the capital-to-labor ratio.

Capitalization rate The rate used to discount expected NOI, which combines the required rate of return on similar properties with an implied constant growth rate.

Capitalized cash flow method In the context of private company valuation, a valuation model based on an assumption of a constant growth rate of free cash flow to the firm or a constant growth rate of free cash flow to equity. Also called *capitalized cash flow model*.

Capped floater Floating-rate bond with a cap provision that prevents the coupon rate from increasing above a specified maximum rate. It protects the issuer against rising interest rates.

Carry arbitrage model A no-arbitrage approach in which the underlying instrument is either bought or sold along with an opposite position in a forward contract.

Carry benefits Benefits that arise from owning certain underlyings; for example, dividends, foreign interest, and bond coupon payments.

Carry costs Costs that arise from owning certain underlyings. They are generally a function of the physical characteristics of the underlying asset and also the interest forgone on the funds tied up in the asset.

Cash available for distribution See *adjusted funds from operations*.

Cash settlement A procedure used in certain derivative transactions that specifies that the long and short parties settle the derivative's difference in value between them by making a cash payment.

Catalyst An event or piece of information that causes the marketplace to re-evaluate the prospects of a company.

CDS spread A periodic premium paid by the buyer to the seller that serves as a return over a market reference rate required to protect against credit risk.

Ceiling analysis A systematic process of evaluating different components in the pipeline of model building. It helps to understand what part of the pipeline can potentially improve in performance by further tuning.

Centroid The center of a cluster formed using the *k*-means clustering algorithm.

Chain rule of forecasting A forecasting process in which the next period's value as predicted by the forecasting equation is substituted into the right-hand side of the equation to give a predicted value two periods ahead.

Cheapest-to-deliver The debt instrument that can be purchased and delivered at the lowest cost yet has the same seniority as the reference obligation.

Classification and regression tree A supervised machine learning technique that can be applied to predict either a categorical target variable, producing a classification tree, or a continuous target variable, producing a regression tree. CART is commonly applied to binary classification or regression.

Clean surplus relation The relationship between earnings, dividends, and book value in which ending book value is equal to the beginning book value plus earnings less dividends, apart from ownership transactions.

Closed DB plan A DB plan that is not accepting new enrollees.

Club convergence The idea that only rich and middle-income countries sharing a set of favorable attributes (i.e., are members of the "club") will converge to the income level of the richest countries.

Cluster A subset of observations from a dataset such that all the observations within the same cluster are deemed "similar."

Clustering The sorting of observations into groups (clusters) such that observations in the same cluster are more similar to each other than they are to observations in other clusters.

Cobb–Douglas production function A function of the form $Y = K^\alpha L^{1-\alpha}$ relating output (Y) to labor (L) and capital (K) inputs.

Coefficient of determination A measure of how well data points fit a linear statistical model, indicated in percentage terms from 0 to 100%. Also known as *R-squared* (R^2).

Cointegrated Describes two time series that have a long-term financial or economic relationship such that they do not diverge from each other without bound in the long run.

Collateral return The component of the total return on a commodity futures position attributable to the yield for the bonds or cash used to maintain the futures position. Also called *collateral yield*.

Collection frequency (CF) The number of times a given word appears in the whole corpus (i.e., collection of sentences) divided by the total number of words in the corpus.

Commodity swap A type of swap involving the exchange of payments over multiple dates as determined by specified reference prices or indexes relating to commodities.

Company fundamental factors Factors related to the company's internal performance, such as factors relating to earnings growth, earnings variability, earnings momentum, and financial leverage.

Company share-related factors Valuation measures and other factors related to share price or the trading characteristics of the shares, such as earnings yield, dividend yield, and book-to-market value.

Comparables   Assets used as benchmarks when applying the method of comparables to value an asset. Also called *comps*, *guideline assets*, or *guideline companies*.

Compiled financial statements   Financial statements that are not accompanied by an auditor's opinion letter.

Complexity   A term referring to the number of features, parameters, or branches in a model and to whether the model is linear or non-linear (non-linear is more complex).

Composite variable   A variable that combines two or more variables that are statistically strongly related to each other.

Comprehensive income   All changes in equity other than contributions by, and distributions to, owners; income under clean surplus accounting; includes all changes in equity during a period except those resulting from investments by owners and distributions to owners. Comprehensive income equals net income plus other comprehensive income.

Comps   Assets used as benchmarks when applying the method of comparables to value an asset.

Concentrated ownership   Ownership structure consisting of an individual shareholder or a group (controlling shareholders) with the ability to exercise control over the corporation.

Conditional convergence   The idea that convergence of per capita income is conditional on the countries having the same savings rate, population growth rate, and production function.

Conditional heteroskedasticity   A condition in which the variance of residuals of a regression are correlated with the value of the independent variables.

Conditional VaR (CVaR)   The weighted average of all loss outcomes in the statistical (i.e., return) distribution that exceed the VaR loss. Thus, CVaR is a more comprehensive measure of tail loss than VaR is. Sometimes referred to as the *expected tail loss* or *expected shortfall*.

Confirmation bias   A type of cognitive bias that makes individuals view information that confirms beliefs they already hold as more salient.

Confusion matrix   A grid used for error analysis in classification problems, it presents values for four evaluation metrics including true positive (TP), false positive (FP), true negative (TN), and false negative (FN).

Conglomerate discount   When an issuer is trading at a valuation lower than the sum of its parts, which is generally the result of diseconomies of scale or scope or the result of the capital markets having overlooked the business and its prospects.

Constant dividend payout ratio policy   A policy in which a constant percentage of net income is paid out in dividends.

Constant returns to scale   The condition that if all inputs into the production process are increased by a given percentage, then output rises by that same percentage.

Contango   Refers to spot price below forward price in a futures market.

Contingent consideration   Potential future payments to the seller that are contingent on the achievement of certain agreed-on occurrences.

Continuing earnings   Earnings excluding nonrecurring components. Also referred to as *core earnings*, *persistent earnings*, or *underlying earnings*.

Continuing residual income   Residual income after the forecast horizon.

Continuing value   The analyst's estimate of a stock's value at a particular point in the future.

Contraction risk   The risk of earlier repayment of a mortgage-backed security than expected.

Control premium   An increment or premium to value associated with a controlling ownership interest in a company.

Convergence   The property by which as expiration approaches, the price of a newly created forward or futures contract will approach the price of a spot transaction. At expiration, a forward or futures contract is equivalent to a spot transaction in the underlying.

Conversion period   The period over which a convertible bond may be exchanged for equity at a predetermined price.

Conversion price   Predetermined share price at which convertible debt may be fully exchanged for common shares during the conversion period.

Conversion rate (or ratio)   For a convertible bond, the number of shares of common stock that a bondholder receives from converting the bond into shares.

Conversion value   The current contingency feature value derived by comparing a convertible bond's price with its value if a bondholder were to exchange bonds for shares.

Convertible bond   A bond that gives the bondholder the right to exchange the bond for a specified number of common shares in the issuing company.

Convexity   The second order, usually a positive change in the price of a bond for a given change in yield, which can be negative for a callable bond such as a high-yield bond.

Core earnings   Earnings excluding nonrecurring components. Also referred to as *continuing earnings*, *persistent earnings*, or *underlying earnings*.

Core real estate   Real estate investments in well-developed, stable-income-producing commercial and residential properties.

Corpus   A collection of text data in any form, including list, matrix, or data table forms.

Cost of carry model   A model that relates the forward price of an asset to the spot price by considering the cost of carry (also referred to as future-spot parity model).

Cost of debt   The required return on debt financing for a company, such as when it issues a bond, takes out a bank loan, or leases an asset through a finance lease.

Cost of equity   The return required by equity investors to compensate for both the time value of money and the risk. Also referred to as the required rate of return on common stock or the required return on equity.

Cost restructuring   Actions to reduce costs by improving operational efficiency and profitability, often to raise margins to a historical level or to those of comparable industry peers.

Country risk premium (CRP)   The additional return required by investors to compensate for the risk associated with investing in a foreign country relative to the investor's domestic market.

Country risk rating (CRR)   The rating of a country based on many risk factors, including economic prosperity, political risk, and ESG risk.

Covariance stationary   Describes a time series when its expected value and variance are constant and finite in all periods and when its covariance with itself for a fixed number of periods in the past or future is constant and finite in all periods.

Covered bonds   A senior debt obligation of a financial institution that gives recourse to the originator/issuer and a predetermined underlying collateral pool.

Covered interest rate parity The relationship among the spot exchange rate, the forward exchange rate, and the interest rates in two currencies that ensures that the return on a hedged (i.e., covered) foreign risk-free investment is the same as the return on a domestic risk-free investment. Also called *interest rate parity*.

Cox-Ingersoll-Ross model A general equilibrium term structure model that assumes interest rates are mean reverting and interest rate volatility is directly related to the level of interest rates.

Creation basket The list of securities (and share amounts) the authorized participant (AP) must deliver to the ETF manager in exchange for ETF shares. The creation basket is published each business day.

Creation units Large blocks of ETF shares transacted between the authorized participant (AP) and the ETF manager that are usually but not always equal to 50,000 shares of the ETF.

Creation/redemption The process in which ETF shares are created or redeemed by authorized participants transacting with the ETF issuer.

Credit correlation The correlation of credit (or default) risks of the underlying single-name CDS contained in an index CDS.

Credit curve The credit spreads for a range of maturities of a company's debt.

Credit default swap A derivative contract between two parties in which the buyer makes a series of cash payments to the seller and receives a promise of compensation for credit losses resulting from the default.

Credit derivative A derivative instrument in which the underlying is a measure of the credit quality of a borrower.

Credit event An occurrence that triggers the settlement of a CDS contract, including failure to make a debt payment, debt restructuring, or a bankruptcy filing.

Credit protection buyer One party to a credit default swap; the buyer makes a series of cash payments to the seller and receives a promise of compensation for credit losses resulting from the default.

Credit protection seller One party to a credit default swap; the seller makes a promise to pay compensation for credit losses resulting from the default.

Credit risk The expected economic loss under a potential borrower default over the life of the contract.

Credit spread The compensation for the risk of default in a debt security, typically measured by the yield-to-maturity difference between a bond and a comparable government benchmark security.

Credit valuation adjustment The value of the credit risk of a bond in present value terms.

Cross-sectional momentum A managed futures trend following strategy implemented with a cross-section of assets (within an asset class) by going long those that are rising in price the most and by shorting those that are falling the most. This approach generally results in holding a net zero (market-neutral) position and works well when a market's out- or underperformance is a reliable predictor of its future performance.

Cross-validation A technique for estimating out-of-sample error directly by determining the error in validation samples.

Cumulative preferred stock Preferred stock that requires that the dividends be paid in full to preferred stock owners for any missed dividends prior to any payment of dividends to common stock owners.

Current exchange rate For accounting purposes, the spot exchange rate on the balance sheet date.

Current rate method Approach to translating foreign currency financial statements for consolidation in which all assets and liabilities are translated at the current exchange rate. The current rate method is the prevalent method of translation.

Curvature One of the three factors (the other two are level and steepness) that empirically explain most of the changes in the shape of the yield curve. A shock to the curvature factor affects mid-maturity interest rates, resulting in the term structure becoming either more or less hump-shaped.

Curve trade Buying a CDS of one maturity and selling a CDS on the same reference entity with a different maturity.

Customer concentration risk The risk associated with sales dependent on a few customers.

Cyclical businesses Businesses with high sensitivity to business- or industry-cycle influences.

Data preparation (cleansing) The process of examining, identifying, and mitigating (i.e., cleansing) errors in raw data.

Data snooping The subconscious or conscious manipulation of data in a way that produces a statistically significant result (i.e., the p-value is sufficiently small or the t-statistic sufficiently large to indicate statistical significance), such as by running multiple simulations and naively accepting the best result. Also known as p-hacking.

Data wrangling (preprocessing) This task performs transformations and critical processing steps on cleansed data to make the data ready for ML model training (i.e., preprocessing), and includes dealing with outliers, extracting useful variables from existing data points, and scaling the data.

Debt service coverage ratio A key indicator of credit performance equal to the ratio of net operating income to debt service.

Dedicated short-selling A hedge fund strategy in which the manager takes short-only positions in equities deemed to be expensively priced versus their deteriorating fundamental situations. Short exposures may vary only in terms of portfolio sizing by, at times, holding higher levels of cash.

Deep learning An area of artificial intelligence in which a system uses neural networks to perform multistage, non-linear data processing to identify patterns. Also called *deep learning nets*.

Deep neural networks Neural networks with many hidden layers—at least 2 but potentially more than 20—that have proven successful across a wide range of artificial intelligence applications.

Default risk See *credit risk*.

Delta The sensitivity of the derivative price to a small change in the value of the underlying asset.

Dendrogram A type of tree diagram used for visualizing a hierarchical cluster analysis; it highlights the hierarchical relationships among the clusters.

Depository Trust and Clearinghouse Corporation A US-headquartered entity providing post-trade clearing, settlement, and information services.

Depreciable base Total construction or original acquisition cost plus any property improvements less the cost of land written down over the estimated useful life, as in the case of a company's fixed assets.

Diluted earnings per share (Diluted EPS) Net income, minus preferred dividends, divided by the weighted average number of common shares outstanding considering all dilutive securities (e.g., convertible debt and options); the EPS that would result if all dilutive securities were converted into common shares.

Dilution   An increase in the number of shares outstanding from share issuance that decreases the percentage of shares owned by existing shareholders.

Dimension reduction   A set of techniques for reducing the number of features in a dataset while retaining variation across observations to preserve the information contained in that variation.

Diminishing marginal productivity   When each additional unit of an input, keeping the other inputs unchanged, increases output by a smaller increment.

Direct capitalization method   Valuation approach that estimates the value of an income-producing property using a discounted cash flow approach based on a single year's net operating income.

Discount   To reduce the value of a future payment in allowance for how far away it is in time; to calculate the present value of some future amount. Also, the amount by which an instrument is priced below its face (par) value.

Discount factor   The price equivalent of a zero rate. Also may be stated as the present value of a currency unit on a future date.

Discount for lack of control   An amount or percentage deducted from the pro rata share of 100% of the value of an equity interest in a business to reflect the absence of some or all of the powers of control.

Discount for lack of marketability   An amount of percentage deducted from the value of an ownership interest to reflect the relative absence of marketability.

Discount function   Discount factors for the range of all possible maturities. The spot curve can be derived from the discount function and vice versa.

Discounted abnormal earnings model   A model of stock valuation that views intrinsic value of stock as the sum of book value per share plus the present value of the stock's expected future residual income per share.

Discounted cash flow method   A valuation method involving a series of income projections discounted to the present with a terminal value.

Discounted cash flow model   A model of intrinsic value that views the value of an asset as the present value of the asset's expected future cash flows.

Dispersed ownership   Ownership structure consisting of many shareholders, none of which has the ability to individually exercise control over the corporation.

Divestiture   When a seller sells a company, segment of a company, or group of assets to an acquirer. Once complete, control of the target is transferred to the acquirer.

Dividend coverage ratio   The ratio of net income to dividends.

Dividend discount model (DDM)   The model of the value of stock that is the present value of all future dividends, discounted at the required return on equity.

Dividend displacement of earnings   The concept that dividends paid now displace earnings in all future periods.

Dividend imputation tax system   A taxation system that effectively assures corporate profits distributed as dividends are taxed just once and at the shareholder's tax rate.

Dividend index point   A measure of the quantity of dividends attributable to a particular index.

Dividend payout ratio   The ratio of cash dividends paid to earnings for a period.

Dividend policy   The strategy a company follows with regard to the amount and timing of dividend payments.

Dividend rate   The annualized amount of the most recent dividend.

Dividend recapitalization   A change in the mix of debt and equity outstanding for an existing corporate issuer which increases leverage via debt-financed dividends or share repurchases to benefit existing shareholders.

Dividend yield   Annual dividends per share divided by share price.

Dividends   Distributions of profits and/or net assets from a corporation to its shareholders. While often in cash, dividends can be also be paid in stock or assets, such as property.

Divisive clustering   A top-down hierarchical clustering method that starts with all observations belonging to a single large cluster. The observations are then divided into two clusters based on some measure of distance (similarity). The algorithm then progressively partitions the intermediate clusters into smaller ones until each cluster contains only one observation.

Document frequency (DF)   The number of documents (texts) that contain a particular token divided by the total number of documents. It is the simplest feature selection method and often performs well when many thousands of tokens are present.

Document term matrix (DTM)   A matrix where each row belongs to a document (or text file), and each column represents a token (or term). The number of rows is equal to the number of documents (or text files) in a sample text dataset. The number of columns is equal to the number of tokens from the BOW built using all the documents in the sample dataset. The cells typically contain the counts of the number of times a token is present in each document.

Dominance   An arbitrage opportunity when a financial asset with a risk-free payoff in the future must have a positive price today.

Double taxation system   Corporate earnings are taxed twice when paid out as dividends. First, corporate pretax earnings are taxed regardless of whether they will be distributed as dividends or retained at the corporate level. Second, dividends are taxed again at the individual shareholder level.

Downstream   A transaction between two related companies, an investor company (or a parent company) and an associate company (or a subsidiary) such that the investor company records a profit on its income statement. An example is a sale of inventory by the investor company to the associate or by a parent to a subsidiary company.

Dual-class shares   Shares that grant one share class superior or even sole voting rights, whereas the other share class has inferior or no voting rights.

Due diligence   Investigation and analysis in support of an investment action, decision, or recommendation.

Dummy variable   An independent variable that takes a value of either 1 or 0, depending on a specified condition. Also known as an *indicator variable*.

Duration   The first-order, linear change in a bond's price for a given yield change in yield, which is a negative or inverse relationship.

Durbin–Watson (DW) test   A test for the presence of first-order serial correlation.

Dutch disease   A situation in which currency appreciation driven by strong export demand for resources makes other segments of the economy (particularly manufacturing) globally uncompetitive.

Earnings surprise The difference between reported EPS and expected EPS. Also referred to as *unexpected earnings*.

Earnings yield EPS divided by price; the reciprocal of the P/E.

Economic profit Equal to accounting profit less the implicit opportunity costs not included in total accounting costs; the difference between total revenue (TR) and total cost (TC). Also called *abnormal profit* or *supernormal profit*.

Economic sectors Large industry groupings.

Economic value added (EVA®) A commercial implementation of the residual income concept; the computation of EVA® is the net operating profit after taxes minus the cost of capital, where these inputs are adjusted for a number of items.

Edwards–Bell–Ohlson model A model of stock valuation that views intrinsic value of stock as the sum of book value per share plus the present value of the stock's expected future residual income per share.

Effective convexity An interest rate risk statistic that measures the non-linear/second-order effect of changes in the benchmark yield curve on a bond's price.

Effective duration The sensitivity of the bond's price to an instantaneous parallel shift in a benchmark yield curve—for example, the government par curve.

Effective gross income Gross rent plus other income minus deductions for vacancies or concessions.

Eigenvalue A measure that gives the proportion of total variance in the initial dataset that is explained by each eigenvector.

Eigenvector A vector that defines new mutually uncorrelated composite variables that are linear combinations of the original features.

Embedded options Contingency provisions found in a bond's indenture representing rights that enable their holders to take advantage of interest rate movements. They can be exercised by the issuer, by the bondholder, or automatically depending on the course of interest rates.

Ensemble learning A technique of combining the predictions from a collection of models to achieve a more accurate prediction.

Ensemble method The method of combining multiple learning algorithms, as in ensemble learning.

Enterprise value A measure of a company's total market value from which the value of cash and short-term investments have been subtracted.

Enterprise value multiple A valuation multiple that relates the total market value of all sources of a company's capital (net of cash) to a measure of fundamental value for the entire company (such as a pre-interest earnings measure).

Equity charge The estimated cost of equity capital in money terms.

Equity dividend rate Equityholder return that considers the first-year return on equity on an income-producing property involving the before-tax cash flow divided by the property purchase price less the mortgage loan outstanding.

Equity investment A company purchasing another company's equity but less than 50% of its shares. The two companies maintain their independence, but the investor company has investment exposure to the investee and, in some cases depending on the size of the investment, can have representation on the investee's board of directors to influence operations.

Equity REITs REITs that primarily own and operate properties and distribute dividends to shareholders.

Equity swap A swap transaction in which at least one cash flow is tied to the return to an equity portfolio position, often an equity index.

Error autocorrelations The autocorrelations of the error term.

ESG integration The inclusion of ESG considerations within financial analysis and investment decisions. This may be done in various ways, tailored to the investment style and approach of the fund manager.

***Ex ante* tracking error** A measure of the degree to which the performance of a given investment portfolio might be expected to deviate from its benchmark; also known as *relative VaR*.

***Ex ante* version of PPP** The hypothesis that expected changes in the spot exchange rate are equal to expected differences in national inflation rates. An extension of relative purchasing power parity to expected future changes in the exchange rate.

Ex-dividend Trading ex-dividend refers to shares that no longer carry the right to the next dividend payment.

Ex-dividend date The first date that a share trades without (i.e., "ex") the right to receive the declared dividend for the period.

Excess earnings method Income approach that estimates the value of all intangible assets of the business by capitalizing future earnings in excess of the estimated return requirements associated with working capital and fixed assets.

Excess tax benefit The amount by which the tax deduction associated with a share-based award exceeds the cumulative share-based compensation expense recognized in accordance with US GAAP or IFRS. Excess tax benefits occur when the value of a share-based award at settlement exceeds the value at the grant date.

Exercise value The value of an option if it were exercised. Also sometimes called *intrinsic value*.

Expanded CAPM An adaptation of the CAPM that adds to the CAPM a premium for small size and company-specific risk.

Expectations approach A procedure for obtaining the value of an option derived from discounting at the risk-free rate its expected future payoff based on risk neutral probabilities.

Expected exposure The projected amount of money an investor could lose if an event of default occurs, before factoring in possible recovery.

Expected shortfall The average loss conditional on exceeding the VaR cutoff; sometimes referred to as *conditional VaR* or *expected tail loss*.

Expected tail loss See *conditional VaR*.

Exploratory data analysis (EDA) The preliminary step in data exploration, where graphs, charts, and other visualizations (heat maps and word clouds) as well as quantitative methods (descriptive statistics and central tendency measures) are used to observe and summarize data.

Exposure to foreign exchange risk The risk of a change in value of an asset or liability denominated in a foreign currency due to a change in exchange rates.

Extendible bond Bond with an embedded option that gives the bondholder the right to keep the bond for a number of years after maturity, possibly with a different coupon.

Extension risk The risk of later repayment of a mortgage-backed security than expected.

Extra dividend A dividend paid by a company that does not pay dividends on a regular schedule, or a dividend that supplements regular cash dividends with an extra payment.

F1 score   The harmonic mean of precision and recall. F1 score is a more appropriate overall performance metric (than accuracy) when there is unequal class distribution in the dataset and it is necessary to measure the equilibrium of precision and recall.

Factor   A common or underlying element with which several variables are correlated.

Factor betas   An asset's sensitivity to a particular factor; a measure of the response of return to each unit of increase in a factor, holding all other factors constant.

Factor portfolio   See *pure factor portfolio*.

Factor price   The expected return in excess of the risk-free rate for a portfolio with a sensitivity of 1 to one factor and a sensitivity of 0 to all other factors.

Factor risk premium   The expected return in excess of the risk-free rate for a portfolio with a sensitivity of 1 to one factor and a sensitivity of 0 to all other factors. Also called *factor price*.

Factor risk premiums   The expected return in excess of the risk-free rate for a portfolio with a sensitivity of 1 to one factor and a sensitivity of 0 to all other factors. Also called factor price.

Failure to pay   When a borrower does not make a scheduled payment of principal or interest on any outstanding obligations after a grace period.

Fair market value   The price, expressed in terms of cash equivalents, at which a property (asset) would change hands between a hypothetical willing and able buyer and a hypothetical willing and able seller, acting at "arm's length" in an open and unrestricted market, when neither is under compulsion to buy or sell and when both have reasonable knowledge of the relevant facts. Fair market value is most often used in a tax reporting context in the United States.

Fair value   A market-based measure of an investment based on observable or derived assumptions to determine a price that market participants would use to exchange an asset or liability in an orderly transaction at a specific time.

Fama–French models   Factor models that explain the drivers of returns related to three, four, or five factors.

Feature engineering   A process of creating new features by changing or transforming existing features.

Feature selection   A process whereby only pertinent features from the dataset are selected for model training. Selecting fewer features decreases model complexity and training time.

Features   The independent variables (X's) in a labeled dataset.

Finance (or capital) lease   A lease that is viewed as a financing arrangement.

Financial buyer   An owner seeking to earn investment returns from an existing company without identifying or capitalizing on synergies from a controlling interest.

Financial leverage   The use of debt in the capital structure. Measured using ratios such as operating income to operating income less interest expense, total assets to total equity, or debt to equity.

First-differencing   A transformation that subtracts the value of the time series in period $t - 1$ from its value in period t.

First-order serial correlation   The correlation of residuals with residuals adjacent in time.

Fitting curve   A curve which shows in- and out-of-sample error rates (E_{in} and E_{out}) on the y-axis plotted against model complexity on the x-axis.

Fixed price tender offer   Offer made by a company to repurchase a specific number of shares at a fixed price that is typically at a premium to the current market price.

Fixed-rate perpetual preferred stock   Non-convertible, non-callable preferred stock with a specified dividend rate that has a claim on earnings senior to the claim of common stock, and no maturity date.

Flight to quality   During times of market stress, investors sell higher-risk asset classes such as stocks and commodities in favor of default-risk-free government bonds.

Float   Amounts collected as premium and not yet paid out as benefits.

Floored floater   Floating-rate bond with a floor provision that prevents the coupon rate from decreasing below a specified minimum rate. It protects the investor against declining interest rates.

Flotation cost   Fees charged to companies by investment bankers and other costs associated with raising new capital.

Forced conversion   For a convertible bond, when the issuer calls the bond and forces bondholders to convert their bonds into shares, which typically happens when the underlying share price increases above the conversion price.

Foreign currency transactions   Transactions that are denominated in a currency other than a company's functional currency.

Forward curve   The term structure of forward rates for loans made on a specific initiation date.

Forward dividend yield   A dividend yield based on the anticipated dividend during the next 12 months.

Forward P/E   A P/E calculated on the basis of a forecast of EPS; a stock's current price divided by next year's expected earnings.

Forward price   Represents the price agreed upon in a forward contract to be exchanged at the contract's maturity date, T. This price is shown in equations as $F_0(T)$.

Forward pricing model   The model that describes the valuation of forward contracts.

Forward propagation   The process of adjusting weights in a neural network, to reduce total error of the network, by moving forward through the network's layers.

Forward rate   An interest rate determined today for a loan that will be initiated in a future period.

Forward rate agreement   An over-the-counter forward contract in which the underlying is an interest rate on a deposit. A forward rate agreement (FRA) calls for one party to make a fixed interest payment and the other to make an interest payment at a rate to be determined at contract expiration.

Forward rate model   The forward pricing model expressed in terms of spot and forward interest rates.

Forward rate parity   The proposition that the forward exchange rate is an unbiased predictor of the future spot exchange rate.

Forward value   The monetary value of an existing forward contract.

Forward-looking estimates   Estimates based on current and expectations. Also referred to as ex ante estimates.

Franchising   A situation where an owner of an asset and associated intellectual property divests the asset and licenses intellectual property to a third-party operator (franchisee) in exchange for royalties. Franchisees operate under the constraints of a franchise agreement.

Franking credit   A tax credit received by shareholders for the taxes that a corporation paid on its distributed earnings.

Free cash flow to equity   The cash flow available to a company's common shareholders after all operating expenses, interest, and principal payments have been made and necessary investments in working and fixed capital have been made.

Free cash flow to equity model   A model of stock valuation that views a stock's intrinsic value as the present value of expected future free cash flows to equity.

Free cash flow to the firm   The cash flow available to the company's suppliers of capital after all operating expenses (including taxes) have been paid and necessary investments in working and fixed capital have been made.

Free cash flow to the firm model   A model of stock valuation that views the value of a firm as the present value of expected future free cash flows to the firm.

Frequency analysis   The process of quantifying how important tokens are in a sentence and in the corpus as a whole. It helps in filtering unnecessary tokens (or features).

Frozen DB plan   A DB plan that is no longer accruing benefits for employee service.

Fulcrum securities   Partially-in-the-money claims (not expected to be repaid in full) whose holders end up owning the reorganized company in a corporate reorganization situation.

Functional currency   The currency of the primary economic environment in which an entity operates.

Fund of funds   Funds that hold a portfolio of hedge funds; also called *funds of hedge funds*.

Fundamental factor models   A multifactor model in which the factors are attributes of stocks or companies that are important in explaining cross-sectional differences in stock prices.

Fundamentals   Economic characteristics of a business, such as profitability, financial strength, and risk.

Funded status   The present value of the DB obligation less the fair value of plan assets (if any).

Funds available for distribution   See *adjusted funds from operations*.

Funds from operations   Net income (computed in accordance with generally accepted accounting principles) *plus* (1) gains and losses from sales of properties and (2) depreciation and amortization.

Futures price   The pre-agreed price at which a futures contract buyer (seller) agrees to pay (receive) for the underlying at the maturity date of the futures contract.

Futures value   The monetary value of an existing futures contract.

FX carry trade   An investment strategy that involves taking long positions in high-yield currencies and short positions in low-yield currencies.

Gamma   A numerical measure of how sensitive an option's delta (the sensitivity of the derivative's price) is to a change in the value of the underlying.

General linear *F*-test   A test statistic used to assess the goodness of fit for an entire regression model, so it tests all independent variables in the model.

Generalize   When a model retains its explanatory power when predicting out-of-sample (i.e., using new data).

Global CAPM (GCAPM)   A single-factor model with a global index representing the single factor.

Going-concern assumption   The assumption that the business will maintain its business activities into the foreseeable future.

Going-concern value   A business's value under a going-concern assumption.

Going-in cap rate   The capitalization rate based on the first year of ownership used to discount the initial annual cash flow from a real estate property.

Goodwill   An intangible asset that represents the excess of the purchase price of an acquired company over the value of the net identifiable assets acquired.

Gordon growth model   A DDM that assumes dividends grow at a constant rate into the future.

Green bond   Bonds in which the proceeds are designated by issuers to fund a specific project or portfolio of projects that have environmental or climate benefits.

Greenmail   The purchase of the accumulated shares of a hostile investor by a company that is targeted for takeover by that investor, usually at a substantial premium over market price.

Greenwashing   The risk that a green bond's proceeds are not actually used for a beneficial environmental or climate-related project.

Grid search   A method of systematically training a model by using various combinations of hyperparameter values, cross validating each model, and determining which combination of hyperparameter values ensures the best model performance.

Gross domestic product   The market value of all final goods and services produced within the economy during a given period (output definition) or, equivalently, the aggregate income earned by all households, all companies, and the government within the economy during a given period (income definition).

Gross potential rental income   Equal to the current market rent of a property at full occupancy.

Gross rent   The average lease or rental price realized per square foot multiplied by the total rentable space.

Ground truth   The known outcome (i.e., target variable) of each observation in a labelled dataset.

Growth accounting equation   The production function written in the form of growth rates. For the basic Cobb–Douglas production function, it states that the growth rate of output equals the rate of technological change plus α multiplied by the growth rate of capital plus $(1 - \alpha)$ multiplied by the growth rate of labor.

Guideline assets   Assets used as benchmarks when applying the method of comparables to value an asset.

Guideline companies   Assets used as benchmarks when applying the method of comparables to value an asset.

Guideline public companies   Public-company comparables for the company being valued.

Guideline public company method   A variation of the market approach; establishes a value estimate based on the observed multiples from trading activity in the shares of public companies viewed as reasonably comparable to the subject private company.

Guideline transactions method   A variation of the market approach; establishes a value estimate based on pricing multiples derived from the acquisition of control of entire public or private companies that were acquired.

Hard-catalyst event-driven approach   An event-driven approach in which investments are made in reaction to an already announced corporate event (mergers and acquisitions, bankruptcies, share issuances, buybacks, capital restructurings, re-organizations, accounting changes) in which security prices related to the event have yet to fully converge.

Harmonic mean A type of weighted mean computed as the reciprocal of the arithmetic average of the reciprocals.

Hazard rate The probability that an event will occur, given that it has not already occurred.

Hedonic index A real estate index that is not based on repeat sales of the same property but, rather, that controls for differences in property characteristics, such as size, age, quality of construction, and location, for the properties sold in each period.

Heteroskedastic When the variance of the residuals differs across observations in a regression.

Heteroskedasticity Non-constant variance across all observations.

Hierarchical clustering An iterative unsupervised learning procedure used for building a hierarchy of clusters.

High-leverage point An observation of an independent variable that has an extreme value and is potentially influential.

Historical exchange rates For accounting purposes, the exchange rates that existed when the assets and liabilities were initially recorded.

Historical scenario analysis A technique for exploring the performance and risk of investment strategies in different structural regimes.

Historical simulation A simulation method that uses past return data and a random number generator that picks observations from the historical series to simulate an asset's future returns.

Historical simulation method The application of historical price changes to the current portfolio.

Historical stress testing The process that tests how investment strategies would perform under some of the most negative (i.e., adverse) combinations of events and scenarios.

Holding period return The single-period internal rate of return for a real estate property that includes property income and the change in property value over the period.

Holdout samples Data samples that are not used to train a model.

Homoskedasticity Constant variance across all observations.

Horizontal ownership Companies with mutual business interests (e.g., key customers or suppliers) that have cross-holding share arrangements with each other.

Household formation An economic statistic which tracks the establishment of new residences as a group of people (or household) decide to live together, which increases housing demand.

Ho–Lee model The first arbitrage-free term structure model. The model is calibrated to market data and uses a binomial lattice approach to generate a distribution of possible future interest rates.

Human capital The present value of an individual's future expected labor income.

Hyperparameter A parameter whose value must be set by the researcher before learning begins.

I-spreads Shortened form of "interpolated spreads" and a reference to a linearly interpolated yield.

Illiquidity discount A reduction or discount to value that reflects the lack of depth of trading or liquidity in that asset's market.

Impairment Diminishment in value as a result of carrying (book) value exceeding fair value and/or recoverable value.

Impairment of capital rule A legal restriction that dividends cannot exceed retained earnings.

Implied volatility The volatility that option traders use to price an option, implied by the price of the option and a particular option-pricing model.

In-sample forecast errors The residuals from a fitted time-series model within the sample period used to fit the model.

iNAVs "Indicated" net asset values are intraday "fair value" estimates of an ETF share based on its creation basket.

Income approach A valuation approach that values an asset as the present discounted value of the income expected from it. In the context of real estate, this approach estimates the value of a property based on an expected rate of return. The estimated value is the present value of the expected future income from the property, including proceeds from resale at the end of a typical investment holding period.

Incremental borrowing rate (IBR) The rate of interest that the lessee would have to pay to borrow using a collateralized loan over the same term as a lease.

Incremental VaR (IVaR) A measure of the incremental effect of an asset on the VaR of a portfolio by measuring the difference between the portfolio's VaR while including a specified asset and the portfolio's VaR with that asset eliminated.

Indenture A written contract between a lender and borrower that specifies the terms of the loan, such as interest rate, interest payment schedule, or maturity.

Independent board directors Directors with no material relationship with the company with regard to employment, ownership, or remuneration.

Index CDS A type of credit default swap that involves a combination of borrowers.

Indexed rents Contractually agreed periodic rent changes based on an observed market variable, such as the consumer price index.

Industry risk premium (IP) The additional return that is required to bear industry-specific risk.

Industry shocks Unexpected changes to an industry from regulations or the legal environment, technology, or changes in the growth rate of the industry.

Industry structure An industry's underlying economic and technical characteristics.

Influential observation An observation in a statistical analysis whose inclusion may significantly alter regression results.

Information gain A metric which quantifies the amount of information that the feature holds about the response. Information gain can be regarded as a form of non-linear correlation between Y and X.

Information ratio The ratio of mean active return to standard deviation (active return).

Insiders Corporate managers and board directors who are also shareholders of a company.

Intangible assets Assets without a physical form, such as patents and trademarks.

Inter-temporal rate of substitution The ratio of the marginal utility of consumption s periods in the future (the numerator) to the marginal utility of consumption today (the denominator).

Interaction term A term that combines two or more independent variables and represents their joint influence on the dependent variable.

Intercept dummy An indicator variable that allows a single regression model to estimate two lines of best fit, each with differing intercepts, depending on whether the dummy takes a value of 1 or 0.

Interest rate risk The risk that interest rates will rise and therefore the market value of current portfolio holdings will fall so that their current yields to maturity then match comparable instruments in the marketplace.

Interlocking directorates Corporate structure in which individuals serve on the board of directors of multiple corporations.

International CAPM (ICAPM) A two-factor model with a global index and a wealth-weighted currency index.

International Fisher effect The proposition that nominal interest rate differentials across currencies are determined by expected inflation differentials.

Intrinsic value See *exercise value*.

Inverse price ratio The reciprocal of a price multiple—for example, in the case of a P/E, the "earnings yield" E/P (where P is share price and E is earnings per share).

Investment value The value to a specific buyer, taking account of potential synergies based on the investor's requirements and expectations.

ISDA Master Agreement A standard or "master" agreement published by the International Swaps and Derivatives Association. The master agreement establishes the terms for each party involved in the transaction.

Joint test of hypotheses The test of hypotheses that specify values for two or more independent variables in the hypotheses.

Joint venture Two or more companies form and control a new, separate company to achieve a business objective. Each participant contributes assets, employees, know-how, or other resources to the joint venture company. The participants maintain their independence otherwise and continue to do business apart from the joint venture, but they share in the joint venture's profits or losses.

Justified (fundamental) P/E The price-to-earnings ratio that is fair, warranted, or justified on the basis of forecasted fundamentals.

Justified price multiple The estimated fair value of the price multiple, usually based on forecasted fundamentals or comparables.

K-fold cross-validation A technique in which data (excluding test sample and fresh data) are shuffled randomly and then are divided into k equal sub-samples, with $k - 1$ samples used as training samples and one sample, the kth, used as a validation sample.

K-means A clustering algorithm that repeatedly partitions observations into a fixed number, k, of non-overlapping clusters.

K-nearest neighbor A supervised learning technique that classifies a new observation by finding similarities ("nearness") between this new observation and the existing data.

Kalotay–Williams–Fabozzi (KWF) model An arbitrage-free term structure model that describes the dynamics of the log of the short rate and assumes constant drift, no mean reversion, and constant volatility.

Key rate durations Sensitivity of a bond's price to changes in specific maturities on the benchmark yield curve. Also called *partial durations*.

kth-order autocorrelation The correlation between observations in a time series separated by k periods.

Labeled dataset A dataset that contains matched sets of observed inputs or features (X's) and the associated output or target (Y).

Labor force Everyone of working age (ages 16 to 64) who either is employed or is available for work but not working.

Labor force participation rate The percentage of the working age population that is in the labor force.

Labor productivity The quantity of real GDP produced by an hour of labor. More generally, output per unit of labor input.

Labor productivity growth accounting equation States that potential GDP growth equals the growth rate of the labor input plus the growth rate of labor productivity.

Lack of marketability discount An extra return to investors to compensate for lack of a public market or lack of marketability.

LASSO Least absolute shrinkage and selection operator is a type of penalized regression which involves minimizing the sum of the absolute values of the regression coefficients. LASSO can also be used for regularization in neural networks.

Law of one price A principle that states that if two investments have the same or equivalent future cash flows regardless of what will happen in the future, then these two investments should have the same current price.

Leading dividend yield Forecasted dividends per share over the next year divided by current stock price.

Leading P/E A P/E calculated on the basis of a forecast of EPS; a stock's current price divided by next year's expected earnings.

Learning curve A curve that plots the accuracy rate (= 1 − error rate) in the validation or test samples (i.e., out-of-sample) against the amount of data in the training sample, which is thus useful for describing under- and overfitting as a function of bias and variance errors.

Learning rate A parameter that affects the magnitude of adjustments in the weights in a neural network.

Lessee Tenant or property user that enters a lease with a property owner or lessor.

Lessor Property owner or manager that leases a property to a tenant or property user.

Level One of the three factors (the other two are steepness and curvature) that empirically explain most yield curve shape changes. A shock to the level factor changes the yield for all maturities by an almost identical amount.

Leverage A measure for identifying a potentially influential high-leverage point.

Leveraged buyout (LBO) A transaction in which a private acquiror uses equity and a high proportion of debt to acquire a public or private company in order to make changes to increase value over an investment period.

Libor–OIS spread The difference between Libor and the overnight indexed swap rate.

Life settlement The sale of a life insurance contract to a third party. The valuation of a life settlement typically requires detailed biometric analysis of the individual policyholder and an understanding of actuarial analysis.

Likelihood ratio (LR) test A method to assess the fit of logistic regression models that is based on the log-likelihood metric that describes the model's fit to the data.

Linear classifier A binary classifier that makes its classification decision based on a linear combination of the features of each data point.

Linear trend A trend in which the dependent variable changes at a constant rate with time.

Liquidating dividend A dividend that is a return of capital rather than a distribution from earnings or retained earnings.

Liquidation value The value of a company if the company were dissolved and its assets sold individually.

Liquidity preference theory A term structure theory that asserts liquidity premiums exist to compensate investors for the added interest rate risk they face when lending long term.

Liquidity premium The compensation for liquidity risk that increases in proportion to the investment's illiquidity.

Loan-to-value ratio A primary measure of leverage involving the ratio of mortgage principal outstanding to the property's current value.

Local currency The currency of the country where a company is located.

Local expectations theory A term structure theory that contends the return for all bonds over short periods is the risk-free rate.

Log odds The natural log of the odds of an event or characteristic happening. Also known as the *logit function*.

Log-linear model With reference to time-series models, a model in which the growth rate of the time series as a function of time is constant.

Logistic regression (logit) A regression in which the dependent variable uses a logistic transformation of the event probability.

Logistic transformation The log of the probability of an occurrence of an event or characteristic divided by the probability of the event or characteristic not occurring.

Long/short credit trade A credit protection seller with respect to one entity combined with a credit protection buyer with respect to another entity.

Look-ahead bias The bias created by using information that was unknown or unavailable in the time periods over which backtesting is conducted. Survivorship bias is a type of look-ahead bias.

Lookback period The time period used to gather a historical data set.

Loss given default The amount that will be lost if a default occurs.

Loss to lease The difference between rental rates on existing leases and current market rents.

Macroeconomic factor model A multifactor model in which the factors are surprises in macroeconomic variables that significantly explain equity returns.

Macroeconomic factors Factors related to the economy, such as the inflation rate, industrial production, or economic sector membership.

Majority shareholders Shareholders that own more than 50% of a corporation's shares.

Majority-vote classifier A classifier that assigns to a new data point the predicted label with the most votes (i.e., occurrences).

Marginal VaR (MVaR) A measure of the effect of a small change in a position size on portfolio VaR.

Market approach Valuation approach that values an asset based on pricing multiples from sales of assets viewed as similar to the subject asset.

Market condition A performance condition that is related to the market price (or value) of the entity's equity instruments such as attaining a specified share price or a specified target based on the market price (or value) of the entity's equity instruments relative to an index of market prices of other companies.

Market conditions Interest rates, inflation rates, and other economic characteristics that comprise the macroeconomic environment.

Market conversion premium per share For a convertible bond, the difference between the market conversion price and the underlying share price, which allows investors to identify the premium or discount payable when buying a convertible bond rather than the underlying common stock.

Market conversion premium ratio For a convertible bond, the market conversion premium per share expressed as a percentage of the current market price of the shares.

Market efficiency A finance perspective on capital markets that deals with the relationship of price to intrinsic value. The traditional efficient markets formulation asserts that an asset's price is the best available estimate of its intrinsic value. The rational efficient markets formulation asserts that investors should expect to be rewarded for the costs of information gathering and analysis by higher gross returns.

Market model A regression model with the return on a stock as the dependent variable and the returns on a market index as the independent variable.

Market value of invested capital The market value of debt and equity.

Mature growth rate The earnings growth rate in a company's mature phase; an earnings growth rate that can be sustained long term.

Maximum drawdown The worst cumulative loss ever sustained by an asset or portfolio. More specifically, maximum drawdown is the difference between an asset's or a portfolio's maximum cumulative return and its subsequent lowest cumulative return.

Maximum likelihood estimation (MLE) A method that estimates values for the intercept and slope coefficients in a logistic regression that make the data in the regression sample most likely.

Mean reversion The tendency of a time series to fall when its level is above its mean and rise when its level is below its mean; a mean-reverting time series tends to return to its long-term mean.

Metadata Data that describes and gives information about other data.

Method based on forecasted fundamentals An approach to using price multiples that relates a price multiple to forecasts of fundamentals through a discounted cash flow model.

Method of comparables An approach to valuation that involves using a price multiple to evaluate whether an asset is relatively fairly valued, relatively undervalued, or relatively overvalued when compared to a benchmark value of the multiple.

Minority interest The proportion of the ownership of a subsidiary not held by the parent (controlling) company.

Minority shareholders Particular shareholders or a block of shareholders holding a small proportion of a company's outstanding shares, resulting in a limited ability to exercise control in voting activities.

Mispricing Any departure of the market price of an asset from the asset's estimated intrinsic value.

Mixed-use development Commercial real estate properties that combine more than one tenant type and economic use.

Model specification The set of independent variables included in a model and the model's functional form.

Molodovsky effect The observation that P/Es tend to be high on depressed EPS at the bottom of a business cycle and tend to be low on unusually high EPS at the top of a business cycle.

Momentum indicators Valuation indicators that relate either price or a fundamental (such as earnings) to the time series of their own past values (or in some cases to their expected value).

Monetary assets and liabilities Assets and liabilities with value equal to the amount of currency contracted for, a fixed amount of currency. Examples are cash, accounts receivable, accounts payable, bonds payable, and mortgages payable. Inventory is not a monetary asset. Most liabilities are monetary.

Monetary/non-monetary method Approach to translating foreign currency financial statements for consolidation in which monetary assets and liabilities are translated at the current exchange rate. Non-monetary assets and liabilities are translated at historical exchange rates (the exchange rates that existed when the assets and liabilities were acquired).

Monetizing Unwinding a position to either capture a gain or realize a loss.

Monte Carlo simulation A technique that uses the inverse transformation method for converting a randomly generated uniformly distributed number into a simulated value of a random variable of a desired distribution. Each key decision variable in a Monte Carlo simulation requires an assumed statistical distribution; this assumption facilitates incorporating non-normality, fat tails, and tail dependence as well as solving high-dimensionality problems.

Multi-class trading An equity market-neutral strategy that capitalizes on misalignment in prices and involves buying and selling different classes of shares of the same company, such as voting and non-voting shares.

Multi-manager fund Can be of two types—one is a multi-strategy fund in which teams of portfolio managers trade and invest in multiple different strategies within the same fund; the second type is a fund of hedge funds (or fund-of-funds) in which the manager allocates capital to separate, underlying hedge funds that themselves run a range of different strategies.

Multi-strategy fund A fund in which teams of portfolio managers trade and invest in multiple different strategies within the same fund.

Multicollinearity When two or more independent variables are highly correlated with one another or are approximately linearly related.

Multiple linear regression Modeling and estimation method that uses two or more independent variables to describe the variation of the dependent variable. Also referred to as *multiple regression*.

Mutual information Measures how much information is contributed by a token to a class of texts. MI will be 0 if the token's distribution in all text classes is the same. MI approaches 1 as the token in any one class tends to occur more often in only that particular class of text.

N-grams A representation of word sequences. The length of a sequence varies from 1 to *n*. When one word is used, it is a unigram; a two-word sequence is a bigram; and a 3-word sequence is a trigram; and so on.

***n*-Period moving average** The average of the current and immediately prior $n - 1$ values of a time series.

Naked credit default swap A position where the owner of the CDS does not have a position in the underlying credit.

Name entity recognition An algorithm that analyzes individual tokens and their surrounding semantics while referring to its dictionary to tag an object class to the token.

Negative serial correlation A situation in which residuals are negatively related to other residuals.

Nested models Models in which one regression model has a subset of the independent variables of another regression model.

Net asset balance sheet exposure When assets translated at the current exchange rate are greater in amount than liabilities translated at the current exchange rate. Assets exposed to translation gains or losses exceed the exposed liabilities.

Net asset value per share Net asset value divided by the number of shares outstanding.

Net liability balance sheet exposure When liabilities translated at the current exchange rate are greater assets translated at the current exchange rate. Liabilities exposed to translation gains or losses exceed the exposed assets.

Net operating income A commonly used measure of income-producing property returns prior to the inclusion of financing costs or income taxes.

Network externalities The impact that users of a good, a service, or a technology have on other users of that product; it can be positive (e.g., a critical mass of users makes a product more useful) or negative (e.g., congestion makes the product less useful).

Neural networks A type of computer program design based on how the human brain learns and processes information.

No-arbitrage approach A procedure for obtaining the value of an option based on the creation of a portfolio that replicates the payoffs of the option and deriving the option value from the value of the replicating portfolio.

No-growth company A company without positive expected net present value projects.

No-growth value per share The value per share of a no-growth company, equal to the expected level amount of earnings divided by the stock's required rate of return.

Non-cash rent An amount equal to the difference between the average contractual rent over a lease term (the straight-line rent) and the cash rent actually paid during a period. This figure is one of the deductions made from FFO to calculate AFFO.

Non-convergence trap A situation in which a country remains relatively poor, or even falls further behind, because it fails to implement necessary institutional reforms and/or adopt leading technologies.

Non-monetary assets and liabilities Assets and liabilities that are not monetary assets and liabilities. Non-monetary assets include inventory, fixed assets, and intangibles, and non-monetary liabilities include deferred revenue.

Non-renewable resources Finite resources that are depleted once they are consumed; oil and coal are examples.

Nonearning assets Cash and investments (specifically cash, cash equivalents, and short-term investments).

Normal EPS The EPS that a business could achieve currently under mid-cyclical conditions. Also called *normalized EPS*.

Normal Q-Q plot A visual used to compare the distribution of the residuals from a regression to a theoretical normal distribution.

Normalized earnings The expected level of mid-cycle earnings for a company in the absence of any unusual or temporary factors that affect profitability (either positively or negatively).

Normalized EPS The EPS that a business could achieve currently under mid-cyclical conditions. Also called *normal EPS*.

Normalized P/E   P/E based on normalized EPS data.

Notional amount   The amount of protection being purchased in a CDS.

NTM P/E   Next 12-month P/E: current market price divided by an estimated next 12-month EPS.

Off-the-run   Seasoned government bonds that are often less liquid.

Offshoring   Refers to relocating operations from one country to another, mainly to reduce costs through lower labor costs or to achieve economies of scale through centralization, but still maintaining operations within the corporation.

Omitted variable bias   Bias resulting from the omission of an important independent variable from a regression model.

On-the-run   Most recently issued, and liquid, government bonds.

One hot encoding   The process by which categorical variables are converted into binary form (0 or 1) for machine reading. It is one of the most common methods for handling categorical features in text data.

One-sided durations   Effective durations when interest rates go up or down, which are better at capturing the interest rate sensitivity of bonds with embedded options that do not react symmetrically to positive and negative changes in interest rates of the same magnitude.

One-tier board   Board structure consisting of a single board of directors, composed of executive (internal) and non-executive (external) directors.

Opportunistic real estate   Real estate investments primarily in commercial and/or residential properties involving major redevelopment, repurposing of assets, taking on large vacancies, or speculating on significant improvement in market conditions.

Opportunity cost   Reflects the foregone opportunity of investing in a different asset. It is typically denoted by the risk-free rate of interest, r.

Option-adjusted spread   Or OAS for a bond is its Z-spread adjusted for the value of an embedded option.

Orderly liquidation value   The estimated gross amount of money that could be realized from the liquidation sale of an asset or assets, given a reasonable amount of time to find a purchaser or purchasers.

Other comprehensive income   Changes to equity that bypass (are not reported in) the income statement; the difference between comprehensive income and net income.

Other post-employment benefits (OPEB)   DB post-employment benefit plans other than plans that pay cash retirement benefits (e.g., retiree medical care benefit plans).

Out-of-sample forecast errors   The differences between actual and predicted values of time series outside the sample period used to fit the model.

Outlier   An observation that has an extreme value of the dependent variable and is potentially influential.

Outsourcing   Shifting internal business services to a subcontractor that can offer services at lower costs by scaling to serve many clients.

Overage rent   Contractual sale-based rental adjustments that result in higher rent if a tenant's sales exceed a pre-agreed minimum target.

Overfitting   When a machine learning model learns the input and target dataset too precisely, making the system more likely to discover false relationships or unsubstantiated patterns that will lead to prediction errors.

Overfunded plan   A DB plan with a positive funded status; the present value of the DB obligation is less than the fair value of plan assets.

Overnight indexed swap (OIS) rate   An interest rate swap in which the periodic floating rate of the swap equals the geometric average of a daily unsecured overnight rate (or overnight index rate).

Pairs trading   An equity market-neutral strategy that capitalizes on the misalignment in prices of pairs of similar under- and overvalued equities. The expectation is the differential valuations or trading relationships will revert to their long-term mean values or their fundamentally-correct trading relationships, with the long position rising and the short position declining in value.

Par curve   A hypothetical yield curve for coupon-paying Treasury securities that assumes all securities are priced at par.

Par swap   A swap in which the fixed rate is set so that no money is exchanged at contract initiation.

Parametric method   A method of estimating VaR that uses the historical mean, standard deviation, and correlation of security price movements to estimate the portfolio VaR. Generally assumes a normal distribution but can be adapted to non-normal distributions with the addition of skewness and kurtosis. Sometimes called the *variance–covariance method* or the *analytical method*.

Partial regression coefficient   Coefficient that describes the effect of a one-unit change in the independent variable on the dependent variable, holding all other independent variables constant. Also known as *partial slope coefficient*.

Parts of speech   An algorithm that uses language structure and dictionaries to tag every token in the text with a corresponding part of speech (i.e., noun, verb, adjective, proper noun, etc.).

Payout amount   The loss given default times the notional.

Payout policy   The principles by which a company distributes cash to common shareholders by means of cash dividends and/or share repurchases.

Payouts   Cash dividends and the value of shares repurchased in any given year.

PEG ratio   The P/E-to-growth ratio, calculated as the stock's P/E divided by the expected earnings growth rate.

Penalized regression   A regression that includes a constraint such that the regression coefficients are chosen to minimize the sum of squared residuals *plus* a penalty term that increases in size with the number of included features.

Pension obligation   The present value, without deducting any plan assets, of expected future payments required to settle the obligation resulting from employee service in the current and prior periods.

Perfect capital markets   Markets in which, by assumption, there are no taxes, no transaction costs, and no bankruptcy costs and in which all investors have equal ("symmetric") information.

Performance condition   A vesting condition comprising a service condition and the meeting of a specified performance target during the service period. A performance target is typically defined as an accounting measure or a market condition.

Performance shares   Shares used in a share-based compensation arrangement that have performance-based vesting conditions.

Perpetuity   A perpetual annuity, or a set of never-ending level sequential cash flows, with the first cash flow occurring one period from now.

Persistent earnings   Earnings excluding nonrecurring components. Also referred to as *core earnings, continuing earnings,* or *underlying earnings.*

Physical settlement   Involves actual delivery of the debt instrument in exchange for a payment by the credit protection seller of the notional amount of the contract.

Point-in-time data   Data consisting of the exact information available to market participants as of a given point in time. Point-in-time data is used to address look-ahead bias.

Portfolio balance approach   A theory of exchange rate determination that emphasizes the portfolio investment decisions of global investors and the requirement that global investors willingly hold all outstanding securities denominated in each currency at prevailing prices and exchange rates.

Positive serial correlation   A situation in which residuals are positively related to other residuals.

Potential GDP   The maximum amount of output an economy can sustainably produce without inducing an increase in the inflation rate. The output level that corresponds to full employment with consistent wage and price expectations.

Precision   In error analysis for classification problems it is ratio of correctly predicted positive classes to all predicted positive classes. Precision is useful in situations where the cost of false positives (FP), or Type I error, is high.

Preferred habitat theory   A term structure theory that contends that investors have maturity preferences and require yield incentives before they will buy bonds outside of their preferred maturities.

Premium leg   The series of payments the credit protection buyer promises to make to the credit protection seller.

Premiums   Amounts paid by the purchaser of insurance products.

Prepayment risk   The risk that the some or all of a mortgage-backed security's principal is repaid at a different speed than expected, either in the form of contraction risk (or earlier repayment than expected) or extension risk (later repayment).

Present value model   A model of intrinsic value that views the value of an asset as the present value of the asset's expected future cash flows.

Present value of growth opportunities   The difference between the actual value per share and the no-growth value per share. Also called *value of growth.*

Presentation currency   The currency in which financial statement amounts are presented.

Price momentum   A valuation indicator based on past price movement.

Price multiples   The ratio of a stock's market price to some measure of value per share.

Price-to-earnings ratio (P/E)   The ratio of share price to earnings per share.

Priced risk   Risk for which investors demand compensation for bearing (e.g., equity risk, company-specific factors, macroeconomic factors).

Principal components analysis (PCA)   An unsupervised ML technique used to transform highly correlated features of data into a few main, uncorrelated composite variables.

Principle of no arbitrage   In well-functioning markets, prices will adjust until there are no arbitrage opportunities.

Prior transaction method   A variation of the market approach; considers actual transactions in the stock of the subject private company.

Private market value   The value derived using a sum-of-the-parts valuation.

Pro forma financial statements   Financial statements that include the effect of a corporate restructuring.

Probability of default   The likelihood that a borrower defaults or fails to meet its obligation to make full and timely payments of principal and interest.

Probability of survival   The probability that a bond issuer will meet its contractual obligations on schedule.

Projection error   The vertical (perpendicular) distance between a data point and a given principal component.

Property classes   A relative ranking of properties based on a combination of features such as location, property age, local income levels, recent property appreciation, and relative condition.

Property maintenance allowance   Expenses incurred to maintain a property's current level of income generation.

Prospective P/E   A P/E calculated on the basis of a forecast of EPS; a stock's current price divided by next year's expected earnings.

Protection leg   The contingent payment that the credit protection seller may have to make to the credit protection buyer.

Protection period   Period during which a bond's issuer cannot call the bond.

Provision for loan losses   An income statement expense account that increases the amount of the allowance for loan losses.

Pruning   A regularization technique used in CART to reduce the size of the classification or regression tree—by pruning, or removing, sections of the tree that provide little classifying power.

Purchasing power gain   A gain in value caused by changes in price levels. Monetary liabilities experience purchasing power gains during periods of inflation.

Purchasing power loss   A loss in value caused by changes in price levels. Monetary assets experience purchasing power loss during periods of inflation.

Purchasing power parity (PPP)   The idea that exchange rates move to equalize the purchasing power of different currencies.

Pure expectations theory   A term structure theory that contends the forward rate is an unbiased predictor of the future spot rate. Also called the *unbiased expectations theory.*

Pure factor portfolio   A portfolio with sensitivity of 1 to the factor in question and a sensitivity of 0 to all other factors.

Putable bond   Bond that includes an embedded put option, which gives the bondholder the right to put back the bonds to the issuer prior to maturity, typically when interest rates have risen and higher-yielding bonds are available.

Qualitative dependent variable   A dependent variable that is discrete (binary). Also known as a *categorical dependent variable.*

Quality of earnings analysis   The investigation of issues relating to the accuracy of reported accounting results as reflections of economic performance. Quality of earnings analysis is broadly understood to include not only earnings management but also balance sheet management.

Quantitative market-neutral   An approach to building market-neutral portfolios in which large numbers of securities are traded and positions are adjusted on a daily or even an hourly basis using algorithm-based models.

Random forest classifier   A collection of a large number of decision trees trained via a bagging method.

Random walk   A time series in which the value of the series in one period is the value of the series in the previous period plus an unpredictable random error.

Rate implicit in the lease (RIIL)   The discount rate that equates the present value of the lease payment with the fair value of the leased asset, considering also the lessor's direct costs and the present value of the leased asset's residual value.

Rational efficient markets formulation   See *market efficiency*.

Readme files   Text files provided with raw data that contain information related to a data file. They are useful for understanding the data and how they can be interpreted correctly.

Real estate cycle   Phases of recovery, expansion, oversupply, and recession that combine short-term adjustments in lease rates and occupancy in response to changing market conditions.

Real estate investment trusts   Investment vehicles that directly own and operate real estate properties or debt investments and distribute dividends and other income to shareholders.

Real estate operating companies   Corporate issuers whose primary activity is in the construction, development, operation, and servicing of real estate.

Real interest rate parity   The proposition that real interest rates will converge to the same level across different markets.

Real options   Refers to the right but not the obligation to take future action. The existence of such options may affect the value of a real estate investment.

Rebalance return   A return from rebalancing the component weights of an index.

Recall   Also known as *sensitivity*, in error analysis for classification problems it is the ratio of correctly predicted positive classes to all actual positive classes. Recall is useful in situations where the cost of false negatives (FN), or Type II error, is high.

Recency bias   The behavioral tendency to place more relevance on recent events.

Reconstitution   When dealers recombine appropriate individual zero-coupon securities and reproduce an underlying coupon Treasury.

Recovery rate   The percentage of the loss recovered.

Redemption basket   The list of securities (and share amounts) the authorized participant (AP) receives when it redeems ETF shares back to the ETF manager. The redemption basket is published each business day.

Reference entity   The borrower (debt issuer) covered by a single-name CDS.

Reference obligation   A particular debt instrument issued by the borrower that is the designated instrument being covered.

Regime   The governing set of relationships (between variables) that stem from technological, political, legal, and regulatory environments. Changes in such environments or policy stances can be described as changes in regime.

Regular expression (regex)   A series of texts that contains characters in a particular order. Regex is used to search for patterns of interest in a given text.

Regularization   A term that describes methods for reducing statistical variability in high-dimensional data estimation problems.

Reinforcement learning   Machine learning in which a computer learns from interacting with itself or data generated by the same algorithm.

Reinvestment rate   A company's rate of investment in working capital and long-term assets necessary to maintain operations and support assumed growth.

Related-party transactions   A business transaction between parties which share economic or other interests and may not take place at fair market value.

Relative valuation models   A model that specifies an asset's value relative to the value of another asset.

Relative value volatility arbitrage   A volatility trading strategy that aims to source and buy cheap volatility and sell more expensive volatility while netting out the time decay aspects normally associated with options portfolios.

Relative VaR   The minimum portfolio loss expected to occur over a given time period at a specific confidence level based on a portfolio containing active positions minus benchmark holdings.

Relative version of PPP   The hypothesis that changes in (nominal) exchange rates over time are equal to national inflation rate differentials.

Relative-strength indicators   Valuation indicators that compare a stock's performance during a period either to its own past performance or to the performance of some group of stocks.

Renewable resources   Resources that can be replenished, such as a forest.

Rental price of capital   The cost per unit of time to rent a unit of capital.

Reorganization   A court-supervised restructuring process available in some jurisdictions for companies facing insolvency from burdensome debt levels. A bankruptcy court assumes control of the company and oversees an orderly negotiation process between the company and its creditors for asset sales, conversion of debt to equity, refinancing, and so on.

Repeat sales index   A real estate price index that relies on multiple sales of the same property.

Replacement cost   Estimate of expenses associated with purchasing land and building a new property on a site with the same features and economic use as a property being appraised.

Required rate of return on equity   The minimum rate of return required by an investor to invest in an asset, given the asset's riskiness. Also known as the required return on equity.

Residual autocorrelations   The sample autocorrelations of the residuals.

Residual income   Earnings for a given period, minus a deduction for common shareholders' opportunity cost in generating the earnings. Also called *economic profit* or *abnormal earnings*.

Residual income model   (RIM) A model of stock valuation that views intrinsic value of stock as the sum of book value per share plus the present value of the stock's expected future residual income per share. Also called *discounted abnormal earnings model* or *Edwards–Bell–Ohlson model*.

Restricted model   A regression model with a subset of the complete set of independent variables.

Restricted stock   A share with selling or other restrictions, commonly used in share-based compensation arrangements with employees.

Restricted stock units (RSUs) An instrument used in share-based compensation plans that represents the right to receive a common share upon vesting. RSUs are not tradeable, nor do they have voting rights or participate in dividends.

Restructuring Reorganizing the capital structure of a firm.

Return on invested capital A measure of the profitability of a company relative to the amount of capital invested by the equity- and debtholders.

Reverse carry arbitrage A strategy involving the short sale of the underlying and an offsetting opposite position in the derivative.

Reverse stock split A reduction in the number of shares outstanding with a corresponding increase in share price but no change to the company's underlying fundamentals.

Reverse stress testing A risk management approach in which the user identifies key risk exposures in the portfolio and subjects those exposures to extreme market movements.

Reviewed financial statements A type of non-audited financial statements; typically provide an opinion letter with representations and assurances by the reviewing accountant that are less than those in audited financial statements.

Rho The change in a given derivative instrument for a given small change in the risk-free interest rate, holding everything else constant. Rho measures the sensitivity of the option to the risk-free interest rate.

Risk budgeting The establishment of objectives for individuals, groups, or divisions of an organization that takes into account the allocation of an acceptable level of risk.

Risk decomposition The process of converting a set of holdings in a portfolio into a set of exposures to risk factors.

Risk factors Variables or characteristics with which individual asset returns are correlated. Sometimes referred to simply as *factors*.

Risk parity A portfolio allocation scheme that weights stocks or factors based on an equal risk contribution.

Risk-based models Models of the return on equity that identify risk factors or drivers and sensitivities of the return to these factors.

Risk-free rate The minimum rate of return expected on a security that has no default risk.

Robust standard errors Method for correcting residuals for conditional heteroskedasticity. Also known as *heteroskedasticity-consistent standard errors* or *White-corrected standard errors*.

Roll When an investor moves its investment position from an older series to the most current series.

Roll return The component of the return on a commodity futures contract attributable to rolling long futures positions forward through time. Also called *roll yield*.

Rolling down the yield curve A maturity trading strategy that involves buying bonds with a maturity longer than the intended investment horizon. Also called *riding the yield curve*.

Rolling windows A backtesting method that uses a rolling-window (or walk-forward) framework, rebalances the portfolio after each period, and then tracks performance over time. As new information arrives each period, the investment manager optimizes (revises and tunes) the model and readjusts stock positions.

Rollover risk The likelihood that a property owner will lose an existing tenant and forgo income until a new one is found.

Root mean squared error (RMSE) The square root of the average squared forecast error; used to compare the out-of-sample forecasting performance of forecasting models.

Sale-leaseback A situation in which a company sells the building it owns and occupies to a real estate investor and the company then signs a long-term lease with the buyer to continue to occupy the building. At the end of the lease, use of the property reverts to the landlord.

Sales comparison approach Real estate valuation approach that considers the price at which similar or comparable properties (comparables) are purchased and sold in the current market; also referred to as the *market approach*.

Sales risk The uncertainty regarding the price and number of units sold of a company's products.

Scaled earnings surprise Unexpected earnings divided by the standard deviation of analysts' earnings forecasts.

Scaling The process of adjusting the range of a feature by shifting and changing the scale of the data. Two of the most common ways of scaling are normalization and standardization.

Scatterplot matrix A visualization technique that shows the scatterplots between different sets of variables, often with the histogram for each variable on the diagonal. Also referred to as a *pairs plot*.

Schwarz's Bayesian information criterion (BIC or SBC) A statistic used to compare sets of independent variables for explaining a dependent variable. It is preferred for finding the model with the best goodness of fit.

Scree plots A plot that shows the proportion of total variance in the data explained by each principal component.

Screening The application of a set of criteria to reduce a set of potential investments to a smaller set having certain desired characteristics.

Seasonality A characteristic of a time series in which the data experience regular and predictable periodic changes; for example, fan sales are highest during the summer months.

Secured overnight financing rate (SOFR) A daily volume-weighted index of rates on qualified cash borrowings collateralized by US Treasuries that is expected to replace Libor as a floating reference rate for swaps.

Security selection risk See *active specific risk*.

Segmented markets theory A term structure theory that contends yields are solely a function of the supply and demand for funds of a particular maturity.

Sell-side analysts Analysts who work at brokerages.

Sensitivity analysis A form of analysis used to determine the impact of a change in one or more key variables affecting investment returns or valuation.

Sentence length The number of characters, including spaces, in a sentence.

Serial correlation A condition found most often in time series in which residuals are correlated across observations. Also known as *autocorrelation*.

Serial-correlation consistent standard errors Method for correcting serial correlation. Also known as *serial correlation and heteroskedasticity adjusted standard errors*, *Newey–West standard errors*, and *robust standard errors*.

Service condition A vesting condition that requires the employee to complete a period of service provision to the employer. A service condition does not require a performance target to be met.

Settled in arrears   An arrangement in which the interest payment is made (i.e., settlement occurs) at the maturity of the underlying instrument.

Settlement   The closing date at which the counterparties of a derivative contract exchange payment for the underlying as required by the contract.

Shadow banking   Lending by financial institutions that are not regulated as banks.

Shaping risk   The sensitivity of a bond's price to the changing shape of the yield curve.

Share repurchase   A transaction in which a company buys back its own shares. Unlike stock dividends and stock splits, share repurchases use corporate cash.

Shareholder activism   A range of actions by a corporation's shareholders that are intended to result in some change in the corporation, typically a change in the board of directors, management, or business strategy.

Shareholders' equity   Assets less liabilities; the residual interest in the assets after subtracting the liabilities.

Short biased   These strategies use quantitative, technical, and fundamental analysis to short overvalued equity securities with limited or no long-side exposures.

Simulation   A technique for exploring how a target variable (e.g. portfolio returns) would perform in a hypothetical environment specified by the user, rather than a historical setting.

Single-manager fund   A fund in which one portfolio manager or team of portfolio managers invests in one strategy or style.

Single-name CDS   Credit default swap on one specific borrower.

Sinking fund bond   A bond that requires the issuer to set aside funds over time to retire the bond issue, thus reducing credit risk.

Size premium (SP)   Additional return compensation for bearing the additional risk associated with smaller companies.

Slope dummy   An indicator variable that allows a single regression model to estimate two lines of best fit, each with differing slopes, depending on whether the dummy takes a value of 1 or 0.

Soft margin classification   An adaptation in the support vector machine algorithm which adds a penalty to the objective function for observations in the training set that are misclassified.

Soft-catalyst event-driven approach   An event-driven approach in which investments are made proactively in anticipation of a corporate event (mergers and acquisitions, bankruptcies, share issuances, buybacks, capital restructurings, re-organizations, accounting changes) that has yet to occur.

Sovereign yield spread   The spread between the yield on a foreign country's sovereign bond and a similar-maturity domestic sovereign bond.

Special dividend   A dividend paid by a company that does not pay dividends on a regular schedule, or a dividend that supplements regular cash dividends with an extra payment.

Specific-company risk premium (SCRP)   Additional return required by investors for bearing non-diversifiable company-specific risk.

Spin off   When a company separates a distinct part of its business into a new, independent company. The term is used to describe both the transaction and the separated component, while the company that conducts the transaction and formerly owned the spin off is known as the parent.

Split-rate tax system   In reference to corporate taxes, a split-rate system taxes earnings to be distributed as dividends at a different rate than earnings to be retained. Corporate profits distributed as dividends are taxed at a lower rate than those retained in the business.

Spot curve   Yields-to-maturity on a series of default-risk-free zero-coupon bonds.

Spot price   The current price of an asset or security. For commodities, the current price to deliver a physical commodity to a specific location or purchase and transport it away from a designated location.

Spot rate   The interest rate that is determined today for a risk-free, single-unit payment at a specified future date.

Spot yield curve   The term structure of spot rates for loans made today.

Stabilized NOI   Normalized or expected long-term level of net operating income level used to value real estate properties.

Stable dividend policy   A policy in which regular dividends are paid that reflect long-run expected earnings. In contrast to a constant dividend payout ratio policy, a stable dividend policy does not reflect short-term volatility in earnings.

Standardized beta   With reference to fundamental factor models, the value of the attribute for an asset minus the average value of the attribute across all stocks, divided by the standard deviation of the attribute across all stocks.

Standardized unexpected earnings   Unexpected earnings per share divided by the standard deviation of unexpected earnings per share over a specified prior time period.

Statistical factor model   A multifactor model in which statistical methods are applied to a set of historical returns to determine portfolios that best explain either historical return covariances or variances.

Steady-state rate of growth   The constant growth rate of output (or output per capita) that can or will be sustained indefinitely once it is reached. Key ratios, such as the capital–output ratio, are constant on the steady-state growth path.

Steepness   The difference between long-term and short-term yields that constitutes one of the three factors (the other two are level and curvature) that empirically explain most of the changes in the shape of the yield curve.

Step-up clauses   Pre-specified contractual future rent increases.

Stock dividend   A type of dividend in which a company distributes additional shares of its common stock to shareholders instead of cash.

Stop-loss limit   Constraint used in risk management that requires a reduction in the size of a portfolio, or its complete liquidation, when a loss of a particular size occurs in a specified period.

Straight bond   An underlying option-free bond with a specified issuer, issue date, maturity date, principal amount and repayment structure, coupon rate and payment structure, and currency denomination.

Straight debt   Debt with no embedded options.

Straight voting   A shareholder voting process in which shareholders receive one vote for each share owned.

Straight-line rent   The average annual rent under a multi-year lease agreement that contains contractual increases in rent during the life of the lease.

Straight-line rent adjustment   See *non-cash rent*.

Stranded assets   A resource that is no longer economically valuable owing to changes in demand, regulations, or availability of substitutes—for example, a newly discovered oil well that will not be brought into production.

Strategic buyer An investor seeking to capitalize on synergies by extending the value creation process initiated by a GP, combining a business with another portfolio company, or taking other actions to increase firm value.

Stress tests A risk management technique that assesses the portfolio's response to extreme market movements.

Stripping A dealer's ability to separate a bond's individual cash flows and trade them as zero-coupon securities.

Stub trading An equity market-neutral strategy that capitalizes on misalignment in prices and entails buying and selling stock of a parent company and its subsidiaries, typically weighted by the percentage ownership of the parent company in the subsidiaries.

Studentized deleted residual A deleted residual divided by its estimated standard deviation.

Studentized residuals t-distributed statistics that are used to detect outliers.

Subject property A real estate property that is being appraised.

Succession event A change of corporate structure of the reference entity, such as through a merger, a divestiture, a spinoff, or any similar action, in which ultimate responsibility for the debt in question is unclear.

Sum-of-the-parts valuation A valuation approach that considers the value of a firm's business segments if they are sold separately.

Summation operator A functional part of a neural network's node that multiplies each input value received by a weight and sums the weighted values to form the total net input, which is then passed to the activation function.

Supernormal growth Above-average or abnormally high growth rate in earnings per share.

Supervised learning A type of machine learning in which the system attempts to learn to model relationships based on labeled training data.

Support vector machine A linear classifier that determines the hyperplane that optimally separates the observations into two sets of data points.

Survivorship bias Relates to the inclusion of only current investment funds in a database. As such, the returns of funds that are no longer available in the marketplace (have been liquidated) are excluded from the database. Also see *backfill bias*.

Sustainable growth rate The rate of dividend (and earnings) growth that can be sustained over time for a given level of return on equity, keeping the capital structure constant and without issuing additional common stock.

Swap curve The term structure of swap rates.

Swap rate The fixed rate to be paid by the fixed-rate payer specified in a swap contract.

Swap rate curve The term structure of swap rates.

Swap spread The difference between the fixed rate on an interest rate swap and the rate on a Treasury note with equivalent maturity; it reflects the general level of credit risk in the market.

Synergies The combination of two companies being more valuable than the sum of the parts. Generally, synergies take the form of lower costs ("cost synergies") or increased revenues ("revenue synergies") through combinations that generate lower costs or higher revenues, respectively.

Systematic risk Risk that affects the entire market or economy; it cannot be avoided and is inherent in the overall market. Systematic risk is also known as *non-diversifiable* or *market risk*.

Tail risk The possibility of extreme losses.

Takeover premium The amount by which the per-share takeover price exceeds the unaffected price expressed as a percentage of the unaffected price. It reflects the amount shareholders require to relinquish their control of the company to the acquirer.

Tangible assets Identifiable, physical assets such as property, plant, and equipment.

Tangible book value per share Common shareholders' equity minus intangible assets reported on the balance sheet, divided by the number of shares outstanding.

Target In machine learning, the dependent variable (Y) in a labeled dataset; the company in a merger or acquisition that is being acquired.

Target capital structure Management's desired proportions of debt and equity financing, usually stated on a book value basis or indirectly using a financial leverage metric, such as net or gross debt to EBITDA or credit rating.

Target payout ratio A strategic corporate goal representing the long-term proportion of earnings that the company intends to distribute to shareholders as dividends.

Taxable REIT subsidiaries Subsidiaries that pay income taxes on earnings from non-REIT-qualifying activities, such as merchant development or third-party property management.

Technical indicators Momentum indicators based on price.

TED spread A measure of perceived credit risk determined as the difference between Libor and the T-bill yield of matching maturity.

Temporal method A variation of the monetary/non-monetary translation method that requires not only monetary assets and liabilities, but also non-monetary assets and liabilities that are measured at their current value on the balance sheet date to be translated at the current exchange rate. Assets and liabilities are translated at rates consistent with the timing of their measurement value. This method is typically used when the functional currency is other than the local currency.

Term frequency (TF) Ratio of the number of times a given token occurs in all the texts in the dataset to the total number of tokens in the dataset.

Term premium The additional return required by lenders to invest in a bond to maturity net of the expected return from continually reinvesting at the short-term rate over that same time horizon.

Terminal cap rate Capitalization rate for a real estate property used to discount a final projected NOI that typically incorporates a constant future growth rate.

Terminal price multiples The price multiple for a stock assumed to hold at a stated future time.

Terminal share price The share price at a particular point in the future.

Terminal value of the stock The analyst's estimate of a stock's value at a particular point in the future. Also called *continuing value of the stock*.

Test sample A data sample that is used to test a model's ability to predict well on new data.

Theta The change in a derivative instrument for a given small change in calendar time, holding everything else constant. Specifically, the theta calculation assumes nothing changes except calendar time. Theta also reflects the rate at which an option's time value decays.

Time series A set of observations on a variable's outcomes in different time periods.

Time-series momentum A managed futures trend following strategy in which managers go long assets that are rising in price and go short assets that are falling in price. The manager trades on an absolute basis, so be net long or net short depending on the current price trend of an asset. This approach works best when an asset's own past returns are a good predictor of its future returns.

Tobin's q The ratio of the market value of debt and equity to the replacement cost of total assets.

Token The equivalent of a word (or sometimes a character).

Tokenization The process of representing ownership rights to physical assets on a blockchain or distributed ledger.

Total factor productivity (TFP) A multiplicative scale factor that reflects the general level of productivity or technology in the economy. Changes in total factor productivity generate proportional changes in output for any input combination.

Total invested capital The sum of market value of common equity, book value of preferred equity, and face value of debt.

Tracking error The standard deviation of the differences between a portfolio's returns and its benchmark's returns; a synonym of active risk.

Tracking risk The standard deviation of the differences between a portfolio's returns and its benchmarks returns. Also called *tracking error*.

Trailing dividend yield The reciprocal of current market price divided by the most recent annualized dividend.

Trailing P/E A stock's current market price divided by the most recent four quarters of EPS (or the most recent two semi-annual periods for companies that report interim data semi-annually). Also called *current P/E*.

Training sample A data sample that is used to train a model.

Tranche CDS A type of credit default swap that covers a combination of borrowers but only up to pre-specified levels of losses.

Transaction exposure The risk of a change in value between the transaction date and the settlement date of an asset of liability denominated in a foreign currency.

Treasury shares/stock Shares that were issued and subsequently repurchased by the company.

Trend A long-term pattern of movement in a particular direction.

Triangular arbitrage An arbitrage transaction involving three currencies that attempts to exploit inconsistencies among pairwise exchange rates.

Trimming Also called truncation, it is the process of removing extreme values and outliers from a dataset.

Two-tier board Board structure consisting of a supervisory board that oversees a management board.

Unbiased expectations theory A term structure theory that contends the forward rate is an unbiased predictor of the future spot rate. Also called the *pure expectations theory*.

Unconditional heteroskedasticity When heteroskedasticity of the error variance is not correlated with the regression's independent variables.

Uncovered interest rate parity The proposition that the expected return on an uncovered (i.e., unhedged) foreign currency (risk-free) investment should equal the return on a comparable domestic currency investment.

Underfunded plan A DB plan with a negative funded status; the present value of the DB obligation is greater than the fair value of plan assets.

Underlying earnings Earnings excluding nonrecurring components. Also referred to as *continuing earnings*, *core earnings*, or *persistent earnings*.

Unexpected earnings The difference between reported EPS and expected EPS. Also referred to as an *earnings surprise*.

Unfunded Post-employment plans for which the sponsor has not set aside assets to pay benefits. Benefits for unfunded plans are paid from company cash

Unit root A time series that is not covariance stationary is said to have a unit root.

Units of comparison Measure used to compare the current market value of real estate properties, such as purchase price per square meter or square foot of leasable area or total area.

Unrestricted model A regression model with the complete set of independent variables.

Unsupervised learning A type of machine learning in which the system tries to learn the structure of unlabeled data.

Upfront payment The difference between the credit spread and the standard rate paid by the protection buyer if the standard rate is insufficient to compensate the protection seller. Also called *upfront premium*.

Upfront premium See *upfront payment*.

Upstream A transaction between two related companies, an investor company (or a parent company) and an associate company (or a subsidiary company) such that the associate company records a profit on its income statement. An example is a sale of inventory by the associate to the investor company or by a subsidiary to a parent company.

Validation sample A data sample that is used to validate and tune a model.

Valuation The process of determining the value of an asset or service either on the basis of variables perceived to be related to future investment returns or on the basis of comparisons with closely similar assets.

Value additivity An arbitrage opportunity when the value of the whole equals the sum of the values of the parts.

Value at risk (VaR) The minimum loss that would be expected a certain percentage of the time over a certain period of time given the assumed market conditions.

Value of growth The difference between the actual value per share and the no-growth value per share.

Variance error Describes how much a model's results change in response to new data from validation and test samples. Unstable models pick up noise and produce high variance error, causing overfitting and high out-of-sample error.

Variance inflation factor (VIF) A statistic that quantifies the degree of multicollinearity in a model.

Vasicek model A partial equilibrium term structure model that assumes interest rates are mean reverting and interest rate volatility is constant.

Vega A measure of the sensitivity of an option's price to changes in the underlying's volatility.

Vertical ownership Ownership structure in which a company or group that has a controlling interest in two or more holding companies, which in turn have controlling interests in various operating companies.

Vesting The process of an employee becoming unconditionally entitled to, and an employer becoming obligated to pay, compensation.

Visibility The extent to which a company's operations are predictable with substantial confidence.

Voting caps Legal restrictions on the voting rights of large share positions.

Web spidering (scraping or crawling) programs   Programs that extract raw content from a source, typically web pages.

Weighted average cost of capital (WACC)   The expected cost of debt and equity weighted by the proportion of each used in a company's capital structure.

Weighted harmonic mean   See *harmonic mean.*

Winsorization   The process of replacing extreme values and outliers in a dataset with the maximum (for large value outliers) and minimum (for small value outliers) values of data points that are not outliers.

Write-down   A reduction in the value of an asset as stated in the balance sheet.

Yield curve factor model   A model or a description of yield curve movements that can be considered realistic when compared with historical data.

Zero   A bond that does not pay a coupon but is priced at a discount and pays its full face value at maturity.

Zero-coupon bonds   Bonds that do not pay interest during their life. They are issued at a discount to par value and redeemed at par. Also called pure discount bond.